Language and Power

Advances in Sociolinguistics
Series Editor: Professor Sally Johnson, University of Leeds

Since the emergence of sociolinguistics as a new field of enquiry in the late 1960s, research into the relationship between language and society has advanced almost beyond recognition. In particular, the past decade has witnessed the considerable influence of theories drawn from outside of sociolinguistics itself. Thus rather than seeing language as a mere reflection of society, recent work has been increasingly inspired by ideas drawn from social, cultural and political theory that have emphasized the constitutive role played by language/discourse in all areas of social life. The Advances in Sociolinguistics series seeks to provide a snapshot of the current diversity of the field of sociolinguistics and the blurring of the boundaries between sociolinguistics and other domains of study concerned with the role of language in society.

Discourses of Endangerment
Ideology and Interest in the Defence of Languages
Edited by Alexandre Duchêne and Monica Heller

Globalization and Language in Contact
James Collins, Stef Slembrouck and Mike Baynham

Language, Culture and Identity
An Ethnolinguistic Perspective
Philip Riley

Language in the Media
Representations, Identities, Ideologies
Edited by Sally Johnson and Astrid Ensslin

Linguistic Minorities and Modernity, 2nd Edition
A Sociolinguistic Ethnography
Monica Heller

Language of Newspapers
Socio-Historical Perspectives
Martin Conboy

Language Testing, Migration and Citizenship
Cross-National Perspectives
Edited by Guus Extra, Massimiliano Spotti and Piet van Avermaet

Languages of Urban Africa
Edited by Fiona McLaughlin

Media Sociolinguistics
Policy, Discourse, Practice
Helen Kelly-Holmes

Multilingualism
A Critical Perspective
Adrian Blackledge and Angela Creese

Semiotic Landscapes
Text, Space, Globalization
Edited by Adam Jaworksi and Crispin Thurlow

Language and Power

An Introduction to Institutional Discourse

Andrea Mayr

continuum

Continuum International Publishing Group
The Tower Building			80 Maiden Lane
11 York Road				Suite 704
London SE1 7NX			New York NY 10038

© Andrea Mayr, David Machin, Tony Bastow and Gill Abousnnouga 2008

All rights reserved. No part of this publication may be reproduced or transmitted in any form or by any means, electronic or mechanical, including photocopying, recording, or any information storage or retrieval system, without prior permission in writing from the publishers.

Diane Pecorari has asserted her right under the Copyright, Designs and Patents Act, 1988, to be identified as Author of this work.

British Library Cataloguing-in-Publication Data
A catalogue record for this book is available from the British Library.

ISBN: 978-08264-8743-8 (Hardback)
      978-08264-8744-5 (Paperback)

Library of Congress Cataloguing-in-Publication Data
The Publisher has applied for CIP data.

Typeset by Newgen Imaging Systems Pvt Ltd, Chennai, India
Printed and bound in Great Britain by MPG Books, Cornwall

Contents

Notes on Contributors   vi

1. Introduction: Power, discourse and institutions   1
   Andrea Mayr

2. Discourses of higher education: Enterprise and institutional change in the university   26
   Andrea Mayr

3. Prison discourse: Enterprising managerialism in a total institution   46
   Andrea Mayr

4. News discourse I: Understanding the social goings-on behind news texts   62
   David Machin

5. News discourse II: Anti-racism and neo-liberalism in the British Regional Press   90
   David Machin and Andrea Mayr

6. Defence discourse I: The visual institutionalization of discourses in war monuments   115
   Gill Abousnnouga and David Machin

7. Defence discourse II: A corpus perspective on routine and rhetoric in defence discourse   138
   Tony Bastow

8. Conclusion: Researching institutional discourse   163
   Andrea Mayr with Tony Bastow

Appendix   178
References   186
Index   199

Notes on Contributors

Gill Abousnnouga teaches on the Language and Communication programme at the University of Glamorgan. Her research interests are in the application of visual communication theories to the analysis of military discourse.

Tony Bastow is a Ph.D. in English corpus linguistics from Birmingham University. He has taught English language and linguistics at the universities of Birmingham, Liverpool and Westminster, and is currently Visiting Lecturer at the Cass School of Education, University of East London.

David Machin works in the School of Journalism, Media and Cultural Studies at Cardiff University. His recent publications include *Global Media Discourse* (2007) with Theo van Leeuwen, and *Introduction to Multimodal Analysis* (2007). He has published numerous journal papers, especially using multimodal discourse analysis, and is co-editor of the journal *Social Semiotics*.

Andrea Mayr is Lecturer in Modern English Language in the School of English at Queen's University Belfast. Her research and teaching interests are in the area of sociolinguistics, critical discourse analysis and media studies. She is the author of *Prison Discourse: Language as a Means of Control and Resistance* (2004). In her most recent research she has focused on media representations of multiculturalism and Reality TV.

1 Introduction: Power, discourse and institutions

Andrea Mayr

This book is about language, power and institutions. It examines language and power across a variety of institutional settings, showing how institutions are shaped by discourse and how they in turn have the capacity to create and impose discourses. In this way, they have considerable control over the shaping of our routine experiences of the world and the way we classify that world. They therefore have power to foster particular kinds of identities to suit their own purposes.

In this book we consider a number of such institutional settings and contexts: the university, the prison, the media and the military. Each chapter deals with one particular case, describing and demonstrating a theoretical and analytical approach within a general critical discourse/multimodal framework. We also include a corpus-based approach to the critical analysis of institutional discourse. Each chapter is intended to give readers an overview of the approach and the practical steps taken in the analysis. In writing this book we see ourselves as contributing to critical voices on institutions and their capacity to produce and disseminate discourses with institutional values, meanings and positions.

Institutions' power and politics are frequently exercised through the discourse of their members. We only have to think of the news media in this respect. On the one hand, we assume that they are obliged to provide impartial and balanced coverage of important political and social events. This is an impression they certainly strive to create. But these are also large organizations that need to maintain themselves and their position. They need to operate as well-oiled machines to process and deal with the stuff of their business. What this means in practice is that to some extent it is the institutional procedures and practices that define what becomes news more so than the events themselves. In addition, these organizations are owned by ever larger corporations who have their own agenda particularly to increase revenue for shareholders. And as they push for more profits this puts new constraints on what kinds of events can become news and creates new opportunities for those organizations which are best able to respond to such changes. So to understand news texts we need to understand them as the result of these institutional processes. It is because of these institutional, practical and financial concerns that news media offer only a partial view of the world that fits with the interests of the socially and economically powerful (e.g. war reporting that excludes acts of violence perpetrated against civilians).

The sourcing and legitimization of news is therefore bound up with the actions, opinions and values of dominant groups in society. In this way, the media tend to function ideologically, not so much due to bias, but simply through the nature of established routine practices. In simple terms this means that we find the news media blame certain social groups for economic and social decline (e.g. single mothers or 'benefit cheats') or for rising crime rates, leaving aside issues of social deprivation that marginalize certain people in the first place. They thereby gloss over and render largely invisible the material conditions of many people.

While the news media play an important role in defining what we think of as crime and criminals, other institutions have the role of processing, punishing and reforming those who break the law. Yet in the same way, these institutions promote and legitimize discourses of who is and is not a good citizen and who are the evil-doers among us. For example, prison systems support current neo-liberal discourses of crime control, which construct crime as an individual rather than structural problem and the individual offender as invested with autonomy, choice and self-responsibility. They do that through the implementation of rehabilitation programmes which target supposed personality defects of offenders. This has the effect thereby of imposing the institutionally based (ideological) assumptions of crime onto those people they process. Some of the people processed, however, might say that criminal behaviour is not always the result of choice and individual agency, and that it is poverty that may cause violent outbursts and not just personality defects and a lack of communication and social skills. Yet, just as news tell us who is bad through the definitions of the powerful who can best act as sources in the institutional value system of news organizations, helping to legitimize the world view of these individuals and the organizations they represent, so do prisons take their place in maintaining the apparent logic of these discourses where crime is simply the act of bad people. And like news organizations, prisons and other institutions are able to *legitimize* their own crucial role in the process.

This book is an investigation of the discourses that dominate institutions, and which they themselves promote. We show that these institutions seek to legitimize their own interests and existence through discourses through which they seek to transform or recontextualize social practices. As Weber (1914) reminds us, in democratic systems, the power of institutions needs to be legitimized and justified to be accepted by people. For example, the invasion of Iraq was justified by the government and the military through the 'rhetoric of military humanism' (Chomsky, 1999), which argued that ridding the world of an evil dictator was necessary to 'liberate' the downtrodden people of Iraq.

There have been three strands of research that have been identified in the study of the relationship between discourse, institutions and power (Mumby and Clair, 1997: 195): (1) the study of how members of oppressed groups can 'discursively penetrate the institutionalized form of their oppression'; (2) how subordinate individuals 'discursively frame their own subordination' thereby perpetuating it; and (3) analysis of how dominant groups 'discursively construct and reproduce their own positions of dominance' (e.g. van Dijk, 1993). It is this third area that we have taken up as our focus here, although we also make occasional reference to the other two. We are particularly concerned with the hegemonic rise of specific institutional discourses over others in 'late modern' or 'new capitalist' societies, such as the discourse of 'enterprise' which espouses a purely economic model as the model for *all* undertakings including previously 'non-economic' public institutions (e.g. the health service) in a wider 'enterprise culture'.

A great deal of contemporary social research has been concerned with the nature and consequences of these changes in the new capitalism (e.g. Giddens, 1991). At the same time, the study of the language aspects of new capitalism has also developed into a significant area of research, particularly for critical discourse analysts. Fairclough (2003: 4) defines the term 'new capitalism' as 'the most recent of a historical series of radical re-structurings through which capitalism has maintained its fundamental continuity'. These restructurings involve dramatic transformations not only of economic, but also political and social domains. For example, in the area of education, there has been a tendency to run universities increasingly like commercial businesses, with students being their 'customers'. This development in turn has been promoted by the government's pro-managerial educational discourses and policies, which espouse an entrepreneurial culture and educational system.

The reason why language plays such a significant role in the new capitalism is because of it being 'knowledge-driven', that is, constantly generating knowledge about the world and how people are to act in the world (e.g. in the workplace). For this, it has to rely on language or discourse, discourse that is 'endowed with the performative power to *bring into being* the very realities it *claims* to describe' (Fairclough, 2003: 203–4; emphasis added). Institutions play a vital role in this as they are primary sites for 'reality construction'. The questions we might ask ourselves are how does this discourse materialize in organizations and institutions, how is it internalized in social practices and how does it define the identities of people ('social actors')?

In the sections that follow, we investigate the relationship between language and institutions in more detail.

Institutions and institutional discourse

Institutions are not easy to define. People usually associated them with physical buildings or institutional settings, such as schools, hospitals, media organizations, prisons or courts of law. Here is an example of a popular definition of 'institution':

1. An established organization or foundation, especially one dedicated to education, public service or culture.
2. The building or buildings housing such an organization.
3. A place for the care of persons who are destitute, disabled or mentally ill. (www.thefreedictionary.com/institution)

As this definition shows, there appears to be a certain overlap in the use of the terms 'institution' and 'organization'. They are also used more or less interchangeably in the sociological and linguistic literature on the topic (e.g. Drew and Sorjonen, 1997; Jablin and Putnam, 2001), although 'organization' seems to be used more for commercial corporations, whereas 'institution' is more associated with the public organs of the state, which is what we are concerned with in the present volume.

Institutions are also seen as inextricably linked to power and serving the interests of certain powerful groups (e.g. the media). Agar's (1985: 164) definition, according to which institutions are 'a socially legitimated expertise together with those persons authorized to implement it' is important here as it suggests that institutions are not restricted to physical settings and can refer to any powerful group, such as the government or the media. Agar's definition also includes the conception of institutions as involving asymmetrical roles between institutional representatives or 'experts' and 'non-experts' or 'clients', who must comply with institutional norms and objectives.

The notion that institutions have immense power which they impose on people has informed many theoretical accounts (e.g. Weber, 1914; Althusser, 1971; Habermas, 1987). Other accounts, however, have adopted a more complex view of institutions and institutional power, in which power is achieved not by mere oppression but also by persuasion and consent and the complicity on the part of people (e.g. Gramsci, 1971; Foucault, 1979). We shall come back to these later.

Linguistic and sociological approaches to the study of institutions and their discourses generally regard language as constitutive of institutions (Deetz, 1982). In this view, language is the principal means by which institutions create a coherent social reality that frames their sense of who they are (Mumby and Clair, 1997). Accordingly, institutions – their employees and others with whom they interact (e.g. the public) – are being constructed and reconstructed in discourse practices. This view of discourse as constituting social reality does not necessarily lead to the view that discourse is all there is, but assigns discourse an important role in shaping reality, creating patterns of understanding, which people then apply in social practices.

There is now an abundance of literature on institutional discourse, interaction and practices which has been concerned with understanding the relationship between discourse, ideology and power (e.g. Mumby, 1988, 2001; Drew and Heritage, 1992; Gunnarsson et al., 1997; Mumby and Clair, 1997; Sarangi and Roberts, 1999; Cameron, 2000; Thornborrow, 2002; Iedema, 2003; Tietze et al., 2003). Issues addressed specifically in Critical Discourse Analysis (CDA) are the discourse of media organizations (Fairclough, 1995a), language and education (Fairclough, 1993, 1995b; Chouliaraki, 1998); communication barriers in institutions (Wodak, 1996); 'new' capitalism and neo-liberalism (Fairclough, 2000), bureaucratic discourses in late modern society (Sarangi and Slembrouck, 1996; Iedema, 1998), racism in the press (van Dijk, 1993, 1997); anti-immigration discourse (Iedema and Wodak, 1999) and the reproduction of class inequalities in media discourse (Richardson, 2007).

Rather than regarding organizations and institutions simply 'as social collectives where shared meaning is produced', these critical studies of organizations/institutions and their discourses see them as 'sites of struggle where different groups compete to shape the social reality ... in ways that *serve their own interests*' (Mumby and Clair, 1997: 182; emphasis added). For example, in new capitalist societies it is in the interest of management to articulate a social reality for employees which emphasizes supposedly egalitarian workplace practices ('teamwork') in which employees take 'ownership' of their work, while at the same time securing commitment from them and being able to realize their institutional goals.

As briefly indicated above, Habermas (1984, 1987) has made an important contribution to the study of institutional discourse. He distinguishes between 'communicative' uses of language – aimed at producing understanding – and 'strategic' uses – oriented to success and making people do things – and the displacement of the former by the latter. Habermas sees this development as a sign of the colonization of people's lives by the systems of the economy and the state. In this way, economic models and discourses have colonized the institutional forms of what Habermas calls the 'life-world', such as education or interpersonal relations. However, this distinction between the 'life-world' ('ordinary' conversation, informality) and the 'system' (institutions, the state, formality) can no longer be upheld, as both spheres now colonize each other and share common discourse practices. This can be observed in the process of 'conversationalization' (Fairclough, 1992), the modelling of formal written and spoken public discourse on informal, face-to-face talk, as, for example, in the bureaucratic field, where institutions in the public and private domain nowadays often rely on promotional discourse reminiscent of advertising to commodify their services and to attract a wide range of people (see Sarangi and Slembrouck, 1996). This is something that has also affected universities and how they interact with students, as we will see in Chapter 2.

So while institutional discourse and power has been studied in terms of Habermas' (1987: 196) notion of the colonization of a 'natural' unspoilt life-world by rational-instrumental social systems expressed in bureaucratic-administrative discourses (e.g. Fairclough, 1992; Wodak, 1996), other studies have pointed to the *productiveness* of institutional discourses, arguing that these encode and construe 'complicity' and 'reciprocal power relations' (Foucault, 1979; Iedema, 1998), which underpin and maintain institutional and hierarchical power. The argument is that to analyse institutional practices and discourses solely from the perspective of domination, oppression and exclusions ignores how these discourses and practices 'enlist subjects to their "natural" cause' (Iedema, 1998: 497). This 'productive' view of institutional power provides an important angle for the analysis of institutional discourse and will be followed up later.

This point was also explored by Giddens (1981) in his 'theory of structuration'. Giddens argues that social actors are not completely overwhelmed by institutional power and dominance and that institutions have a potential for domination as well as emancipation. For instance, new workplace practices (e.g. teamwork), which favour a more egalitarian relationship between the management and the workforce, are often said to give workers more space to exercise their abilities and to fulfil themselves. In this way, workplaces would be enabling as well as constraining. However, while this may apply to institutional locations where domination of one group over the other is partial and contested, such as management and shop floor, in more coercive institutions, such as the prison, power relations are very real and cannot be ignored. In this respect, Giddens may therefore have marginalized considerations of objective power relations.

So far we have discussed the centrality of discourse in the critical study of institutions. It is now time to examine the term itself in more detail.

Discourse

'Discourse' is a difficult and fuzzy concept as it is used by social theorists (e.g. Foucault, 1972; 1977), critical linguists (e.g. Fowler et al., 1979) and finally, critical discourse analysts (e.g. van Dijk, 1990), all of whom define discourse slightly differently and from their various theoretical and disciplinary standpoints. We will now elaborate on the meanings of the term and how we intend to use it in this book.

Discourse is often defined in two different ways: according to the formalist or structuralist paradigm, discourse is 'language above the clause' (Stubbs, 1983: 1). This approach to discourse focuses on the form which 'language above the sentence' takes, looking at structural properties such as organization and cohesion, but paying little attention to the social ideas that inform the way people use and interpret language.

This social aspect of language is emphasized by the second, so-called functionalist paradigm, which states that discourse is 'language in use' (Brown and Yule, 1983: 1) and should be studied as such. Brown and Yule state that

> [. . .] the analysis of discourse is, necessarily, the analysis of language in use. As such, it cannot be restricted to the description of linguistic forms independent of the purposes or functions which these forms are designed to serve in human affairs.

According to the functionalist paradigm, the analysis of language cannot be divorced from the analysis of the purpose and functions of language in human life. Discourse is therefore seen as a culturally and socially organized way of speaking. As Richardson (2007: 24; emphasis in original) notes, researchers who adopt this definition of discourse 'assume that language is used to *mean* something and to *do* something' and that this 'meaning and doing' is linked to the context of its usage. If we want to interpret a text properly, 'we need to work out what the speaker or writer is *doing* through discourse, and how this "doing" is linked to wider interpersonal, institutional, socio-cultural and material contexts.' 'Text' refers to 'the observable product of interaction', whereas discourse is 'the process of interaction itself: a cultural activity' (Talbot, 2007: 9).

This view of language as action and social behaviour is emphasized in CDA, which sees discourse – the use of language in speech and writing – as a form of *social practice*. It is this definition of discourse as a social practice that is the most useful for our analysis of institutional discourse, as it implies a two-way relationship between a 'discursive event' (i.e. any use of discourse) and the situation, institution and social structure in which it occurs: discourse is shaped by these, but it also shapes them (Fairclough, 1992: 62). In other words, language represents and contributes to the (re)production of social reality. This definition of discourse establishes a link to our view of institutional discourse as engaged in 'reality construction'.

A different view of discourse that has also been incorporated into the theoretical framework of CDA, especially the one developed by Fairclough (1992), is by Foucault. This is because he offers important theoretical concepts for understanding institutions as sites of discursive power. Foucault does not think of discourse as a piece of text, but as 'practices that systematically form the objects of which they speak' (Foucault, 1972: 49).

By discourse, Foucault means 'a group of statements which provide a language for talking about – a way of representing the knowledge about – a particular topic at a particular historical moment' (Hall, 1992: 291). Discourse, Foucault argues, *constructs* the topic. It governs the way that a topic can be meaningfully talked about. It also influences how ideas are put into practice and used to regulate the conduct of others. This in turn means that discourse (or discourses in the social theoretical sense) can limit and restrict other ways of talking and producing knowledge about it (e.g. discussing working-class crime as an individual problem in the media can marginalize an alternative conception of it being a social problem).

Critical Discourse Analysis

Critical Discourse Analysis (CDA) is 'a theory and method analysing the way that individuals and institutions *use* language' (Richardson, 2007: 1; emphasis in original). Critical discourse analysts focus on 'relations between discourse, power, dominance and social inequality' (van Dijk, 1993: 249) and how discourse (re)produces and maintains these relations of dominance and inequality'. Because of their concern with the analysis of the 'often opaque relationships' between discourse practices and wider social and cultural structures, CDA practitioners take an 'explicit socio-political stance' (ibid.: 252). In this respect, CDA is different from the other main, and more descriptive, approach to institutional discourse, Conversation Analysis (CA).

CDA places particular emphasis on the interdisciplinary study of discourse, mediating between the linguistic and the social and regarding the social more than a mere contextual backdrop to texts (e.g. Chouliaraki and Fairclough, 1999; Weiss and Wodak, 2003). Unlike CA, CDA therefore addresses broader social issues and attends to external factors, including ideology, power, inequality, etc. and draws on social and philosophical theory to analyse and interpret written and spoken texts. As Fairclough (2001: 26; emphasis in original) puts it:

> CDA analyses texts and interactions, but it does not *start* from texts and interactions. It starts rather from social issues and problems, problems which face people in their social lives, issues which are taken up within sociology, political science and/or cultural studies.

CDA researchers therefore typically examine how the microstructures of language are linked with and help to shape the macrostructures of society.

There is not just one way of doing CDA and the various methodologies reflect the theoretical and philosophical orientations of the researchers (Fairclough, 1992; van Dijk, 1993; Wodak, 2001). Fairclough (1992) works from a broadly Marxist perspective, arguing that the task of CDA is to identify how relations of domination and inequalities, which arise from neo-capitalist societies, are produced and reproduced in discourse. Van Dijk (1993, 2001), on the other hand, has developed a socio-cognitive framework which theorizes the relationship between social systems and social cognition. Wodak's discourse-historical approach is intent on tracing the historical (intertextual) history of phrases and arguments (see, for example, van Leeuwen and Wodak, 1999) and centres on political issues such as racism, integrating all available background information in the analysis and interpretation of the different layers of a text. An application of the discourse-historical approach can be found in Chapter 5 in our analysis of institutionalized discourses of multiculturalism in a British regional paper.

As we indicated above, CDA maintains that discourse – the use of language in speech and writing – should be regarded as a social practice. Fairclough (1992: 10) argues that every instance of language use has three dimensions: 'it is a spoken or written language text; it is an interaction between people involving processes of producing and interpreting the text; and it is a piece of social practice. Describing discourse as social practice implies dealing with issues that are important for social analysis such as the *institutional* circumstance of the discursive event and how that shapes the nature of the discursive practices and the constitutive effects of discourse (Fairclough, 1992). For example, take the discursive event of a newspaper article about 'benefit scroungers' or 'hordes of immigrants'. The article has not been written in a social vacuum, but is shaped by situational, institutional and social structures. But it also helps to *shape* them, because it may (re)produce certain (anti-immigration) attitudes or help to transform them. So the analysis of discourse as a social practice implies the analysis of the 'social and cultural goings-on which the communicative event is part of' (Fairclough, 1995a: 57). So with regard to institutional discourses, we might ask ourselves what are the wider institutional practices in which they are produced and in what ways do they help to perpetuate or help to stop undesirable social practices (e.g. racism).

Although the general thrust in CDA has been towards an analysis of linguistic structures, which are attributed a crucial function in the social production of inequality, power, ideology and manipulation, other scholars have emphasized the importance of incorporating visual images into concepts of discourse and moved towards broader *multimodal* conceptions (Kress and van Leeuwen; 1996; Machin and van Leeuwen, 2007), because several forms of representations, linguistic and non-linguistic, are used in its construction. For example, while political and ideological views of newspapers can be expressed in the choice of different vocabularies (e.g. 'resistance fighters' vs. 'insurgents') and different grammatical structures (e.g. active vs. passive constructions), the same applies to the visual representation of events, of what Kress and van Leeuwen (1996) have termed 'the grammar of visual design'. Just as linguistic structures, visual structures also express (ideological) meanings and contribute to the overall meaning of texts. Most research in the area of institutional discourse has largely ignored multimodal aspects of meaning-making (see Grant and Iedema, 2005). We therefore address this issue in Chapters 4 and 5, where we demonstrate through a multimodal analysis of media discourse that images are 'entirely within the realm of ideology, as means – always – for the emergence of ideological positions' (Kress and van Leeuwen (1996: 13).

Ideology

Since CDA is concerned with exposing the often hidden ideologies that are reflected, reinforced and constructed in everyday and institutional discourse, the concept of ideology is crucial. Like the concepts of discourse and power, ideology is probably the one that most defies precise definition. Definitions usually fall into two broad categories: a relativist definition, denoting systems of ideas, beliefs and practices, and a critical definition, allied with Marxist theory, which sees it as working in the interests of a social class and/or cultural group. When critical discourse analysts argue that discourse embodies ideological assumptions, they use the term ideology in a 'critical' sense. Fairclough (1992: 87) understands ideologies to be

> significations/constructions of reality (the physical world, social relations, social identities) which are built into various dimensions of the forms/meanings of discursive practices, and which contribute to the production, reproduction or transformation of relations of domination.

This critical conception of ideology, which is based on Gramsci's (1971) concept of hegemony (domination by consent), links it to the process of sustaining asymmetrical relations of power and inequalities – that is to the process of maintaining domination. In the words of Fairclough (1995b: 14), ideology is 'meaning in the service of power'. Critical discourse analysts see ideologies as serving the interests of certain groups with social power, ensuring that events, practices and behaviours come to be regarded as legitimate and *common-sense*. Ideologies do this subtly, because they inform the way people interpret the world around them, hence hegemony.

Social power is defined as power belonging to people who have privileged access to social resources, such as education, knowledge and wealth. However, analysts do not see power and dominance merely as imposed from above on others, but maintain that, in many situations, power is 'jointly produced', for example, when people are led to believe that dominance is legitimate in some way or other.

The question what power is, where it is located and how it can be studied in or as language has been an important question in many critical language studies. We therefore set out to provide an overview of some of the concepts of power which have informed sociological and linguistic research on institutions.

Power: key concepts

Although power is pervasive in social systems and their institutions, its conceptualization has remained a matter of disagreement (see Lukes, 1974). Scott (2001) makes a useful distinction between what he terms the 'mainstream' and 'second-stream' traditions of power research. The mainstream tradition has tended to focus on the corrective forms of the power of the state and its institutions, whereas the second-stream has been mainly concerned with the significance of its persuasive influence. As both are important for an understanding of centrality of discourse in the workings of institutions, we will review them here.

The mainstream tradition of power research: power as domination

The classic account of the mainstream tradition goes back to Weber (1914) and his analysis of authority in modern and pre-modern states through the varying abilities of actors to secure the compliance of others, even against their resistance. Weber made the important point that power not only resides within the state, but also in other sovereign organizations, such as businesses and the church. In democratic systems, power needs to be legitimate to be accepted by people. This is generally expressed in symbolic forms by means of language: institutions legitimate themselves with regard to citizens. It is discourse that justifies official action of an institution or the institution itself. At the same time, legitimation implies that opposing groups will be delegitimated. For example, in his work on racism and the press, van Dijk (1991) found that accusations of racism on the part of ethnic minorities in newspaper reports were not only construed as doubtful and therefore as less legitimate, but they also did not go unchallenged by the (white) authorities.

The mainstream tradition culminates in Lukes' (1974) critique of power studies as limited to those forms of power that could be seen. Lukes describes three different views or 'faces' of power, two of which he found inadequate: a one-dimensional view which focuses on decisions over which there is some observable conflict of interest. This view was developed by Dahl (1957, 1961), who argued that power was a matter of individual agency, residing in individuals rather than in institutions. According to this view, power only exists in so far as it can be observed empirically in visible instances of decision-making.

This somewhat simplistic one-dimensional view, which focuses on conscious and explicit decision-making, was criticized by Bachratz and Baratz (1962). They emphasized a 'second face' to the exercise of power that prevents issues from coming to the point of decision through what they termed 'non-decision-making'. Non-decision-making may work in that the powerful do not attend or listen to demands articulated by the less powerful. The two-dimensional view focuses on mechanisms which prevent decisions from being reached on issues where conflicts of interest are apparent, thereby introducing the notion of 'bias' and defending the interests of the powerful. A case in point is how powerful groups in society use the news media for securing their powerful position.

Finally, the three-dimensional and Luke's own view is concerned with ways in which issues are kept out of politics altogether and where conflicts of interest are latent rather than actual. The third aspect is therefore far more concerned with the importance of the real interests of which actors may not be aware. If institutions are able to shape the values of people, then they may be able to make them do things that are against their true interests. Luke's view then stresses the ways in which people, but above all groups and institutions, succeed in keeping conflict over potential issues from arising in the first place, which he sees as the most effective use of power. As Lukes (1974: 34) puts it, 'A exercises power over B when A affects B in a manner contrary to B's interest'. This happens mainly through discourse and the capacity of power to act ideologically.

Luke's conception of power as an ideological phenomenon has been prominent in many accounts on the interconnectedness between language, power and institutions. Althusser (1971) was one of the first to describe power as a discursive phenomenon and stressed the significant roles of ideologies in reproducing or changing political relations through so-called 'ideological state apparatuses', such as the church, the legal system, the family, the media and the educational system. One current example of this is the construction of citizens as 'consumers', for instance, in the language of public health materials in late modernity which construct readers as 'consumers' who should take personal responsibility for their health through proper 'life-style choices'. By accepting the role of subjects with personal choices in a consumer culture, people are reproducing the ideology of consumerism and the construction of health problems as individual rather than public or structural problems that need collective solution.

The second-stream of power research: power as persuasion

The persuasive form of power associated with the second-stream of research has provided important insights into the limitations of first-stream, orthodox accounts of power. Here the focus is not so much on specific organizations of power, but rather on strategies and techniques of power, in which language is given a central role.

A central figure in the development of this second-stream is Gramsci (1971), whose concept of *hegemony* highlights the mechanisms through which dominant groups in society succeed in persuading subordinate groups to accept their own moral, political and cultural values and their institutions through ideological means. Power is therefore not exercised coercively, but routinely. It is because CDA explores how discourse constructs ideological (hegemonic) attitudes, opinions and beliefs that often appear as common sense that it is such an important concept for critical analysis.

Like Althusser, Gramsci took the view that it is through the cultural formations of individuals ('subjects') by the institutions of civil society (the family, the educational system, churches, courts of law, the media) that dominant groups in society can gain a more stable position for themselves than through the repressive powers of the state. An important factor in this process is 'consent': subordinate groups are said to consent to the existing social order because it is effectively presented by the state and its institutions as being universally beneficial and commonsensical. As a practice of power, hegemony operates largely through language: people consent to particular formations of power because the dominant cultural groups generating the discourse represent them as 'natural'.

This may give rise to a view of hegemony as total consent. However, domination is only ever achieved partially and temporarily, as an unstable equilibrium. As Gramsci (1971) points out, dominant groups have to work at staying dominant. They attempt to secure domination first, by constructing a 'ruling group' through building and maintaining political alliances; second, by generating consent ('legitimacy') among the population; and, third, by building a capacity for coercion through institutions such as the police, the courts and the legal system, prisons, and the military to create 'authority'. The more legitimacy dominant groups have, the less coercion they need to apply. Each of these three hegemonic functions relies on language and communication, which involves the dissemination of 'representations which inculcate identities, beliefs and behaviours confirming the practices and discourses of the ruling group' (Louw, 2005: 98).

The more commonsensical ('naturalized' in the words of Marx) the discourses and practices appear, the greater is the capacity for dominant groups to rule by 'consent'. To take an example from the media, Richardson (2007) points out that the work of mainstream journalism supports hegemony by naturalizing or taking for granted the inequalities of contemporary capitalism, mainly reporting events as they are seen by officials and sidelining other voices. However, such dominance 'arises as a property of the system of relations involved, rather than as the overt and intentional biases of individuals' (Hall, 1982: 95; quoted in Richardson, 2007: 36). This is a point elaborated in Chapter 4 on news as institutional discourse, where some of the professional and institutional practices of journalism are examined.

The other central figure to provide us with important insights into the study of the relationship between power, knowledge and institutional practices is Foucault. Foucault sees institutions as sites of disciplinary power and disciplinary 'micropractices' (Mumby, 2001: 607). In this view, power is not solely exercised from above in terms of repression and ideology through the state and other sovereign institutions. In fact, Foucault refuses to identify any particular institution or set of practices as a constant source of power (e.g. a framing of all power relations within a capitalist system of domination). Instead, he sees power as far more diffused and dispersed, and describes it as a 'productive network which runs through the whole social body' (Foucault, 1980: 131), and which is characterized by a complex and continuously evolving web of social and discursive relations. Power, Foucault (1977: 194) says, 'produces reality, it produces domains of objects and rituals of truth' and it produces discourse. These rituals of truth can be understood as rules for what counts as true or false in any society. For example, in the more recent cultural and economic changes of late modernity, the reorganization of workers into teams has changed the way power is exercised in institutions. Control shifts from managers to workers themselves through the establishment of work teams that engage in 'self-surveillance'. In this way, 'power is produced from the bottom up through the everyday discursive practices that construct team members' identities' (Mumby, 2001: 607). This demonstrates how power does not just prohibit and negate but *produces*: it produces identities, knowledge and possibilities for behaviour and it does this through discourse.

Power, then, is inextricably linked with knowledge: 'power and knowledge directly imply each other . . . there is no power relation without the correlative constitution of a field of knowledge, nor any knowledge that does not presuppose and constitute at the same time power relations' (Foucault, 1977: 27). Foucault shows us how knowledge can be put to work through discourse practices in specific institutional settings to regulate the conduct of its members and the general public. Imprisonment, for example, can be seen as the prime example of the symbiotic relationship between knowledge and power, in that the disciplinary surveillance of the prison creates a new kind of 'knowledge' of the prisoner's body and mind which in turn creates a new kind of power. A body of knowledge about the nature of criminals is essential to justify rehabilitation and discipline.

As with Gramsci's notion of hegemony, power, for Foucault, is 'secured not so much by the threat of punishment, but by the internalization of the norms and values implied by the prevailing discourses within the social order' (Mesthrie et al., 2000: 324). People are formed as 'subjects', that is, free but disciplined individuals. This process occurs in modern capitalist societies mainly through the work of 'experts' who are empowered by their formation of scientific and technical forms of discourse. Expertise has become an important feature of disciplining populations and is central to the dynamics of power in modern societies and their institutions (Scott, 2001: 92). Of course, resistance to, just as much as compliance with, institutionally preferred discourses and disciplinary practices, is to be expected (see, for example, Silverman, 1997; Houghton, 1995; Pelissier-Kingfisher, 1966).

Foucault's views on externally imposed discipline in the form of regimentation, classification and surveillance are already well-developed in Weber's (1914) work on modern authority and administration. However, his work on how the techniques of discipline attempt to produce internal self-discipline is an important contribution to the discussion of institutional power. Experts inculcate practices of self-reflection and self-control in those they deal with. A notable development in this respect is the emergence of 'discourse technologists' in the workplace and other institutional settings who offer people guidance in linguistic and social tools ('social and communication skills training') and which are often based on therapeutic models of 'co-operative' talking. Examples of discourse technologies will be discussed in Chapter 2 on universities and Chapter 3 on prison discourse.

All the accounts covered here contain conceptualizations of language and power in institutions which are relevant to the institutional locations and contexts we cover in this book. In the next section, we introduce a practical framework for linguistic analysis that we will apply in the chapters that follow.

A practical framework for Critical Discourse Analysis

It was stated above that CDA is concerned with exposing the often hidden ideologies that are reflected, produced and reproduced in everyday and institutional discourse. To achieve this, a multifunctional view of discourse is necessary. The most influential theory of language in CDA that is socially oriented and informed is Systemic Functional Linguistics (SFL). As Chouliaraki and Fairclough (1999: 139) state

> It is no accident that critical linguistics and social semiotics arose out of SFL or that other work in CDA has drawn upon it – SFL theorizes language in a way which harmonizes far more with the perspective of critical social science than other theories of language.

While there are undoubtedly other theoretical models that are also critical, SFL is useful for CDA precisely because it sees language as meaningful behaviour and interprets language as a process of making meanings: 'it is not only text (what people mean) but also the semantic system (what they can mean) that embodies the ambiguity, antagonism, imperfection, inequality and change that characterize the social system and the social structure' (Halliday, 1978: 114). It is because SFL provides insights into the ways in which language is socially constructed and embedded in culture that it becomes useful for its application in CDA.

One of the most important claims of SFL is that language is a resource for making three types of meaning or 'metafunctions' at a time:

1. Language is used to organize, understand and express our perceptions of the world. This function is called the *ideational* function. In analysing this function we would be asking ourselves how is the social world represented? Who is presented as responsible for actions in important events (e.g. wars)? How are beliefs and ideologies encoded in language?
2. Language is also used to enable us to communicate with other people, to take on roles (e.g. expert – lay person, parent – child, teacher – student) and to express and understand feelings, attitudes and judgements. This is called the *interpersonal* function. Questions we might ask here are what kind of relationship is expressed between speakers or between readers and text, for example, between universities and students in student prospectuses? Is the discourse formal or informal?
3. Finally, language is used to create coherent and cohesive texts, both spoken and written. This *textual* function concerns how bits of information are foregrounded or backgrounded, taken as given or presented as new, chosen as 'topic' or 'theme'. What interests us here is not just what aspects of information are foregrounded or backgrounded but also why this happens (e.g. the foregrounding of a business model for Higher Education).

These simultaneous meanings can be identified in linguistic units of all sizes: in words, phrases, clauses, sentences and texts. They are not there accidentally, according to Halliday, they are there because those are the three types of meaning people need to make with each other and they are related to a particular grammatical system.

These three metafunctions of language are realized in three more or less independent systems at the sentence or clause level.

1. The system of *Transitivity,* involving 'processes' (= verbs), 'participants' (= nouns) and 'circumstances' (= prepositional phrases) relates to the ideational metafunction.
2. The system of *Mood,* involving types of clause structure (declarative, interrogative), degrees of certainty or obligation, use of tags, attitudinal words, politeness markers, etc.) relates to interpersonal meaning.
3. The system of *Theme,* involving patterns of foregrounding of certain elements in texts, relates to textual meaning. Together, these three

systems represent the meaning potential of a language, from which the language user makes contextually motivated choices. We shall now look at the three grammatical systems of Transitivity, Mood and Theme in more detail. These categories will be used in the analysis of institutional discourse in the chapters that follow, particularly in Chapter 3.

Transitivity: ideational function

The description of the ideational strand of meaning involves one major category, that of Transitivity. Transitivity has been a focus of attention in Critical Linguistics (Fowler et al., 1979) and CDA (e.g. Fairclough, 1992). The idea behind analysing Transitivity is to explore what social, cultural, ideological and political factors determine what Process type (verb) is chosen in a particular type of discourse. Relations of power may be implicitly inscribed by the relationship between *Actor* and *Goal*: 'processes' can be active, as in

Table 1.1 Transitivity: process types and participants

Process type	Participants	Example (process types in italics; participants in bold)
Material	Actor (A), Goal (G) Beneficiary (B)	**She** (A) *moved* **the table**. (G) **He** (A) *gave* **me** (B) **a present**. (G)
Mental	Senser (Se), Phenomenon (P)	**He** (Se) *saw* **the accident**. (P)
Behavioural	Behaver (B), Phenomenon	**They** (B) *watched* **the game**. (P) **Peter** (Be) *smiled*.
Verbal	Sayer (S) Sayer, Verbiage (V)	**Mary** (S) *didn't reply*. **Mary** (S) *said* **this wasn't true**. (V)
Relational: (1) Attributive	Carrier (C), Attribute (A)	**Helen** (C) *was* **clever**. (A) (not reversible: 'clever was Helen')
(2) Identifying	Token (T), Value (V)	**Oxford** (T) *is* **the best university**. (V) (reversible: 'The best university is Oxford')
Existential	Existent (E)	**There** *were* **many changes**. (E)

'Police (Actor) shot demonstrators' (Goal), or passive, as in

'Demonstrators (Goal) were shot by police' (Actor).

In passive constructions, the actor may be deleted, as in

'Demonstrators were shot'.

In media reports of important events, this can be significant, because it means that agency and responsibility can either be made clear or left vague. The systemic view of language emphasizes that the grammar of a language is a system of 'options' from which speakers choose according to social circumstances, and that the choice of certain linguistic forms always has a meaning. This makes it not only a powerful basis for analysing what is *in* texts, but also for what is *absent* or *omitted* from them. In media accounts of 'riots', responsibility of authorities and police may be systematically omitted, leaving agency and responsibility implicit, for example, by use of passive constructions and nominalizations (Fowler et al., 1979; Fowler, 1991). This is what is meant by news not being a mere reflection of reality, but a product shaped by political, economic and cultural forces.

The transitivity of a clause is its process type (verb), of which there are six: *material, mental, behavioural, verbal, existential and relational*. Table 1.1 is a summary of Transitivity.

It has to be said that these processes and participant types do have no particular (ideological) function out of context. But, as we can see from the examples above, the relationship between *Actor* and *Goal* can be ideologically significant if agency is backgrounded, obscured ('Demonstrators were shot by police') or completely omitted ('Demonstrators were shot'). So one of the most important ways in which language can represent power is through manipulation of agency at the grammatical level. This can be achieved through the use of nominalization (turning verb processes into nouns), as in 'investment', 'adaptability', 'problem-solving', 'change orientation', 'The *introduction* of variable tuition fees marked a new era in Higher Education provision', where agency is omitted. Relational processes ('be', 'have', 'represent', 'mark', etc.) are often used in discourse presenting 'facts' as they suggest a certain certainty ('It *is* the University's policy to enhance the employability and capability of all our students').

Modality: interpersonal function

Modality has to do with the different ways in which people can temper or qualify their messages and express attitudes and judgments of various kinds. If we employ a fairly broad notion of modality, as in

Fairclough (1992: 158–62), we may include any unit of language that expresses the writer's/speaker's affinity with what s/he writes/says. Therefore modality can be said to adopt a variety of grammatical forms, such as modal verbs ('can', 'must', 'should', etc.); modal adverbs ('obviously', 'clearly', 'probably', 'possibly', 'perhaps', 'definitely', with their equivalent adjectives 'it is likely'/probable/possible that, etc.); copular verbs ('is', 'seems', 'appears') and verbs of cognition ('I think/believe/feel'). These all express the speaker's/writer's judgment regarding the relevance of the message. Modality can also express certainty and strong obligation ('high' modality: 'must', 'should', 'always', 'definitely') or uncertainty and weak obligation ('low' modality: 'could', 'maybe', 'possibly', 'sort of').

Theme: textual function

The definition of Theme as given by Halliday (1985: 38) is that it is the element which serves as 'the point of departure of the message: it is that with which the clause is concerned'. Theme typically contains familiar or 'given' information, that is, information which has already appeared somewhere, or is familiar from the context. For example, in the sentence '*Loughborough* is an enterprise-rich university', 'Loughborough' is the given information or Theme, which always comes first in the clause. The remainder of the message, '. . . *is an enterprise-rich university*', the part in which the Theme is developed, is called the 'Rheme'. It typically contains unfamiliar or 'new' information.

If the Theme of a declarative sentence is also the subject, as in the sentence above, then the Theme choice is neutral or 'unmarked', that is, it has no special prominence. However, when a different clause element is Theme (e.g. an adverbial phrase) it becomes 'marked' and gains a greater textual prominence. The following example contains a marked Theme:

> *A world-renowned centre of excellence*, Oxford understands and values its increasingly important role in the powerhouse of the nation's economy.

Writers choose marked Themes to add coherence and emphasis to their texts. But the choice of a marked Theme can also serve an ideological function. In the example above, which comes from a website of the University of Oxford, the University advertises itself to its potential customers, the students, stressing that its status places it in a particularly privileged position to fulfil its increasingly market-oriented role. These (imposed) market-oriented values are informed by a managerialist ideology, in which education has become a commodity with the primary aim of making students employable.

Lexical items and lexical cohesion

The selection of vocabulary or lexical items, whether seemingly neutral or emotionally loaded, signals the speaker's or writer's attitude about a certain topic. Lexical items are therefore the most obvious and most thoroughly studied forms of (ideological) expression. In the words of Richardson (2007: 47), 'words convey the imprint of society and of value judgments in particular – they convey connoted as well as denoted meanings'.

Lexical cohesion refers to the lexical and semantic means of linking sentences together (Halliday and Hasan, 1976) and is not simply an objective and neutral property of texts. For instance, ideology can be expressed at the semantic level through the choice of one word over another. An example of an ideologically based lexicalization is the choice of 'prison riot' over 'prisoner protest' in news coverage following prisoner protest at various British prisons in the late 1980s, thereby denying the possible legitimacy of these acts.

Lexical cohesion can be achieved through simple repetition of words in texts and the linking of words and expressions in meaning relations, such as synonyms or near synonyms (sameness of meaning), as in *enterprising/innovative/entrepreneurial*; and antonyms (two or more lexical items having a different meaning), as in *enterprising universities/'do-nothing' universities*).

Intertextuality

In CDA, textual analysis involves both linguistic and intertextual analysis. Intertextuality refers to the way in which discourses are 'always connected to other discourses which were produced earlier as well as those which are produced synchronically or subsequently' (Fairclough and Wodak, 1997: 276). Institutions develop and change over time and so do their discourses. So if we want to understand the reasons for institutional practices we need to look at the development of certain discourses within that institution over time.

Intertextuality is of particular concern to CDA because of its preoccupation with the transformation of institutional discourse practices ('orders of discourse') and the colonization of one discourse practice by another. 'Orders of discourse' (a term appropriated from Foucault) refer to different ways of writing and talking in different institutional settings, such as schools, universities, government agencies, the family, etc.

In the institutional setting of a university, for example, discourse types would include teacher-student interaction, written communication between the university authorities and the tutors, the language of staff meetings, job advertisements, etc. Examples of intertextuality would be the inclusion of terms and expressions of managerial or corporate discourses in the various discourses at universities. For example, the design of university prospectuses can be said to reflect pressures on universities to 'sell' their courses, using discourse techniques borrowed from advertising, so that the boundaries between information ('The University was founded in 1900 and currently has 15,000 students') and persuasion ('The University is set in a *beautiful* 200 acre parkland campus'; 'Graduates of the University are *greatly in demand by employers*') are blurred. This inevitably results in a more 'consumer-oriented' relationship between students and universities, for better or for worse.

New discourse practices and discourse mixes are always a sign of and an important factor in discursive and cultural change. The resulting hybrid discourses are an example of what Bernstein (1990) has termed 'recontextualization'. This concept allows us to show how the discourses of one social practice are 'recontextualized', that is, drawn upon and incorporated, into another. In this way, the incorporation of managerialist discourses into the university and other public institutions can be seen as a recontextualization of managerial discourses and models and in the wider sense of the new capitalist and neo-liberal order.

We will return to the concept of recontextualization in Chapter 5, where we discuss how the social practice of multiculturalism is recontextualized in news discourse.

The structure of the book

In this opening chapter we have begun to establish the concepts and approaches that are core to this volume. These are developed throughout the following chapters based on specific institutional contexts.

Chapter 2 discusses the increasing orientation of universities towards a managerial model for running universities as businesses which compete for student numbers, and places in league tables by 'selling' knowledge and education. This has resulted in major institutional and discursive changes manifested most clearly in business-related vocabulary. The rhetoric of the market is now firmly embedded in the discursive repertoire of academic leaders, informs university policy documents on teaching and learning, and therefore influences relations between university management and staff who in the discursive hegemony of the market are increasingly constructed as self-motivated and 'enterprising' individuals.

Chapter 3 examines the way that prisons and their discourses of rehabilitation serve to legitimize broader societal ideologies where crime is blamed on the individual and not on structural factors such as poverty, deprivation and lack of opportunity through education and work. This chapter describes a move within the crime control system towards a managerial approach to imprisonment and offender rehabilitation and demonstrates how the institutional discourse of a cognitive-behavioural rehabilitation programme for offenders justifies intervention by constructing individual offenders as cognitively deficient. A vocabulary of helping and treating is used by 'experts' to define, categorize and restrict 'clients', who are deemed 'irresponsible' and 'irrational' due to a lack of cognitive skills. The Course does not address the social contexts in which crime occurs, focusing instead on the individual offender and his or her supposed defects. It thereby helps to reproduce the current neo-liberal and managerialist discourses of crime control promoted by governments over the past two decades.

Chapter 4 turns to media discourse to show that media organizations are oriented to produce particular representations of the world due to institutionalized practices which align them to particular kinds of sources and ideological frames. The chapter demonstrates that news texts can only be understood in the context of these practices. The chapter looks at the way that commercial changes have swept the newsroom, leading to certain kinds of texts that are generated with the consumer in mind. News organizations have historically come to rely on a limited range of news values, that determine what becomes news more so than the events themselves. But these have now become integrated with the need to meet advertiser-oriented market groups. The chapter shows how the images and footage we frequently see in news is also partly explained by these commercial changes as much comes from commercial archives. The result is that news becomes increasingly bound up with pre-existing frames of reference. We cannot understand the nature of the language of news texts without understanding these processes.

Chapter 5 is concerned with how the news media recontextualize social practices. Again we see how the media try to conceal structural issues such as poverty, deprivation and unemployment. In this case the chapter shows how the practice of multiculturalism becomes recontextualized in a British 'model' regional newspaper that has moved towards a positive representation of immigration and multicultural cohesion. But this model of multiculturalism and antiracism has to be understood primarily as part of the commercial role of the newspaper to promote an image of the city as a business and investment centre. What this means in practice, is that multiculturalism becomes recontextualized in a form that is disconnected from socio-economic issues that often lie behind marginalization and racial conflict. Instead, multiculturalism is represented as involving the communities talking to each other and 'sharing' culture and festivals. Conflict is a result not of unemployment and deprivation, but of choice and failure to communicate. Stripped of this important detail, this model deflects responsibility away from authorities, from broader social organization and economic issues onto individuals. The discourses therefore remove the role of the government in social welfare and merge multiculturalism with discourses of consumer choice and individual responsibility.

Chapter 6 is concerned with the ways that discourses of war commemoration have become institutionalized in British society. The chapter shows how the authorities and powerful groups in society were concerned about the working-class reaction to the First World War in the context of rising Bolshevism throughout Europe. As well as linguistically representing the pointless squalid deaths of millions of young working-class men in terms of sacrifice to God and country, these discourses were represented visually by the building of monuments throughout Britain. These monuments and the discourses of which they are a part are still alive in present day commemorations where we hear military and nationalistic music and see modern day soldiers in regimentals along with national leaders. This chapter looks at the history of the building of the monuments along with the political decision-making and fear that was part of this. Then it goes on to provide a multimodal discourse analysis of the monuments themselves. It shows that the monuments have helped to institutionalize discourses not found linguistically but which equally powerfully serve to justify war and protect the interests of the powerful in society.

Chapter 7 presents a corpus methodology of the analysis of defence speeches by the American military. The chapter offers a critical analysis of the speeches showing the strategies used to align the interests of the military to those of ordinary decent citizens. It shows the use of metaphor in the speeches to obscure concrete political and ideological issues. But as well as revealing some of the linguistic techniques used by the military the aim of the chapter is to show how corpus analysis can be one useful approach for the process of CDA. It considers some criticisms of CDA that only a handful of texts are chosen that may support the kind of conclusions intended by the analyst. In response, it shows that it may be useful to carry out corpus analysis where we compare large collections of data against language use in standard English, looking for comparisons of frequency of specific lexical choices, for example. This allows a more systematic and less ideologically guided approach to institutional texts.

Chapter 8, the final chapter, offers some guidance on designing projects for analysing institutional discourses, provides a brief overview of qualitative and quantitative methods of analysis and makes some suggestions for corpus analysis. The advice is mainly intended for final-year undergraduate and MA students, although Doctoral students may find some of the suggestions for research useful too.

2 Discourses of higher education: Enterprise and institutional change in the university

Andrea Mayr

Introduction

Since the 1980s, universities in Britain and elsewhere have increasingly come under pressure to operate like commercial companies, competing with each other to attract the highest number of students and interacting with both staff and students in ways that were earlier more characteristic of business and commerce. These changes, first introduced by the Thatcher government, but continued and expanded during the years of New Labour, have resulted in far-reaching structural, cultural and discursive changes at universities. The rhetoric necessary to effect these institutional changes has been provided by the 'discourse of enterprise', a form of strategic, managerial discourse, which has been heavily influenced by the 'enterprise culture' (Keat and Abercrombie, 1991), a term often used to describe more recent economic, political and social shifts in late modern Western capitalist societies. 'Enterprise discourse' can now be detected in many areas of social life, as it has been transported from political discourse, mainly Labour's 'Third Way discourse' (Fairclough, 2000) into the public services in general, the health services, the criminal justice system (see Chapter 3) and Higher Education.

Cuts in government funding and the concomitant reliance of universities on external, often corporate, funding sources have resulted in universities adopting a form of 'enterprising managerialism', which in turn has been promoted by New Labour's pro-market managerialist educational agenda (e.g. Blunkett, 2000). For example, in 2001, the then Chancellor Gordon Brown spoke of the need 'to spread the spirit of enterprise from the classroom to the boardroom' and the vital role universities had to play in generating ideas and providing high-level skills crucial for Britain's productivity and growth: 'If we are to have the deeper and wider entrepreneurial culture we need, we must start in our schools and colleges'. He further stated that

> We want every young person to hear about business and enterprise in school, every college student to be made aware of the opportunities in business – and to start a business, every teacher to be able to communicate the virtues and potential of business and enterprise. (http://news.bbc.co.uk/1/hi/education/1394674.stm, 18 June 2001)

The Government therefore sees its role in creating an 'enterprise culture' by delivering through the state education system the skills and qualities companies will want their 'enterprising' workers to have. And while the teaching of 'knowledge' used to be the area of expertise of schools and universities, it is now the business world that increasingly dictates what type of knowledge is necessary for 'self-managing knowledge workers' (Jacques, 1998: 270), who through 'life-long learning' are expected to continually adapt, change and learn new skills. As universities become more and more drawn into new capitalist business practices and discourses, they are also compelled to adopt modes of learning and teaching that are in line with these practices.

In this chapter, we will look at some of the institutional 'enterprise' discourse practices that continue to develop in the social and cultural reorganization of universities and which are now pervasive in official documents (mission statements), website information, student prospectuses and the teaching of academic and non-academic staff in 'communication skills'. First, however, it is necessary to say a few words about what is meant by the term 'enterprise culture'.

Enterprise culture and discourse

While enterprise culture is generally regarded as the symbol and goal of Thatcherism, it means something broader that has gone beyond the economic, political and institutional reform process of Britain during the years of the Conservative government. From the start, it was also a moral undertaking, in which economic reconstruction was to be supplemented with cultural reconstruction.

Keat (1990) distinguishes two main meanings of the term: the first can be glossed as the Conservative government's programme of economic and institutional reform, evidenced in the transfer of state-owned industries and public utilities to the private sector and the reorganization in the areas of education, health, local government, etc. The task of creating an enterprise culture has therefore involved the reconstruction of a wide range of institutions along business lines, institutions that previously were not run along those lines (in a British context, these are the railway network, hospitals, schools and universities). This process was characterized by the adoption of specific marketing techniques and the discourses associated with them, particularly a focus on and reference to the 'consumer', a term that has more or less displaced the words 'student', 'patient' or 'client'. Meeting the demands of the consumer has become the overriding institutional imperative and even universities now tend to regard their students more as 'consumers' who get 'value for money' with the courses they choose. Keat (1990: 12–13) regards this assimilation of universities to the commercial enterprise and the 'appeal to consumer sovereignty' as 'politically double-edged', since the 'inequalities of "consumer-power" generated by the free market are at odds with the supposed equality of democratic citizens'. What was previously a 'right' has now become a commodity with all its implications for justice and equality. What, for example, will the introduction of the market into the educational system mean for people who have little or no economic and political power? Those in favour of enterprising universities, on the other hand, refer to the need to make universities and other educational institutions more accountable, arguing that according students the status of consumers has the effect of giving them more rights and more control over the course of their studies and not less.

To understand what is implied by the construction of an enterprise culture, the second, quite distinct, meaning of the term needs to be explained. In this second meaning, enterprise culture defines the conduct of the individual, who should develop and exhibit 'enterprising' qualities, such as personal responsibility, independence, resourcefulness and self-discipline, all regarded as human and moral values in an enterprise culture. As Keat (1990: 3–4) remarks, in the discourse of enterprise, the 'institutional' and the 'ethical' are intimately linked. And not only are individuals expected to behave like this in the public sphere, but they are even to extend these qualities to their private lives. This has gone hand in hand with enterprise culture and its discourses shifting responsibilities from the state to the individual. People are now expected to work on their selves to make themselves happier, healthier, more productive and successful (e.g. by acquiring 'job-getting skills').

To make them more enterprising, people also have to receive training in these 'enterprising' qualities. Hence the introduction of government schemes such as 'Enterprise in Education' and of now wide-spread institutional practices such as assertiveness and management training, student-centred learning, non-directive counselling, etc., all of which are in many ways congruent with the political rhetoric of enterprise: the (discursive) construction of an active, self-motivated, 'enterprising' individual who monitors his or her performance on the road to success.

It is important to note though that enterprise culture is not simply a matter of the government imposing business values and practices on 'non-economic' institutions. It also represents a *culture* change within business from bureaucratic to 'entrepreneurial' styles of management and to 'the new forms of work-based identity it tries to forge among all members of an organization' (du Gay, 1996: 57). What is more, enterprise has become an approach capable 'of addressing the totality of human behaviour, and thus, of envisaging a coherent, purely economic method of programming the totality of governmental action' (Gordon, 1991: 43; quoted in du Gay, 1996: 57). It now permeates management discourse, which in turn has colonized the discourse of universities and many other public institutions.

It is in this socio-political context that the 'enterprising' or 'entrepreneurial university' is embedded.

The entrepreneurial university

The term 'entrepreneurial university', a 'previously unthinkable adjective-noun combination' (Mautner: 2005: 96) can be attributed to Clark's (1998) definitive account on the restructuring of universities for the twenty-first century. Clark (ibid.: 3–4) defines 'entrepreneurial' in the following terms:

> 'Entrepreneurial' is taken . . . as a characteristic of social systems; that is, of entire universities and their internal departments, research centers, faculties, and schools. The concept carries the overtones of 'enterprise' – a willful effort in institution-building that requires much special activity and energy . . . An entrepreneurial university . . . seeks to work out a substantial shift in organizational character so as to arrive at a more promising posture for the future. . . . Institutional entrepreneurship can be seen as both process and outcome.

As we shall see below, the terms 'enterprising' and 'entrepreneurial' are often used together in the texts universities use to describe and advertise themselves. To arrive at 'a more promising posture for the future', universities need to display 'enterprising' qualities. So while 'entrepreneurial' refers more specifically to business acumen, 'enterprising' also includes a more general innovativeness (Mautner, 2005: 103–4).

Critical (linguistic) research, notably by Fairclough (1992; 1993; 2001) Trowler (2001), Webster (2003), Owen (2004) and Mautner (2005) has drawn attention to and examined the 'marketization' of the university sector and the 'entrepreneurial university'. Whereas Chouliaraki and Fairclough (1999) have referred to these trends as a 'colonization' of academia by the market and its discourse practices, Mautner (2005: 106) argues that academic entrepreneurialism goes beyond mere commercialization and is 'a pervasive institutional transformation, targeting staff and students, and aiming to achieve in them not just behavioural, but also cognitive and "emotional" changes'. A good example of this is the following statement from a website of the University of Oxford, stating (perhaps worryingly) that 'Oxford seeks to foster a culture of entrepreneurialism *at all levels and within all disciplines*' (emphasis added). The website further informs that

> Among UK universities, Oxford is at the forefront of *encouraging enterprise among students, teachers and researchers*. It prides itself on its success in transforming enquiry and invention into *commercial ventures* that create innovative products, new skills, jobs and wealth. A world-renowned centre of excellence, Oxford understands and values its increasingly important and *dynamic role in the powerhouse of the nation's economy* (www.ox.ac.uk/aboutoxford/community.shtml; emphasis added).

This shows how firmly embedded the spirit of enterprise is in current university discourse and practice. One might think that it is the 'post 1992' 'new' universities, which started out as Polytechnics and have been traditionally more vocationally oriented that are more 'entrepreneurial' than the older and more prestigious universities. However, as the above example demonstrates, it is often the older universities which, because of their status, are in a better position to pursue their entrepreneurial aspirations (Mautner, 2005).

The four texts analysed here are taken from British universities, but the phenomenon of enterprising/entrepreneurial universities is by no means limited to Britain. In recent decades, universities around the world have been undergoing sweeping changes which can be described as a trend towards 'the adoption of a free-market or corporate-business perspective' (Webster, 2003: 85), with implications for teaching, research and administration. As the linguistic analysis of four texts from British universities will demonstrate, this 'corporate-business perspective is evident in universities' websites (e.g. their mission statements), in job advertisements for academics, and in communication training for academic and non-academic staff.

Text 1

Text 1, taken from the website of Loughborough University, in the East Midlands of England, contains the first two paragraphs from the welcoming message by the Vice-Chancellor. It is an affirmation of the institutional values Loughborough subscribes to and at the same time an exercise in self-promotion. This is how the Vice Chancellor describes the University:

1. Loughborough University is a dynamic, forward looking institution, committed to being a centre of excellence in teaching, learning and enterprise. We have much to be proud of – surveys

in the media consistently rate Loughborough as a top university. In June 2006 the Times Good University Guide ranked Loughborough University the sixth highest university in the UK, the highest outside Oxbridge and London. In September 2005 Loughborough was again short listed for University of the Year by the Sunday Times, and, most recently in November 2006 Loughborough was voted Best Student Experience out of 97 UK universities by the Times Higher Awards.
2. The introduction of variable tuition fees marked a new era in Higher Education provision. By committing to do a university degree, you are making a vital investment in your future. The University is pleased to offer a range of bursaries to support those in financial need and widen participation in higher education, as well as scholarships to help students who choose to study selected subjects. However, we appreciate that you will want to be reassured that you are getting value for your money.
3. At Loughborough we can demonstrate that our graduates do gain rewards over and above their financial investment. The University is ranked among the best universities for graduate employment, with our graduates being consistently targeted by the UK's top recruiters.[. . . .]
4. Loughborough is an enterprise-rich University, proud of its strong links with industry, commerce and the professions and with a long history of international research. This cutting-edge research, designed to solve real world problems and improve quality of life, informs the teaching content of many degrees, directly benefiting students. (www.lboro.ac.uk/prospectus/ug/general/university/welcome/index.htm; paragraph numbers added)

One of the first things to notice in this text is that the University advertises itself as a desirable product, using positive lexis, such as '*dynamic*', '*forward looking*', which can be said to be near-synonyms of 'enterprising'. It uses superlatives ('the *sixth highest* university in the UK, the *highest* outside Oxbridge and London') and describes itself as a '*centre of excellence*' in the three areas of 'teaching, learning and *enterprise*'. One might expect 'research' as the third area of excellence, since this has traditionally been one of the pillars of a 'good' university. The university also invokes authority by quoting external sources that testify to its excellence ('*The Times Good University Guide*'), thereby adding to its market value. Quality is assessed from elsewhere rather than being a claim that universities can make for themselves ('*The Times Good University Guide ranked Loughborough University the sixth highest university in the UK . . .*'). This is also expressed grammatically by 'Loughborough being made the *Goal* of sentences e.g. ('Loughborough (Goal) was again short listed . . . by the Sunday Times' (Actor)). The fact that Loughborough was voted '*Best Student Experience*' by the Times Higher Awards testifies how serious the University is about its customer-focused approach to students.

The second paragraph broaches a more serious topic, the introduction of 'variable' tuition fees. The sentence '*The introduction of variable tuition fees marked a new era in Higher Education provision*' does not mention the Government, who are behind the introduction of tuition fees. The active material process 'introduce' has been turned into a nominalization, 'the introduction', which attenuates the feeling of activity and at the same time makes for a certain impersonality. Those affected by the introduction, students, are mentioned only in the sentences that follow and then it is to reassure them that the university has the financial means to assist poorer ('*those in financial need*') students. Fairclough (2003) notes that the choice of a relational process, in this case 'to mark' (a near-synonym of 'to be') instead of an active material process ('to introduce') can remove important political implications, in this case camouflaging the active role of the Government. Instead, the introduction of study fees is represented metaphorically as 'marking a new era', which sounds almost positive or at least has a certain sense of inevitability about it.

In terms of interpersonal relations, the use of pronouns is revealing. In the first three paragraphs the text veers between presenting Loughborough formally as an institution ('*the University*') and personalizing it by the use of first person 'we', constructing a corporate identity for it. Students are on the one hand made part of the enterprise by the use of the possessive pronoun 'our' ('At Loughborough, we demonstrate that *our* students do get rewards . . .). On the other hand, students are also addressed as potential customers and individuals by the use of second person singular 'you'. ('By committing to do a university degree, *you* are making a vital investment . . .'; 'However, we appreciate that *you* will want to be assured that *you* are getting value for *your* money'). Fairclough (1989) has termed this use of informal 'you' in mass communication, particularly advertising, as 'synthetic personalization', a simulated personal address in an attempt to handle masses of people, that is, students, as if they were individuals.

Paragraph 4 finally describes Loughborough as an 'enterprise-rich' University. Here the text reverts to its more formal tone, representing 'the University' again as an institution. Although the text as a whole presents Loughborough as an 'enterprising' and pro-entrepreneurial university, (it is replete with business and enterprise buzzwords, such as 'dynamic', 'forwardlooking', 'value for your money', 'rewards over and above their financial investment', 'enterprise-rich', etc.), pointing to its 'long-standing links with industry and the professions' it is also careful to retain a kinder and more compassionate image, offering support to 'those in financial need' and attempting to attract students from lower socio-economic groups ('... *widen participation*'). Equally important, though, is its 'no-nonsense', vocational-oriented approach to university education, which benefits students '*directly*' by enhancing their chances of immediate employment due to the University's '*strong links with industry* . . .', of which it is 'proud'. As Mautner (2005) points out, universities are now at pains to stress that they are no longer unaccountable and otherworldly 'ivory towers', but firmly rooted in today's world with '*cutting-edge* research, designed to solve *real world* problems', therefore '*directly* benefiting students'.

Loughborough's 'enterprising' attitude is also expressed grammatically in the use of active material processes, such as '*demonstrate*', '*solve*', '*improve*', '*offer*', '*support*', '*help*', although on the whole relational processes (to 'be' and synonyms; to 'have') dominate, lending the text an impersonal and uncontestable factual tone and constructing the University as a serious corporate body ('Loughborough *is* . . .'; 'we *have* much to be proud of'). In line with this being a rather formal text, there are also many noun constructions (*'enterprise', 'centre of excellence', 'industry', 'commerce'*) and nominalizations (*'teaching', 'learning', 'introduction', 'provision', 'investment', 'participation', 'employment'*). The pattern of nominalizations together with the mention of abstract qualities, such as 'best student experience', 'rewards over and above their financial investment', contribute to the construction of education as 'product' rather than process, of which students are beneficiaries.

To sum up, by using positive lexis reminiscent of advertising the University presents itself as a marketable commodity and at the same time, while careful to retain a 'caring' image with its students, also constructs them as potential customers ('. . . you are making a *vital investment in your future*'). We could also say that students are turned into 'marketable products', '*being consistently targeted by the UK's top recruiters*'.

Text 2

Text 2 is taken from the Employability Policy and Strategy (2005–2008) document of the University of Salford, Manchester. Like Lougborough, Salford 'prides itself on being an innovative and enterprising university with a real world focus – so research and teaching concentrate on issues that directly affect people's daily lives'. (www.salford.ac.uk/about/special/enterprising)

> Employability Policy and Strategy (2005–2008)
>
> As an Enterprising University it is our goal to produce graduates with the skills, creativity, confidence and adaptability to succeed in the labour market and to make a meaningful contribution to society. [...]
>
> It is the University's policy to enhance the employability and capability of all our students to enable them to thrive in a competitive, knowledge-based, global economy.
>
> Principles: Our Employability Policy and Strategy are shaped by our Learning and Teaching Strategy and by the following principles:
>
> Employability and Enterprise: The University of Salford's Learning and Teaching Strategy places significant importance on enterprise in our approach to learning and teaching. We recognize Salford's distinctive strengths in this regard, that consideration of employability in the Salford context must also embrace enterprise and entrepreneurship and that whilst *enterprise and entrepreneurship* may be most manifest in the form of self-employment, the creativity, problem solving and change orientation implied is also relevant to those working *within* organizations. (University of Salford, Employability Policy and Strategy 2005–2008; www.tal.salford.ac.uk/documents/Employability_PS_Final.doc; emphasis in original)

Just as the previous text, this text is replete with business-related lexis (e.g. '*competitive*', '*employability*', '*thrive*'). Like a commercial company producing goods, Salford's role is to '*produce* graduates with the skills, creativity, confidence and adaptability to succeed in the labour market'. Does this mean that only knowledge that helps graduates 'succeed' in the labour market is useful knowledge? If learning and teaching is predominantly geared to the labour market, is the teaching and acquisition of non-utilitarian knowledge, which has been one of the more traditional purviews of universities, now obsolete? 'Creativity and confidence' is coupled with '*adaptability*', another buzzword in the new capitalism. As Gee et al. (1996: 19) point out, in the fast-changing environment of the new capitalism, 'workers must be "eager to stay" but also "ready to leave"'. An 'adaptable', 'flexible' and multi-skilled workforce is needed, so that in an economic downturn labour can be reduced and taken back on again if demand rises. The moral and social implications of these business practices, such as increasing job insecurity for employees, are omitted from a discourse that is based on pragmatism and instrumentalism. As Cameron (2000: 12) puts it, 'the capitalist's flexibility is the worker's insecurity'.

Not only is it university policy to enhance the employability of students, but also to 'enable them *to thrive in a competitive, knowledge-based, global economy*'. The term 'knowledge-based' economy (or 'knowledge-driven' economy) is highly ideological, as it implies that it is 'knowledge' that shapes the direction of the market, whereas it is 'the social relations that characterise the economy (and specifically the forces and relations of production)' that 'direct and shape knowledge' (Richardson, 2007: 33). This can be observed in the example above and in the use of language at universities in general, the discursive construction of students as consumers with enterprising and entrepreneurial skills and Departments as producers of capable graduates ('. . . it is our goal to *produce* graduates . . .'). At the level of university policy and practice, this is evidenced in the introduction of tuition fees 'in line with classic demand-supply economic logic' (ibid.: 33).

Here the hegemonic aspirations of neo-liberal business-speak become apparent: global economic change is represented as an inevitable process; it is an assumed and taken-for-granted background against which university graduates (and employees in general) must compete for jobs in the global market place. But what about students who are not comfortable with the proposed business model, who do not want to 'thrive' in a competitive global economy? It is one of the features of neo-liberalism to claim 'universal status for this particular representation and vision of economic change' (Fairclough, 2003: 45). Other representations of this economic order might focus on the injustices and inequalities created in the 'global' job market. Absent also is a conceptualization of students as 'real, diverse, responsive individuals who might react in different ways to the policies proposed. Instead, we are offered the totalizing category of the "market" and "market need"' (Trowler, 2001: 187). What matters most these days is that Universities 'enhance the *employability and capability*' of students.

The final paragraph stresses Salford's vocational approach to education and the significance of 'enterprise' in it. Here '*enterprise and entrepreneurship*' are named together and in italics to emphasize Salford's strong commitment to 'enterprise'. Strong obligation is placed on the university ('. . . *must* embrace enterprise and entrepreneurship). Although it concedes that enterprising qualities are more important '*in the form of self employment*', the reader is left in no doubt that these are necessary requirements for 'all those working organizations'. Those who have to be 'change-oriented' are mentioned ('all those working *within* organizations'), but they are kind of backgrounded. This is also expressed grammatically in the text by making students the beneficiaries of actions performed by the university ('it is our goal to produce *graduates*'); 'It is the University's policy . . . to enable *them* to thrive.

In terms of interpersonal relations, the University is again at times personalized by the use of first person 'we' and the possessive 'our' ('*our* goal is . . .'), and students also are part of the enterprise ('. . . all *our* students'). There is no direct engagement with students, they are not directly addressed. This is because the text is an official document. Hence the high number of nouns ('*creativity*', '*employability*') and nominalizations ('*problem-solving*', '*change orientation*', '*learning and teaching*'), some of which are typical new capitalist buzzwords, which background agency. These are coupled with mostly active material processes ('produce', 'succeed', 'make', 'enable', 'place importance on', 'embrace') that exemplify Salford's 'enterprising' character.

Text 3

Text 3 is an extract from a job description for the post of Lecturer in English and Educational Studies at Sheffield Hallam University from the year 2006, taken from the academic recruitment website jobs.ac.uk. Four paragraphs from the 'Main Duties' section are reproduced here, which outline the requirements for the future postholder:

> Research and Scholarly Activity
>
> Identifies and conducts research and scholarly activity which is relevant to the lecturing role. Integrates research into teaching and learning. Identifies opportunities for income generation and entrepreneurialism through research, consultancy or professional practice.
>
> Team Work and Communication
>
> Works effectively with colleagues at all levels and contributes to the achievement of team objectives. Develops collaborative relationships across teams and between Schools/Departments. Maintains dialogue with managers in the performance of post responsibilities. Develops network of useful contacts both within and outside the University.
>
> Personal effectiveness
>
> Seeks ways to improve efficiency and quality and motivates and encourages others. Contributes to achievement of organizational goals.
>
> Business effectiveness
>
> Engages in income generation and develops an understanding of marketing and business needs. Contributes to business enhancement and maintenance of customer-focus.

The first paragraph, 'Research and Scholarly Activity', starts off with one of the traditional requirements for academic staff, namely, to engage in scholarly research and, ideally, to make their teaching research-led. It then becomes clear, however, that research is being subjected to commercial pressures in that the future postholder is expected to identify '*opportunities for income generation and entrepreneurialism through research, consultancy or professional practice*'. Some have argued (e.g. Webster, 2003) that to encourage academics to attract external commercial funding may in the long run result in a threat to their intellectual freedom, which includes the freedom to criticize.

The second paragraph focuses on the importance of 'teamwork'. In the new capitalist work order, employees must take responsibility for their work, usually in teams. 'Teamwork', another buzzword in the new capitalist work order and taken over by the enterprising university, is meant to constitute a move away from hierarchical to supposedly more egalitarian workplace cultures, in which employees all work together for the good of the company. Here, academic and non-academic staff ('*at all levels*') are meant to work together to achieve particular institutional goals ('*team objectives*'). 'Team work' is paired with '*communication*'. Although not specified here, to work successfully in teams, employees are often deemed to be in need of training in the more 'co-operative' ways of communicating, such as negotiation, which should enable them to develop '*networks of useful contacts both within and outside the University*'). Hence the proliferation of 'communication skills' straining in the (university) workplace (see following text).

'Motivation' is another important and desirable quality not only for team work but also for general '*personal effectiveness*'. A good team worker is highly motivated, but also '*motivates and encourages others*'. Implied here is the notion of the 'enterprising' employee. Grammatically this is expressed throughout the text in exclusive use of active material processes (e.g. '*identifies*', '*develops*', *seeks*', '*motivates*', '*contributes*', etc.), all denoting an active and self-motivated 'enterprising' employee.

The sentence '*Contributes to the achievement of organizational goals*' embodies the logic of management discourse: that employees can be made more efficient and productive if they are taught to think like managers and instilled with 'management-chosen values and practices' (Webster, 2003: 87), thereby promoting a strong corporate culture. As du Gay (1996: 62–3) puts it, the aim of management is that staff 'make the goals and objectives of their employing organization their own personal goals and objectives'. That there might be a conflict of interest or cultural differences between management and employees which also involves power issues is ignored.

The requirement '*maintains dialogue with managers in the performance of post responsibilities*' is open to interpretation. While 'maintaining dialogue with managers' sounds very neutral and innocuous, it could also refer to imported new speech events in the university workplace, such as appraisal, a method for evaluating the performance of staff. Fairclough (2001) notes that appraisal is widely resented by university staff because of its representation as apparently oriented to their needs, whereas at the same time personal objectives and needs are adjusted to the institutional goals and objectives of the university, thereby undermining academic freedom.

Reading the final requirement, under the heading *'Business effectiveness'*, one might be forgiven for thinking that this is not an outline for a university post at all, but indeed a commercial company (*'Contributes to business enhancement and maintenance of customer-focus'*).

The whole text is redolent with managerialist vocabulary and tight lexical cohesion is created by repetition of lexical items (*'income generation'*), use of (near) synonyms (*'effectiveness'/'efficiency'*; *'motivates'/'encourages'*; *'achievement of team objectives'/'achievement of organizational goals'*; *'income generation'/'business enhancement'/'entrepreneurialism'*). The stress on 'personal' as well as 'business' effectiveness' seems to serve to counteract the popular notion that universities and the people working within them have been anything but effective in the past.

Text 4

Our last example to illustrate the encroachment of universities with business models is taken from 'negotiation skills training' material used for staff in the university. Although this text is different in that it does not explicitly refer to 'enterprise', it nevertheless is infused with the same business-related lexis and logic and is clearly an importation from the commercial sector. The material presented here includes some of the overheads used and some comments made by the trainer.

'Communication' – in the sense of spoken interaction – and training of staff in communication in particular has become a growing concern in the commercial sector in more recent economic changes. These changes have been brought on by the 'knowledge-driven' economy, in which new knowledge and hence new discourses are continuously produced, circulated and applied as commodities. Knowledge and information are now ordered into what Giddens (1991: 18) has termed 'expert systems': 'modes of technical knowledge which have validity independent of the practitioners and clients who make use of them'. This means that these discourse practices are relatively context-free and as such can be applied to a variety of settings (see also Chapter 3). The training of various 'communication skills', such as assertiveness and negotiation, is one typical example of this trend, where the knowledge of how to conduct communication, including the language to be used, is produced and sold as a commodity by management consultants. Drawing on Foucault, Fairclough (1992: 215) has referred to this kind of discourse as being 'technologized':

> We can usefully refer to 'discourse technologies' and to a 'technologization of discourse' . . . Examples of discourse technologies are interviewing, teaching, counselling and advertising . . . [I]n modern society they have taken on, and are taking on, the character of trans-contextual techniques, which are seen as resources and toolkits that can be used to pursue a wide variety of strategies in many diverse contexts. Discourse technologies . . . are coming to have their own specialist technologists: researchers who look into their efficiency, designers who work out refinements in the light of research and changing institutional requirements, and trainers who pass on their techniques.

Teaching 'communication skills' can be said to qualify as a 'transcontextual technique' with the skills seen as useful and often indispensable for a variety of purposes, situations and institutions. Cameron (2000) points out that the specialists ('discourse technologists') who teach these 'communication skills' are hardly ever linguists, who tend to adopt a *de*scriptive approach to language; their expertise is rarely referred to. Instead, more *pre*scriptive, 'therapeutic' models of communication training are preferred. These suggest that communication training can result in morally and socially advantageous behaviour, such as conflict resolution through assertiveness and enhanced negotiation skills. For example, the 'skills' to be used in 'negotiation' and communication training in general often include 'active' listening and providing 'constructive' feedback, both of which are reminiscent of counselling techniques. So these 'therapeutic' models have become institutionalized in workplace settings that have nothing to do with therapy.

The instructional material presented here is taken from a one-day Negotiation Skills Training Course for academic and non-academic staff at Queen's University in Belfast. It was run by an outside training consultancy, which has a strong working relationship with universities, colleges and research institutes and offers courses in management and office skills, team work and interpersonal skills.

The topics and skills taught were: the ability to 'negotiate'; demonstrating rapport and empathy; asking questions; 'active' listening; avoiding conflict; and interpreting body language. These skills are the focus of many communication training courses designed for different audiences and purposes and are considered to be as important for professional as well as personal life. We now turn to what is said about some of these skills in the negotiation training materials:

'Negotiation' was defined as

- the process by which a mutually acceptable solution is reached between 2 or more parties
- it is about getting the best possible deal in the circumstance
- a social as well as a business skill
- can be learned!

This definition of negotiation and what it is for ('getting the best possible *deal*') is of course based on a business model that is deemed to be applicable to the university context also. Negotiation is a 'skill' which can be acquired. The assumption that 'skills' are detachable from people's individual personalities and can be taught and learned is common in many prescriptive communication training materials. But it is debatable whether it is possible or even desirable, as talk is an expression of people's individual personalities.

For Fairclough (2001: 35), the concept of 'skill', pervasive in the new capitalism, is only 'superficially ethically neutral' and 'can be construed as benefiting people . . . not only in work but also in citizenship and personal relationships' ('a *social* as well as business skill'). But to Fairclough, 'the application of skills in the conduct of social relationships is ethically objectionable' as it 'incorporates and legitimizes a manipulative and instrumentalist relationship to others'. For example, to become 'skilful' negotiators, trainees are advised to show '*rapport and empathy*' by using several behavioural steps:

- open on a neutral subject to allay hostility
- assure the other party of your commitment to a mutually agreeable solution – especially when holding back
- demonstrate respect for the process and the opposition
- explain where you are coming from
- really put yourself in their shoes – understand where they are coming from.

In this way, by '*opening on a neutral subject to allay hostility*', trainees ('delegates') are instructed to use small talk strategically to establish rapport. This can be done by claiming common ground, as in casual conversation, but ultimately serves to make communication 'effective', thereby achieving institutional goals. The last two instructions on the list,' ('*Explain where you are coming from*', and '*Really put yourself in their shoes*') again remind of techniques used in counselling.

Hardly surprising, 'communication' is presented as a 'key skill for negotiators' and is defined as 'the transfer of an idea/information from one individual/group to another'.

According to this rather reductionist model of communication, which sees language simply as an efficient transfer of information, some rules for '*effective* 2-way communication' are to

- ask questions
- listen actively to every word
- speak the same language.

Communications skills training materials often suggest that skilled communicators know how to ask the right questions in order to control the behaviour of other speakers (see Cameron, 2000). Usually a distinction is made between 'open' (wh-questions) and 'closed' ('yes-no'-questions) along with a list of their purposes. According to the overheads, 'Questioning techniques' can be

- Closed
  –elicit facts
  –yes/no questions
- Open
  –elicit information
  –feelings
  –opinions – What? How? Why? etc.
- Probing
  –often takes further e.g. 'in what ways do you think we could . . .'
  –'give me an example of . . .'

It is not surprising that people should receive instructions on the subject of asking questions, since the 'question-answer' routine forms a significant part of talk in institutional settings (Drew and Heritage, 1992). Again, questions should be asked not just to obtain information, but also to demonstrate an interest in the other person, make them feel 'at ease' and make the interaction resemble an informal dialogue, even 'elicit feelings', as if in a counselling session.

The overheads also stress that 'active' listening is yet another skill that can be acquired and that is not only very important for the negotiation process but also '*vital to communication*' and a skill '*we tend to practice* [sic] *rather badly*'. 'Active' listening involves

- eye contact
- mirroring posture and speech
- encouraging
- summarizing
- clarifying.

The view that people are inadequate when it comes to listening appears to be widespread in the communication training literature. Its use of 'explicit or implicit deficit models' (Cameron, 2000: 47) emphasizes the notion that people are deficient in their own language and particularly in listening to talk in their own language. '*Mirroring posture and speech*' and '*encouraging and summarizing*' are another example of the application of therapeutic models of communication as a 'transcontextual technique'.

This intense preoccupation with the regulation of speech patterns and non-verbal behaviour (body language) or the 'aesthetics of verbal interaction' has been referred to by Cameron (2000: 86) as 'styling': staff talk is 'styled' to make it as pleasant and as 'effective' as possible. Talk is strategically used to establish rapport and to reduce interpersonal distance. But as Cameron (2000: 76) remarks, one problem with this 'synthetic personalization' (Fairclough, 1989) is that 'people may perceive it as more synthetic than personal'.

'Avoiding conflict' is regarded as another important skill in negotiation. Trainees are advised not to

- be insulting/provocative
- use time constraints – unless essential
- let the opposition lose face
- say 'gotcha' in any shape or form
- lose sight of the whole deal
- push too hard.

Conflict is therefore seen as undesirable and a sign of inappropriate conversational behaviour, leaving out its possible causes or its possible legitimacy in given situations. According to Cameron (2000: 69), conversational instructional material is 'no tool for understanding what goes on in an interaction, but has an ideological agenda – one that fits particularly well with the goals and values of the enterprising organization'.

Trainees are advised to use 'inclusive' language (such as 'I understand; 'I appreciate') and to use phrases such as

- 'as things stand'
- 'I may be able to help you'
- 'there might be . . .'
- 'I'll be honest with you'
- 'a small point'
- 'frankly'.

These phrases range from 'discourse markers' or minimal responses (e.g. 'frankly'), basically supportive utterances used strategically to enhance the positive outcome of a negotiation.

During the actual training session the trainer commented that 'language and how to use it is key' and that it 'is all about *rehearsing* the language' and that one had 'to use the right language to be attractive'. This shows that the training of negotiation skills, just as other communication skills training, is 'talk strategically designed and inculcated through training' (Fairclough, 2001: 34).

The training session was followed by a negotiation skills role-play which was supposed to demonstrate the 'skilled performance of the "delegates"' who had just received training in negotiation. The group role-play consisted of a situation in which the participants were divided into 'buyers' and 'sellers' and had to negotiate the selling/buying of motorway construction machines. This again demonstrates the implicit belief of the applicability of a business context for negotiation to a completely different setting, in this case a university.

However, how much of this communicative ideal is inculcated and reflected in actual practice is another matter. Both du Gay (1996) and Cameron (2000) comment on the fact that people negotiate and resist (linguistic) behaviours imposed on them by linguistic prescription in the workplace. It is precisely because many people believe that talk is an expression of their individual personality that they regard training in communication skills as only marginally useful (Cameron, 2000).

The above is a good example of how much importance is attached to language and communication in contemporary management contexts. It illustrates the widespread belief (among managers) that linguistic regulation can be used systematically to implement institutional change and to control people. The increased focus on 'acculturation training' is driven by the need of institutions to develop a 'shared mindset' in the workforce and to train employees to their vision, values and culture.

Conclusion

This chapter has provided examples of the increasingly marketized and managerialist orientation of many British universities, expressed and (re) produced in a variety of their discourses. These espouse a reductionist attitude to learning and knowledge, in which the role of Higher Education is primarily vocational and learning is commodified, with students turning into 'customers' and marketable products. Academics in turn are no longer so much scholars committed to teaching and research but increasingly 'enterprising' and 'self-promoting entrepreneurs or knowledge workers' (Webster, 2003: 87) who are expected to engage in 'income generation' and 'possibilities for entrepreneurialsim'. Academic and non-academic staff receive training in 'discourse technologies' to equip them with the linguistic 'toolkits' deemed necessary for 'effective' communication in the university workplace. Trowler (2001: 187) states that 'like all ideologies, managerialism embodies a reductionist understanding to social life. It simultaneously simplifies and occludes'.

What is completely omitted from governmental and university management discourse is the question whether it is morally right to promote consumerism and managerialism as the only viable model in academia. Individual academics and the Higher Education research community may voice their scepticism about the adoption of business models into the university, but they do not have the power to translate their sentiments into action. It is the proponents of academic entrepreneurialism, the university management and the government, who have the power to implement the institutional and discursive changes.

It is because of the neo-liberal, consumerist and universalizing characteristics of corporate discourse that its adoption into Higher Education is problematic. It is simply assumed that the current market-oriented orthodoxies are 'universally applicable', in other words, what is good for business is just as good for universities and the public sector, employers and employees. In this model, profit is the main measure of success and all services, including health care and education, have a market value and are best run as businesses. Here the problem might be that knowledge will increasingly be judged on the basis of its market performance and that less 'marketable' subjects, such as the Humanities, will fare badly.

However, we should maybe reject the notion that people working in academic institutions are simply 'captured' by the discourse of enterprise. Trowler (2001: 197) refers to a 'discursive struggle, or sometimes accommodation, rather than simply discursive capture'. It is also possible for people to employ different (and conflicting) sets of discourse in different contexts (e.g. the lecture; the job interview, appraisal, etc.). Studies of managers and managerialism in Higher Education have shown that managers 'often adopt a form of 'bilingualism' in relation to the use of managerialist and other discourses' (ibid.: 197), depending on context. So inspite of the capacity of institutional discourses to construe 'complicity' and enlist people to their agenda, as Foucault has suggested, people also have the capacity to subvert and resist these discourse practices.

Finally, the justification for embracing entrepreneurialism and its discourses in Higher Education is based on 'new hegemonic managerial discourse' (Thrift, 1997: 36), which portrays the global business context as hyper-competitive, unstable and largely unpredictable and insists that any business wanting to survive must adapt to these market conditions. We should maybe resist this market logic. As Webster (2003: 88) has put it, by adopting corporate models and their discourses, the university will be 'less concerned with future visions as a maker of history, and more with simply struggling for survival in the free-market conditions that it has convinced itself it is helpless against and which it has itself contributed to'.

3 Prison discourse: Enterprising managerialism in a 'total institution'

Andrea Mayr

Introduction

In Chapter 2, we pointed out that economic thinking and discourse practices originating from the economic sphere are now pervasive in various institutional settings, citing the university as one example. In this chapter, we turn to yet another institution, the prison, to show that prisons and the rehabilitation of offenders are now also subject to managerialist ideologies and strategies. Managerialism in crime control and its associated discourse of enterprise rests upon the assumption that modern managerial techniques, such as the ones used in private sector businesses, can be successfully applied to the problems of crime and punishment (see Wozniak, 1994; Garland, 2001). Managerialism is now a pervasive feature of the crime control system in Britain.

In this chapter, we look at a cognitive rehabilitation programme for prisoners in a Scottish prison, which can be seen as one application of the managerial approach to crime. Claiming to be 'directly rehabilitative', the Programme focuses primarily on addressing offenders' 'dysfunctional' behaviour, teaching them 'how to think' through the use of cognitive skills. Through a critical analysis, we will explore some of the ways in which the institutional discourse of the Programme constructs (ideological) meanings about prisoners by labelling their behaviour as irrational and 'anti-social' due to a lack of social and cognitive skills.

The prison as a 'total institution'

The prison is an institution that plays an important part in rehabilitating prisoners and defining new selves for them. Prison services throughout the world have always made claims about rehabilitative ideals, teaching values and forming therapeutic communities, although in essence, they are bureaucratic institutions whose main concern is *managing* the place. For Goffman (1961: 6) one of the central features of what he calls 'total institutions', such as the prison, is the 'handling of many human needs by the bureaucratic organization of whole blocks of people – whether or not this is a necessary or effective means of social organization'. These bureaucratic imperatives create conditions and practices within the prison which are at odds with its rehabilitative aims and initiatives, and which therefore have to be subsumed under the larger needs of the prison as an institution. Goffman's (1961) rather pessimistic conclusion was that an institution like the prison 'stripped' the inmates of any meaningful manifestations of self and justified this through reasonable-sounding security and rehabilitation objectives.

Discourses about imprisonment and the rehabilitation of prisoners are not value-free and respond to changes in government and public policy. As part of these changes in government associated with neo-liberalism in recent decades, major transformations in penal policy and practices have been taking place in which criminal justice systems in Canada, the USA and Britain have increasingly turned to a managerial approach to offender rehabilitation.

Enterprising managerialism in the crime control system

Here we focus on the adoption of managerialism into the Scottish prison system. In the late 1980s, the Scottish Prison Service (SPS) experienced a serious crisis in the form of overcrowding, prisoner unrest ('riots') and hostage-taking of prison officers by prisoners. This resulted in the adoption of a new corporate philosophy with a more management-oriented approach to the running of its prisons and to the rehabilitation of offenders. This move was characterized by institutional and discursive changes in a number of policy documents and the construction of the SPS as an enterprising organization with a 'customer-focused' approach. The customers in this case are not, as one might expect, the public, but its prisoners. This thinking is particularly exemplified in *A Shared Enterprise* (SPS, 1990b; para. 7.2), one of the policy documents of the SPS, the priorities of which are to 'improve the quality of service to prisoners, so as to provide them with as full, active and constructive a life as possible', while at the same time 'develop the appropriate organizational structure and management style to deliver the service as efficiently, effectively and economically as possible'.

These developments and the concomitant reformulation of discourses within the SPS and the crime control system in general are seen by the criminologist David Garland (2001: 76) not only as the outcome of changes in criminological thinking but also of the social, economic and cultural changes in late modernity, and changes in social and economic policy – a combination of free-market neo-liberalism and social conservatism in the UK and across the Atlantic. As a result of these changes, 'the practice of rehabilitation is increasingly inscribed in a framework of 'risk' and is represented as a 'targeted intervention', its overriding concern being the 'efficient enhancement of social control' (Garland, 2001: 176). 'Social control' can be understood as 'all organized responses to crime, delinquency and allied forms of deviance – whether sponsored directly by the state or by institutions such as social work and psychiatry, and whether designated as treatment, prevention, punishment or whatever' (Cohen, 1983: 102).

Connected to these developments is the construction of the offender in the SPS policy documents as 'responsible, despite the fact he or she may have acted irresponsibly many times over in the past' (*Opportunity and Responsibility, SPS*, 1990; quoted in Adler and Longhurst, 1994: 226). The concept of individual responsibility is based on a highly voluntaristic conception of human agency, which downplays the relevance of social conditions in determining individual action. Such constructions of the prisoner as an autonomous being with choice and responsibility are also prominent in the cognitive behavioural approach to offender rehabilitation.

Offender rehabilitation: the cognitive approach

Unlike sociological approaches to deviance, which regard crime largely as a result of poverty or desperate social conditions, the cognitive approach considers criminal activity to be a result of the individual making faulty (i.e. criminal) decisions. This school of thought is based on cognitive development theory (Piaget, 1958; Kohlberg et al., 1975) and neo-liberal perspectives on deviance.

The Cognitive Skills Programme we will analyse in this chapter, *Reasoning and Rehabilitation*, is based on the 'Cognitive Skills Deficit Model', developed by Ross and Fabiano (1985), two Canadian psychologists. Taught by prison officers, the Programme was first introduced in one Scottish prison in 1995 and was subsequently rolled out to other Scottish prisons. It is an example of more pragmatic, '*directly* rehabilitative' types of programme, which focuses primarily on addressing offending behaviour rather than on prison education as 'empowerment' and therefore fits well into the current managerialist climate: managing offenders' minds and behaviours has become a favourite tool in their rehabilitation. The change in thinking and behaviour is to be brought about by a combination of training cognitive, communicative and social skills and introspection on part of the prisoner. Here Foucault's (1977) concept of 'discipline' comes to mind, to characterize the attempt to transform the 'soul' of the prisoner. Prisoners are confined and disciplined so they can gain an awareness of their own state and an alteration of their minds can be achieved. This attempt at transforming the self of the prisoner is however open to contestation from prisoners.

Methodology

I employed a combination of Critical Discourse Analysis (CDA) and Systemic Functional Linguistics (SFL) to shed light on the ways in which offenders are constructed as 'cognitively deficient' in the written and spoken discourse of the Cognitive Skills Programme. For the analysis of written 'crime-control' discourse, I analysed sections from *Reasoning and Rehabilitation: A Handbook for Teaching Cognitive Skills* (Ross et al., 1989), which is the teaching guide complete with lesson plans for the cognitive skills trainers. The sections I have chosen for analysis are 'Objectives of Training' and 'Assertive Communication'. Not only do these put the classroom interactions we will look at into context, but they also serve to draw attention to some of the linguistic means by which certain (ideological) assumptions about offenders' thinking and behaviour patterns are presented as 'common sense'.

I used a participant-observation method, observing and taking part in the Cognitive Skills classes at Prison X with the permission of the SPS, the prison officers/teachers and the inmates attending the Course. I interacted with the participants and took part in group discussions and exercises and also occasionally operated the video camera set up in the classroom. Many Cognitive Skills classes were videotaped, to be used either as feedback for the inmates after performing role-plays or as part of the tutors' teaching assessment by the founders of the Programme in Canada. After being present in the recorded sessions as a mere observer for the first two of my eight weeks of fieldwork, the officer and the inmates allowed me to use some of the classroom tapes for transcription and analysis.

Prison X is a short-term prison with a capacity for 400 male adult prisoners sentenced to up to four years for mainly drug-related offences. The Cognitive Skills Programme, *Reasoning and Rehabilitation* (Ross et al., 1989) consisted of 35 2-hour classes taught at a rate of 3 per week, covering cognitive, social and self-control skills (anger management), creative thinking and critical reasoning and communication skills such as negotiation and assertiveness. Prisoners are advised or referred to the Course by prison officers or other prison staff, although they often express an interest in the Course themselves. All potential participants undergo a semi-structured interview with the officer teaching the Course to assess their 'cognitive functioning' and their need for the Programme. The prison officers teaching the Programme have to undergo several weeks training to qualify as teachers. One of the reasons for using prison officers to teach the Course is to improve relations between inmates and officers, but there is also the more pragmatic motivation of greater cost-effectiveness.

Having explained the wider cultural and institutional changes which have lead to a managerial approach to offender rehabilitation, we now move on to the analysis of some of the written texts from *Reasoning and Rehabilitation: A Handbook for Teaching Cognitive Skills* (Ross et al., 1989). This Handbook is based on the original account of the cognitive approach to offender rehabilitation, *Time to Think* (Ross and Fabiano, 1985) and is therefore a recontextualization. It provides lesson plans for training offenders in the cognitive skills deemed necessary for their 'adequate social adjustment'. The reason for choosing these two texts is that they provide an outline of the cognitive model and its approach to offender rehabilitation and also put the samples of spoken classroom interactions below into context. We shall analyse the two texts for the following systems used in SFL: Transitivity, Mood, Theme and Cohesion. The first text, 'Objectives of Training', explains the purpose of the training and the philosophy behind it:

Text 1: 'Objectives of Training'

(1) The cognitive training sessions are designed to target the specific cognitive skills deficits which are discussed in detail in *Time to Think*: interpersonal cognitive problem-solving, consequential thinking, means-end reasoning, social perspective-taking, critical reasoning, abstract reasoning, creative thinking and values. (2) Deficits in these skills constitute a serious personal handicap which puts the individual at risk of developing an anti-social lifestyle. (3) Cognitive training focuses on modifying the impulsive, egocentric, illogical and rigid thinking of offenders and on teaching them to stop and think before acting, consider the consequences of their behaviour, conceptualize alternative ways of responding to interpersonal problems and consider the impact of their behaviour on other people (including their victims). (4) Rather than viewing the offender's anti-social behaviour as a reflection of some presumed underlying psychopathology, cognitive training is based on two premises: offenders tend to be under-socialized – they lack the values, attitudes, reasoning and social skills which are required for pro-social adjustment; such skills can be taught. (5) The purpose of the cognitive training sessions is to foster the

offender's cognitive development and to teach them specific cognitive skills (Ross et al., 1989: 3; sentence numbers added).

The first thing to notice in this text is the heavy use of nouns and nominalizations through which the objective, quasi-scientific side of cognitive training is being presented (e.g. *'interpersonal cognitive problem-solving', 'consequential thinking means-end reasoning', 'social perspective-taking'; 'critical/abstract reasoning', 'creative thinking, pro-social adjustment'; 'deficits'*). Nominalizations, unlike clauses with a process verb, are not tied to any specific time in relation of speaking. Therefore, meaning about offenders can be presented as if it has some external objective reality. Another important function of nominalizations is that a judgmental or evaluative adjective can be added to it, as in '*pro-social* adjustment', '*impulsive/egocentric/illogical/rigid* thinking', '*serious* personal handicap', '*anti-social* lifestyle', turning them into terms with a rather fixed, non-negotiable meaning.

Reference to offenders is backgrounded. If we look at *Transitivity,* we can see that offenders are rarely referred to as agents and occur only twice in the informationally important part of the sentence, as its Theme ('... *offenders* tend to be under-socialized ... *they* lack the values ...' (4)). Instead, 'offenders' are construed as being acted upon, as objects of intervention rather than subjects. They typically occur as Goals or Beneficiaries in action clauses, as in 'Cognitive training focuses on ... teaching *them* to stop and think ...' (3). Offenders' actions and thinking processes, '*stop* and think before *acting*', '*consider* the consequences of their behaviour', '*conceptualize* alternative ways of responding to interpersonal problems' (3), are embedded in main clauses that represent them as Beneficiaries of actions performed by the cognitive training process. There seems a certain 'subject/object dichotomy' (Duguid, 2000a, b) in that the imprisoned criminal becomes an 'object' in the sense of being subjected to the authority of the crime control system. In the Cognitive Skills Course, however, he is expected to reflect on his criminal past and behaviour – such reflection clearly requires the skills and attributes of a subject. Hence, the prisoner as object of intervention is nevertheless asked to make a (temporary) shift to being a subject.

The text further constructs offenders as rigid and irrational in their thinking due to a lack of cognitive skills, and cognitive training (or its trainers) as acting by taking concrete steps, such as '*target* the specific cognitive skills deficits' (1), 'Cognitive training *focuses* on *modifying* the impulsive ... thinking of offenders' (3), 'The purpose of the cognitive training sessions is to *foster* the offenders' cognitive development and to *teach* them specific cognitive skills' (5), which are all material processes to signal that something can be done about this.

Moving on to interpersonal meaning and *modality,* we can see that the text uses the present tense to make rather categorical statements about the quality of the Course and about offenders. The present tense expresses what is called in SFL 'categorical modality', for example, 'Deficits in these skills *constitute* a serious personal handicap which *puts* the individual at risk . . .' (2); '. . . they *lack* the values . . .' (4). The text makes rather unmitigated statements about the behaviour of offenders, presenting it as a straight fact, although this certainty is not unusual for textbooks, which treat their topic as fully understood and unproblematic. Only one sentence in the text is modalized: '. . . such skills *can* be taught' (4), which suggests that offenders' faulty thinking is not beyond control and can be changed for the better. One of the features of crime control discourse is that it always tries to convey change and progress in dealing with crime and criminals (Cohen, 1985).

Looking at the textual dimension of *Theme*, we can see that most Themes are unmarked subject Themes, such as 'the cognitive training sessions', 'deficits in these skills', 'cognitive training', 'the purpose of the cognitive training sessions'. This foregrounding of cognitive training serves the important function of evaluating the Course positively. It is treated as 'given', not new information, which is particularly significant, as evaluative words or nominal groups which are placed in sentence initial position make it more likely that the reader will accept them as a valid evaluation (Hoey, 2000). And once the information in Theme position is accepted, as in 'Deficits in these skills', the subsequent Rheme, 'constitutes a serious personal handicap', is more likely to be accepted also. We can see that the focus is on the individual offender and his or her alleged 'personal defects'.

There is one marked Theme, a whole subordinate clause, '*Rather than viewing the offender's anti-social behaviour as a reflection of some presumed underlying psychopathology, . . .*' (4), which can be seen as a rhetorical strategy by the Handbook writers to distance themselves from more extreme psychological schools of thought. '*Offenders*' are mostly in Rheme ('new' information) position, which shows that all activity is focused on them. Only twice are *offenders* made the Theme of a clause: '. . . *offenders* tend to be under-socialized – *they* lack the values . . .' (4), which is when their alleged moral defects are enumerated.

As for *lexical cohesion,* the text uses Theme repetition, which contributes significantly to the text's overall cohesion. Expressions such as 'serious personal handicap', 'anti-social life-style/behaviour', 'impulsive, egocentric, illogical and rigid thinking', 'anti-social behaviour', etc. serve to evaluate offenders in negative terms. All these become authoritative quasi-scientific explanations which call for intervention. By employing a 'language of individual pathology' (Edelman, 1977), offenders' failure to conform is presented as a reflection on their inadequacies rather than those of the social system. In other words, the text directs attention away from a conceptualization which could lead to the social system being questioned and not just offenders' cognitive (mal)functioning.

Text 2: 'Assertive Communication'

This text contains the instructions for Cognitive Skills tutors (i.e. prison officers) for teaching assertiveness. In the following excerpt from the 'Instructions for Trainers', it is claimed that teaching offenders assertive conversational skills will help them to avoid unpleasant conflicts:

> (1) You will be teaching them that the manner in which they attempt to implement a solution will determine the success of their problem-solving effort; that some ways of implementing a possible solution will be effective, some ineffective and some may magnify the problem.
> (2) Your goal will be to have each client understand that he must communicate his proposed solutions precisely and accurately and in such a manner that people clearly understand how he feels and he must do so without antagonizing others or violating their rights. (3) In effect, he must learn to express his feelings, his views and his suggestions in an *assertive* manner.
> (4) Many offenders tend to *avoid* expressing their views, whereas many others express them *aggressively*; neither approach is likely to achieve the goal of making others understand or appreciate their suggestions. (5) You will teach them to understand why avoidance or aggressive approaches are ineffective because of their effect on other people – and you will help them to learn and practise *assertive* responses – communicating their views clearly without antagonizing people (Ross et al., 1989: 92; emphasis in original; sentence numbers added).

'Assertive Communication' for offenders focuses on techniques for turning a confrontational conversation into an assertive, collaborative one. With its emphasis on the rational and pragmatic (attempting to change offenders' dysfunctional thinking and behaviour rather than looking for its deeper causes), 'Assertive Communication' is similar to other assertiveness training courses that have been widely implemented to train those who are considered to be 'socially inadequate'. They are an integral part of programmes designed to combat social problems such as drug-taking and crime, in which assertiveness is taught to 'enable' people to resist peer pressure or, as in the Cognitive Skills

Course, to 'enable offenders to interact positively with peers, teachers, parents, employers or other authority figures (including correctional officers)' (Ross et al., 1989: 107).

In this text, the 'trainer' (i.e. the prison officer teaching the session) is directly addressed ('you') and instructed how to teach 'them', that is, the prisoners, assertiveness. This text is therefore far more interactive than the previous text.

Looking at the text in terms of *Transitivity,* offenders are again more objects of intervention, or the Goals or Beneficiaries, with the trainer acting upon them ('You will be teaching *them* . . .'; 'Your goal will be to have *each client* understand . . .'; 'You will teach *them* to understand . . . and you will help *them* to learn . . .') than active subjects. When they do act, they might do so by '*antagonizing* others or *violating* their rights'. It uses fewer noun constructions than the previous text, for example, '*problem-solving effort*', which is another example in which a verb construction ('their effort to solve their problems') has been condensed into a new lexical item.

Turning to *Modality*, most sentences in this are modalized with 'will' (e.g. 'You *will b*e teaching them that the manner in which they attempt to implement a solution *will* determine the success . . .'). This is coupled with strong obligation being placed on the offender: 'Your goal will be to have each client understand that he *must* communicate his proposed solutions precisely . . . and he *must* do so without antagonizing others . . .'. ('In effect he *must l*earn to express his views . . .')

Since this text addresses the Cognitive Skills trainer, it is hardly surprising that s/he is made the topical *Theme* in most sentences (Theme reiteration). Once, the topical Theme is a brief nominal group (*your goal*; sentence 2), also referring to the Cognitive Skills tutor. Then there is a short pattern of thematic shifting, in which the 'offender' is made Theme: '*he*', referring back to the '*client*' (i.e. the offender; sentence 3). In sentence 4, '*many offenders*', followed by 'many others' is the Theme, which is when their communicative abilities are evaluated negatively.

Looking at *lexical cohesion*, as in the previous text, there is extensive use of lexical repetition here, which contributes significantly to the text's cohesion: *to implement a (possible) solution* (2x); *ineffective* (2x); *solution(s)* (4x); *understand* (2x); *antagonize* (2x); *express* (2x); *communicate* (2x); *avoid/avoidance, goal* (2x). Cohesion is also achieved through contrast or antonymy (*effective/ineffective; aggressive approaches/assertive responses*) and synonymy (*precisely/ accurately; antagonize/violate; feelings/views; understand/appreciate*). These serve to negatively evaluate offenders' ways of communicating and to positively evaluate assertiveness training. To account for the value-laden nature of evaluation, Hunston (1985) suggests that 'what is good' can be defined in terms of goal-achievement: 'your *goal* will be to have each client understand that . . .'; 'neither approach is likely to *achieve the goal* of making others understand . . .' (2). Assertiveness is the Goal the prisoner has to strive for to be 'successful' and therefore has to be strategically employed in interaction, following a number of behavioural steps as we shall see below.

Having looked at the written instructions on how to teach assertiveness, we will now turn to an actual 'Social Skills' training session, where assertiveness was taught and in particular 'Responding to complaints'. The class was attended by a group of five inmates who had been on the Course for three weeks. The officer is instructed in the Handbook (Ross et al., 1989: 109) to make up a scenario and demonstrate to the group in a role-play with a selected group member 'how an unskilled person would behave in various situations'. This demonstration is meant to 'approximate the inappropriate and ineffective behaviours' that some group members 'might typically evidence in such situations' (ibid.: 109).

In the following classroom interaction, the officer, following the instructions of the Handbook, addresses one of inmates in a mock aggressive way. The inmates do not know what is coming:

1	Officer:	Hey hey
2	Rab:	Hey what? Hey what hey fuckin what?
3	Officer:	Every time ye cough ye spread yer fuckin germs [over me
4	Rab:	[well stand back fae them then
?:		hahaha
5	Officer:	Right how do ye feel about that eh?
		[pause]
6	Jamie:	Blooter him or punch him
7	Rab:	Naw
8	Officer:	Wud ye not jis clam up if somebody shouts at ye like that?
9	Rab:	Nah [?]
10	Officer:	Right that type ay thing. The thing is there's a way ay nae daein it, the way ay nae daein it the aggressive way ye get an aggressive response. {*approaches another two inmates*} if ye are up tae anybody and say 'stoap fuckin sittin back in that chair you', ye're not gettin annoyed? Right see you're not happy [Tam: Aye] That type ay thing.

In this exchange, the officer has to attempt twice to get the desired reaction from the inmates. When he approaches the first inmate, Rab, Rab just reacts with an ironic comment ('Well stand back fae them then'), which makes the others laugh. When the officer asks him how he 'feels' about this aggressive complaint, he pauses for an answer, and another inmate, Jamie suggests to 'blooter or punch him', which is probably the reaction the officer was hoping for. Rab's reply ('naw') seems to indicate that he can take an aggressive complaint quite calmly. The officer then says there is a right and a wrong way to communicate ('there's a way ay daein it and there's a way ay no doin it') and underscores this by demonstrating aggressive behaviour with a different inmate who agrees with the officer. The whole exchange, although it looks quite serious on paper, was quite humorous with Rab making fun of the officer ('Hey what? Hey what hey fuckin what?'). He also tripped the officer up as he stepped back to the board. All this was taken in good humour by the officer. Ma\king fun of what the officer says and thereby subverting official definitions of them, is one way in which inmates try to steal back bits of freedom from an institutional regime that attempts to train, improve and transform them.

After the demonstration given by the officer, the inmates were asked to role-play in pairs certain situations (which they could either select from role-playing scenario cards provided or make up themselves). They were asked to first perform the role-play in an 'unskilled' and then in a 'socially skilled' manner using the following steps listed on the flipchart:

1) Listen carefully to the complaint
2) Ask for more information
3) Decide if the complaint is justified
4) Decide if you should accept or deny responsibility and what should be done
5) Express your view and your suggested solution
6) Ask for his/her reaction. (Ross et al., 1989: 124)

In the following role-play, one inmate is complaining in a 'socially unskilled manner' to another about the way he has parked his car, a scenario the two inmates created themselves:

1. Rab: Tell me what's yer car parked here for? Ah was in here first and ye're blockin us from getting oot
2. Tam: Cos ye parked yer car where mine should be
3. Rab: No Ah was here first but
4. Tam: That's what well that's what Ah'm sayin (Ah parked ma car in this space)

5.	Rab:	Dae ye pay for that space? Dae ye pay for that [Tam: listen!] space? Ah paid for that space
6.	Tam:	Ah don't give a fuck what ye've paid for it. Ah've parked ma car and there's nothing ye can do aboot it
7.	Rab:	(?) Ah fuckin Ah jis steal it and smash it intae a wall.
8.	Tam:	Ye canny dae that because ye will get lifted.

The two inmates then repeat the role-play in a more 'skilled' way:

1.	Rab:	Dae ye want tae move yer car out of the road for me to get oot I won't be able to get past you?
2	Tam:	{to Officer} That's the easy one. Ah'll jis' go with that no problem {to Rab} We 're oanly gonna be here for a wee while.
3	Rab:	How how long are ye gonna be?
4.	Tam:	What about an hour?
5	Rab:	An hour? Naw Ah need tae be at the hospital in the afternoon with ma wife, she's just come out of Tecso Tesco's
6	Tam:	Ye give us five minutes then is that awright?
7	Rab:	Nae bother
8	Officer:	Perfectly acceptable. Ah can jis' imagine you Tam in a motor tryin tae get in.

We can see that the two inmates are perfectly capable of 'performing' an interaction in a 'socially unskilled' and a 'socially skilled' way set within the parameters of what constitutes such behaviour by the Course. The question is whether this type of training can really bring about attitudinal change in inmates. More to the point, it is questionable that 'appropriate' communicative behaviour will 'enable' them to overcome systemic inequalities.

In another excerpt from a 'socially unskilled' role-play performed by another pair of inmates, at one point one inmate does not know what to say next.

1.	Colin:	What am Ah supposed tae dae [now?
2.	Officer:	[you respond tae it, be angry
3.	Colin:	Angry?
4.	Officer:	Respond tae him the way you were doin in (?) the other day
5	Colin:	Aye?
6.	Officer:	Aye
7.	Colin:	{to Neil} Talkin tae me pal?
8.	Neil:	Aye Ah'm talkin tae ye
9.	Colin:	Ah break yer fuckin nose

Here the inmates are actually instructed to react in an aggressive way by the officer ('react to him in the way you were doing (?) the other day') for the sake of performing the role-play successfully. But what is the point of making inmates rehearse 'good' and 'bad' behaviour?

Ross et al. (1989: 110) argue that breaking the behaviour down into steps aids the learning process as it helps offenders realize that they need to 'communicate their position clearly, while acknowledging the needs of others'. However, as criminologists Wilson and Reuss (2000) point out with regard to cognitive skills training it is somewhat artificial to assist offenders in rehearsing both 'unskilled' and new behaviour and new thinking skills using overheads, role-plays and scenarios.

The motivations underlying the teaching of cognitive and communicative skills for offenders are problematic in several other respects. The Cognitive Skills Course is based on the assumption that social, cognitive and communication skills can be isolated and described, and that inadequacies in these skills can be overcome by teaching offenders to use them. A particular, non-confrontational model of communication and behaviour is preferred, backed up by psychological expertise and conveyed by the officer as right versus wrong, good thinking versus bad thinking and acceptable versus unacceptable behaviour, irrespective of context. As Cameron (1995: 218) has put it:

> [T]he norms of 'assertive' or 'effective' communication [ ] all function (among other things) to tidy up messy or troublesome realities. The rules affirm basic distinctions like true/false, good/bad, correct/incorrect, and they insist that those distinctions are categorical absolutes, not matters of opinion or arbitrary convention, and not contingent judgements that could vary with the context.

The basic assumption of 'Assertive Communication' is that it is for prisoners' own benefit when they are taught 'communicating their views clearly without antagonizing people' (Ross et al., 1989: 92), 'people' meaning not only their peers, but also prison officers and others in positions of authority. But is it? After all, the training is very much in the interest of the prison system, too, in that it aims at making prisoners more compliant with the prison regime. It may marginalize prisoners' grievances by reducing them to problems that are supposedly due to their personal (communicative) defects. The idea that prisoners may have legitimate complaints and that their anger can be an expression of reason as well as irrationality is ignored. As Scraton et al. (1991: 67) point out, 'prisoners' violence is often part of the symbol, ritual and reality of a male hostile environment. However, it can also be . . . the individual or collective expression of anger, fear and frustration . . . fed by personal anxieties and institutional injustices.' These issues are largely left aside by the Cognitive Programme.

The basic rationale of the Cognitive Skills Course that if prisoners learn 'how to think' and communicate less aggressively, they may be less prone to recidivism, suffer less personal misery and less social disadvantage, is debatable. This is because the practice and delivery of the Course tends 'to ignore the *life-history and personal identity of the prisoner*' (Reuss, 2000: 174; emphasis in original).

The Cognitive Skills Course could be an example of what Cohen (1985: 150) has called the 'new Behaviourism' in crime control. Behaviour modification is suited to prison settings, where you can observe behaviour in ways you cannot observe insights. This makes both managerial and ideological sense. Cohen offers four reasons for why the new Behaviourism is so ideologically perfect: it is uninterested in causes for crime; it is compatible with management, control and surveillance; it offers the possibility of changing behaviour rather than people; it works at the 'realistic' level of situations or physical environments and does not criticize the social order. As long as offenders behave, using the cognitive and social skills they have been taught, something has been achieved. It is thus the behaviour patterns of offenders and not so much their thoughts that are targeted for change by teaching them social and thinking skills through traditional behaviourist techniques, accompanied by the rhetoric of cognition.

Conclusion

In the current climate of Managerialism, programmes for the rehabilitation of prisoners are often measured against rates of recidivism to determine their effectiveness, as opposed to a more radical interpretation of education as empowerment. The Cognitive Programme we have looked at in this chapter is a good example of this: it is mainly an exercise in behaviour modification and social control and the discipline of the mind, rather than enriched identities. One could argue that the disciplinary character of the Programme does not negate its virtue if indeed it helps reducing reoffending rates. But crime is a function of the *interaction* between the individual and their environment. From this it would follow that attempts to change offenders' thinking and behaviour patterns must also be concerned with changes to their environment.

Nevertheless, although essentially a 'correctional' programme, the Cognitive Skills Course raises the question of the possibility of personal change for inmates. If Giddens (1981) is right in that social actors are never completely overwhelmed by institutional power and dominance and have an enabling function too, then the prison would also have a capacity for domination as well as transformation and change of self. So the Course may mark the first step in a potentially transformative education for prisoners. This seems to be reflected in comments inmates themselves made about the Course, although what they found most rewarding was not the acquisition of a number of cognitive, communicative and social skills, but the social benefits of working together as a group and experience a Course that would relieve them from prison routine for a while.

It has also been the aim of this chapter to show that a detailed critical discourse analysis can shed light on how various grammatical and syntactical forms and professional terms can be used to express meanings about prisoners, as 'common sense' and justified, disguising their political and ideological character. Crime control ideology is significant in so far as it succeeds in presenting as natural, acceptable or even just and humane, an institutional system that is basically coercive. However, as Cohen (1983: 126) reminds us, crime control discourses have to be understood not as mere ideological proclamations but as 'working or practice languages' for those operating within the system. By inventing new names and announcing new programmes that convey change, progress and rational decision, professionals and administrators are engaged in giving the impression to the population that the crime problem is not totally out of control.

Transcription key

In representing the classroom interactions in written form, I have decided to transcribe the spoken texts in a way which attempts to be faithful to the Scottish dialect. I used moderate non-standard spellings for the classroom interactions, which are also accessible to readers unfamiliar with the dialect. Prisoners' names have been changed. The transcription key and a gloss of dialect features is provided below:

Symbol	Meaning
[	overlapping utterances: two speakers talking at the same time
(?)	question mark in round bracket indicates inaudible words
{non-verbal}	description of non-verbal behaviour (e.g. changes in posture) appear before or after the segment of talk in curly brackets
[hh]	chuckle
[hhh]	laughter

...	three dots in transcripts indicate pauses of less than three seconds
[pause – 4 secs]	indication of inter-turn pause length exceeding 3 seconds

Glossary

'fae' = from
'jis' = just
'ay' = of
'daein' = doing
'tae' = to
'aboot' = about
'oot' = out
'naw' = no
'nae bother' = no bother

4 News discourse I: Understanding the social goings-on behind news texts

David Machin

Introduction

The consensual view of the role of the journalist is a seeker of truth, the eyes and ears of the people. Michael Grade, in his 2005 inaugural Hugh Cudlipp Lecture at the London College of Communications, said of the BBC: 'The BBC has a duty to set a gold standard in news reporting, in accuracy, in impartiality, in creating a better understanding' (www.bbc.co.uk). Kevin Marsh, editor of BBC Radio 4s *Today* programme, in a speech to the Society of Editors in Autum 2004, said that some of the important characteristics of good journalism were: 'Curiosity. Persistence. Toughness . . .. Ruthlessness with fact'. Similarly, The American Project for Excellence in Journalism states on its website (www. journalism.org) that journalism is: 'a discipline of verification' whose 'first obligation is to the truth'.

In this model, journalism is about bravely finding the facts and delivering them to the public with neutrality so that the truth can be known. The public does not have the time or the resources to be able to find out about why wars are fought, where there are current famines in the world, or what dangers lie outside the home in the form of crime. So reporters dig around to investigate and reveal on the public's behalf. They select the events that are most relevant to people, find ways to investigate them further and identify sources that can shed light on the central issues.

This consensual view of news holds the view that journalists have an important role to play in a democratic society in creating informed citizens aware of what is going on in society and also what those they elect to govern them are doing in relation to these things. In this 'Fourth Estate' role, journalists have responsibility to report on the most important and relevant news events truthfully, accurately and impartially. Problems only arise where journalists are biased and the 'ruthlessness with the facts' required by the public, the representation of the 'truth' is compromised.

One of the core activities of Critical Discourse Analysis (CDA) has been the analysis of news texts to reveal journalistic bias in the case, for example, of racism (van Dijk, 1993), the representation of Muslims (Richardson, 2006), anti-immigration (Wodak and Reisigl, 1999) and other political ideology (Kress, 1983). However, in this chapter we question the very idea that we can reasonably think about news as being able to represent truth at all. News should be understood not as a simple window of the world and should certainly not be judged in terms of whether it is accurate or biased, as this overlooks the fundamental way that the institution of the news organization and news gathering procedures themselves shape what becomes news as much as the events themselves. The kinds of distortions that we often call 'bias' are trivial in the context of how news is manufactured. In fact, thinking about news in terms of 'truth' and 'bias' serves to distract our attention from the fundamentally institutional nature of news.

All institutions, such as schools, hospitals and news organizations, shape, categorize and transform reality to make it predictable and more easily manageable. Each sets up systems, which allow them to manage reality. Schools need to place children in age groups and ability categories. Sociologists have taught us that what we call ability is in fact based on factors such as social class and having access to certain cultural codes, which questions the validity of these categories. In addition, all children have complex individual needs. Yet schools overlook this due to the need to process students through the system. An institution like a school can simply not deal with each student as an individual, unique case, nor consider them in the light of complex socio-cultural factors. In this chapter, I explore these kinds of processing in the case of news, showing how the texts we read, see or hear, the photographs and news footage we see, should be thought about first not as about representing reality but as the products of an institution. I start with a number of examples, showing how these raise certain questions both about the idea of news as a mirror on reality and the weakness of the notion of truth versus bias. I go on to look at some of the factors that better explain how these news texts get produced in the way that they do.

Fairclough (1995a), in his account of what kind of approach constitutes Critical Discourse Analysis, pointed to the importance of understanding production processes that lie behind texts to understand their nature. He said that if we analyse texts without considering the contexts of production, then we carry out only textual analysis and not Discourse Analysis. In other words, we need to know the broader discursive practices of which texts are a part. Only by considering production can we understand texts as they are part of social relations (Richardson, 2007). As Fairclough (1995a: 57) argues, CDA should know 'the social and cultural goings-on' which the text is a part of. Verschueren (1985) has argued that much language analysis of the work of journalists is ignorant of how journalists and news organizations operate, what in fact drives the nature of the texts that are produced. These texts are the outcome of specific institutional and professional practices. If we wish to understand what they represent, how they represent and what they do not represent, we need to understand them in the context of these institutional and professional practices.

Some clues to the institutional nature of news

To begin with, here are some examples from an average daily diet of news which indicate the problem with thinking about news in terms of truth or bias and how we need to understand, as Fairclough says 'the social and cultural goings-on' that lie behind these texts. These goings-on include institutionalized habits, procedures, values and the way that these are deeply influenced by financial matters.

Radio news

One morning at 6 a.m. you put on the radio and hear the following news bulletin about a hurricane:

> Tens of thousands of people are on the move in America with Hurricane Isabel just hours away. Airlines have been forced to cancel flights – and the White House is battening down the hatches. Reporter Robert Moore's on the north Carolina coast where Isabel's expected to hit first . . . (11 secs of audio from ITN's Robert Moore)

An hour later at 7 a.m. you hear the following:

> Hurricane Isabel's racing towards the east coast of America – forcing thousands to leave their homes. A state of emergency's been declared in Washington and four other states. The White House has been partly boarded up and schools and businesses have closed. It's expected to hit North Carolina in the next few hours – CNN reporter Keith Oppenheim is there . . . (15 secs voices from Oppenheim)

The second bulletin is slightly different. Lexical items have been changed to create a sense of immediacy. Words such as 'racing', 'forcing thousands', 'declared' and 'hit', connote action, drama and impending threat. The vocabulary is highly charged and active in comparison with the 6 a.m text. In addition, we have greater specificity in lexical items.

In the 6 a.m. bulletin, we have non-specific actions to describe the effects of the hurricane: 'people are on the move' whereas in the second bulletin we find 'forcing thousands to leave their homes'. What is being done by the actors is also much more precise. 'A state of emergency's been declared' replaces the abstraction of the White house is 'battening down the hatches'. There is also a change in category of those affected. In the first, we are only told that flights have been cancelled. In the second 'schools and businesses have closed'. This is specific as regards the kinds of disruption and is much more about city life rather than general travellers.

Through analysis of these texts, we can see that the same story has been dressed up differently. In the second case, there is more energy and specificity. But why has this been done? And which of the two best fits our 'truth' or 'mirror of reality' model of news? Where is the 'real' version of the events? To understand why this is the case we need to understand some very basic things about how news gets made. These news bulletins have been produced by the same commercial news organization, Independent Radio News (IRN), which supplies tailor-made news for commercial radio throughout Britain and Europe. IRN produces the bulletins mindful of the market audience for each station, which will itself vary throughout the day. In this case, the news events are selected and shaped accordingly. IRN will use details about the listeners in terms of opinions, lifestyle and consumer behaviour to create bulletins that speak to them. To create the bulletins, the raw materials will be taken from other news agencies. No investigation or corroboration will be done by the IRN news team.

In the case of the 7 a.m. news bulletin, no additional information had been gathered or received by the newsroom editor, but they skilfully remodelled the text to address a different target audience. But is it not wrong that news is here being processed according to market defined factors? In other words, is it right that news is written for consumers rather than for a public? Is this the worst form of journalistic bias? We will explore this in more detail shortly to consider how *commercial factors* can help us to understand news texts. First we consider another example:

What follows is a news bulletin, again produced by IRN, again tailor-made for the target group. Afterwards we see the original news agency feed from which IRN generated the bulletin:

> A man's been jailed for life for helping to plan and carry out the Bali bombings. Twenty-six Britons were among more than two hundred people killed in the attack in October last year. Ali Imron was spared the death sentence handed down to other suspects because

he expressed remorse and cooperated with the Indonesian authorities. (Thursday, 18 September 2003)

APTN feed as received by IRN:

> One of the few suspects to express remorse over his alleged involvement in last year's bombings on Indonesia's Bali island arrived at court on Thursday to hear his sentence. Ali Imron is facing a possible death penalty, but prosecutors have asked that he receive 20 years in prison because he has shown regret and cooperated with investigators. Imran's older brother Amrozi bin Nurhasyim, and another key defendant, Imam Samudra, already have been sentenced to face firing squads for their roles in the attack, which killed 202 people – mostly foreign tourists. The copy goes on to describe Imron, 33, as a school teacher and the investigation's progress.

The IRN rewrite of the agency copy uses strong, unambiguous language to signpost the importance of the story to the listener – Bali is a holiday destination . . . 26 Britons . . . spared death sentence. The bomber is depersonified to make the story simpler and to ensure a simple good versus bad binary. The bomber ceases to be simply a 'suspect', but he is represented as having planned and carried out the bombings. The rewrite sets the tone by starting the story in a colloquial way, that is, 'A man's been . . .'. Halliday's (1985) categories of 'Theme' and 'Rheme' assist in explaining this linguistic difference. In the APTN version, the Theme is 'One of the few suspects to express remorse over his alleged involvement in last year's bombings on Indonesia's Bali island'. In the IRN version it is 'A man'. There has been massive simplification here. In the first case we have 20 words, in the second two words, to communicate the Theme. In Hallidayan linguistics these groupings of information around the Theme are called 'nominal groups'. Each of these two descriptions of our Theme is a single nominal group. Clearly, in the first instance, more information is packed into the nominal group. When little information is present, or where the information is removed, there may be an ideological effect. In this example, terms that tell us more about the 'head' of the nominal group ('*suspects*' in the first case, '*man*' in the second) are not present.

This simplification by journalists allows news events to be placed into easily recognizable frames of reference for the listener. Market research will have identified the broader and specific world views of the target listener. And more broadly, members of the public are generally aware of typical news themes or 'news frames' (Gans, 1980; Bennett, 2005). In this IRN example, we can see that the story has been simplified into a simple theme about a terrorist being caught. On the one hand, this is done by removing additional information about the 'head' of the nominal group. And it is done by the removal of court-type legal information such as 'suspects', 'alleged' and 'sentence'. This legal terminology would cloud the simple news-frame.

This process is revealing of the institutional nature of news. In a world where journalists had the time to carry out further investigation, they might ask which court and under whose justification. They might have found out more information about the suspect and how it is that they have been arrested. But journalists have always had a massive reliance on other institutional sources, as they provide readily accessible and predictable sources of news. We are familiar with news being a definition of reality that comes from a very limited range of official sources and bureaucratic institutions. We often now hear of suspected terrorist prisoners awaiting trial without hearing about the evidence for this or being clear under whose jurisdiction. But in terms of news itself these texts speak of the routine way that information is processed and dealt with in a standardized way.

We can again return to our questions about the nature of the text above. Clearly, it is not enough to explain what we find in this text as simply 'bias'. Stories are being chosen and shaped so that they fulfil certain expectations held by the public – in other words so that they can be readily recognizable as newsworthy. But if so, this challenges the very idea of news as being something new, and certainly as being representative of the most important things going on in the world of which the public should know to be informed citizens. In fact, there are two factors that determine what becomes news more so than the events themselves. One is 'news values'. These are the institutionally and historically established themes and features that all journalists learn to perceive what is newsworthy or what can be made newsworthy. Two is the incredible dependence on official sources and other bureaucratic organizations that are used to give news its legitimacy. The problem here is that what becomes news is an official definition of reality, and one that itself reflects the bureaucratic concerns of those organizations more than anything in the real world. We explore these issues in greater detail shortly. First I wish to give two more examples.

Newspapers and photojournalism

In the newspaper, in front of you as you eat your breakfast, you see a story about conflict in Afghanistan. There are two photographs accompanying the story. One shows a soldier looking thoughtful, another shows a mother and a child, doe-eyed, in portrait, looking at the viewer. Yet these photographs, on closer inspection are sourced as 'Getty Images'. These images have not been commissioned for this particular story but have been bought from Getty, a commercial image archive. In fact, the photographs were not taken in Afghanistan at all, but depict a soldier in East Africa and a mother and child from a National Geographic collection taken some years before in India (Machin, 2004). Therefore, these images are not documents of the actual people in Afghanistan referred to in the story, but are used to convey a sense of a thoughtful/confused soldier and a vulnerable child. They represent the ambiguity of the conflict and the innocent victim of the conflict, respectively.

The two examples (Figures 4.1 and 4.2) shown below are images taken from the Getty collection. These are the kinds of images that we now see used in advertisements and throughout our newspapers especially in supplements, as they are cheap and easy to use, searchable and downloadable in a few minutes. A multimodal discourse analysis of these images gives us some clues as to the way that they symbolize rather than record reality.

We can apply Kress and van Leeuwen's (1996/2006) modality scales. Just as there are resources in language, the modal auxiliaries, for expressing certainty or less certainty such as the verbs 'may', 'will' and

Figure 4.1 'Business women'.

Figure 4.2 'Woman architect'.

'must' and adjectives such as 'possible', 'probable' and 'certain', Kress and van Leeuwen believe there are such resources in visual communication. They produced eight scales to measure such levels of certainty, to assess the modality configuration, of an image. This can allow us to assess how images represent in a way that resembles how we would have seen something had we been there, or if they are 'less certain', or 'more certain'. Another way of putting this is where there is ambiguity, concealment or exaggeration: where there is reduction we have abstraction and where there is increase we have exaggeration.

- *Degrees of the articulation of detail* – a scale from the simplest line drawing to the sharpest and most finely grained photograph. So we can think of this as a continuum.
- *Degrees of articulation of the background* – ranging from a blank background, via lightly sketched in or out of focus backgrounds, to maximally sharp and detailed backgrounds.
- *Degrees of depth articulation* – ranging from the absence of any depth to maximally deep perspective, with other possibilities (e.g. simple overlapping) in between.

- *Degrees of articulation of light and shadow* – ranging from zero articulation to the maximum number of degrees of 'depth' of shade, with other options in between.
- *Degrees of articulation of tone* – ranging from just two shades of tonal gradation, black and white (or a light and dark version of another colour) to maximum tonal gradation.
- *Degrees of colour modulation* – ranging from flat, unmodulated colour to the representation of all the fine nuances of a given colour.
- *Degrees of colour saturation* – ranging from Black and White to maximally saturated colours.

In both of these images, the articulation of the detail of the backgrounds has been reduced. This serves to decontextualize the subjects of the photograph. The women sit in the office space (Figure 4.1), although it is simply a blank wall and a window without a view. We can think of this as the visual equivalent of the linguistic 'it might be'. The articulation of the detail of the other features of the photograph has also been reduced. This would have formerly been done through overexposure, where light was used to wash out details, often thought of as soft focus, although of course this can now be done electronically. This gives the images a clean look and makes the skin and clothing appear perfect. The natural range of light and shadow is reduced to give a bright and optimistic feel to the image. The colours are also not as we would expect to see them had we been present. They are flat and unmodulated, appearing almost as if in a cartoon, where we do not see all the nuances where light plays upon folds in material on clothing, for example. The colours also appear saturated and therefore more than real. Kress and van Leeuwen (1996/2006) see this effect as creating a 'sensory modality'. This is often a quality of children's toys or used to colour products in adverts. This is used to enhance the emotional or sensory quality of the item.

The image of the woman classified by Getty as 'woman architect' (Figure 4.2) has all of these same qualities: flat, saturated colour, decontextualization, high-key lighting. As with the women in the office, the decontextualization allows the objects in the frame, the laptop computer, the cell phone and the drawing board to have greater symbolic value. Both images have the 'meaning potential' to be used with a range of stories to do with women at work, being busy, colleagues, ambition, careers, job interviews, insurance policies, etc.

In summary, these images are unrealistic. They are not as we would expect them to look were they taken in everyday circumstances. Through this removal from reality, they are able to do their symbolic work.

Machin and Thornborrow (2003: 455) described this less-than-real photographic world as akin to the fairytale world of children's stories described by the psychologist Bruno Bettelheim. They point out that

> historically and cross culturally many of the texts that tutor us in dealing with life's problems have been set in imaginary worlds (e.g. fairytales–(cf. Bettelheim 1976) or worlds that are distant in time and space (e. g. Biblical stories) and classical Hollywood movie narrative (Bordwell, 1985).

Such distancing allows what van Leeuwen (1996) has called 'overdetermination'. Therefore, these images are given greater genericity and hence have a greater potential for adaptation to a range of local circumstances and application to a range of real-life practices. In other words, Machin and Thornborrow (2003: 455) suggest, 'they provide models which are not meant to be followed literally but only in spirit'. On the one hand, these images appearing in our newspaper are useful as they are cheap. But why they are appealing to page editors, as our multimodal discourse analysis tells us, is that they have greater genericity and of course they are technically of a high quality. The saturated colours and overexposed appearance help to create a buoyant, positive mood, which makes the page look good and harmonizes with advertisements. This goes not only for the 'creative' images we analysed above but also for the news photographs of soldiers and civilians that appear accompanying news items on war (Machin, 2007).

But is this what we would expect from journalism? What is happening here is the visual equivalent of what we saw in the IRN examples. These images are cheap and can be used to create a designed look to the newspaper important to attract particular target groups. But importantly, these images are designed to fit with particular news frames.

Machin and Jaworski (2006) have described the video archive collections that are equally made available for use in news bulletins and have the same generic nature, designed to fit with the well-trodden themes of established news frames. They discuss the ITN news footage archive. As with the case of photographs, footage can be searched and accessed cheaply and quickly saving the costs of equipment, camera operators, sound technicians and travel expenses. When we watch news bulletins, we will regularly see footage that has not been filmed for the specific story but has been taken from an archive. In the same way as the Getty images, this footage symbolizes rather than documents and is also characterized by the same genericity and overdetermination.

The ITN archive can be searched under different categories. One of these is 'Crime and Punishment'. Under this heading the sub-categories are Anonymous Crime, Courts and Trials, Hooligans, 11 September, Hijack, Myra Hindley. On the one hand, this list can appear ideological and therefore biased. There is nothing on the site about corporate crime, for example, which research shows is many hundreds of times more expensive for society than individual working-class crimes, such as burglary. There is no mention of state crime. But Machin and Jaworski (2006) argue that this list is not ideological as such, as the footage is simply a collection designed with the established news frames in mind. My own interviews with Getty management (Machin, 2004) suggested that anything could be included that would sell. However, due to the nature of news frames and the way news is closely aligned to other bureaucratic organizations this is the kinds of footage that is most required. We can see this by the kinds of material ITN lists under 'Anonymous Crime':

A collection of generic pictures where people and places cannot be easily identified is intended for use in crime stories. Shots have been selected which make recognition of individuals difficult and in most cases impossible. The collection includes anonymous shots of police officers on patrol (. . .) stations and incident rooms, drug preparation and taking, dealing, busts and hauls, prostitutes, etc. (Machin and Jaworski, 2006: 251)

The result of this is of course that the news does not, so much, report reality as repeat well-trodden themes. And since what news gets chosen also depends on whether or not there is available footage, the kinds of events that are reported will tend to depend on such archives. Machin and Jaworski (2006: 351) suggest that we can think of these news frames as established discourses in the manner described by Fairclough (2001) and Foucault (1972). As they say, 'when events in the world are chosen as news they must to some degree fit with such existing accepted discourses or news frames'. So in our societies what we view as 'crime', our dominant discourse for thinking about crime, is largely in terms of working-class crime, such as burglary, prostitution, drugs, and not crimes against society by corporations, government policy, privatization that devastates lives and communities, etc. Such discourses therefore are not commonly found as news frames.

Perhaps more importantly, the list of footage available for 'crime' reveals the way that news is closely tied to bureaucratic organizations such as law enforcement. While it might seem logical that we should let the police define what crime is, this means that much about crime will never be reported. I will discuss this in more detail shortly. Now I want to explore specifically what is meant by 'news values'. I will then move on to look at the journalistic dependence on other bureaucratic organizations.

News values: what gets to be news

Imagine an evening news bulletin starting like this:

> This is the evening national and international news. A man in Beirut has planted a tree in his garden in commemoration to his family. In Burkina Faso there was a power cut related to government repayment of international loans. And in the North a local man is still unemployed after 20 years where we relate levels of crime to urban deprivation.

Of course, this is not what we would expect from a news bulletin that claimed to give us national and international news. As news audiences we expect to be receiving important events from around the world in our newspapers, our radio and television broadcasts and on our web pages. By important we mean important to everyone. Stories about an unknown man in Beirut are not of importance to the rest of the world. A story about an event in a small African country doesn't seem important to everyone, even if it may be connected to pressures being placed by international financial organizations, which for important reasons generally do not appear on the journalistic radar.

Of course, each day in the world many, many things happen. Even if most of them were important, a news bulletin is only so long. A newspaper can only carry so many stories. So we rely on the journalist to select those that are most important for us to know.

Among experienced journalists, it is often said that a new reporter must develop a 'nose for a story'. Editors we interviewed spoke of a 'news instinct'. These descriptions are used to describe the way that journalists, through experience, are able to acquire a sophisticated sense of what comprises a newsworthy event, of what kinds of things should be revealed to the public and in what kinds of ways. When a news team have a morning meeting to discuss, which of the day's stories should be followed or developed, they will generally have a shared sense of what kinds of newsworthiness different stories carry. This will guide them in how they decide what is the lead story and what should follow. But sociologists of news have shown that newsworthiness is less to do with an instinct and more to do with internalizing a set of arbitrary values that have become established over time through institutionalized practices.

It was Galtung and Ruge who first described the kinds of values that underpinned the way that certain international events and not others come to be chosen as news. Studying the coverage of international news, they identified 12 recurring criteria that determine whether or not a story was published.

- *Frequency*: how close a story happens to the moment of publication.
- *Threshold*: the level the event must reach in terms of scale for it to stand out.
- *Unambiguity*: the story should be clearly understood.
- *Meaningfulness*: the story should be relevant to the readers' frame of reference.
- *Consonance*: the build-up to an expected event.
- *Unexpectedness:* how unpredictable an event is.
- *Continuity:* a big story will remain in the news for days or weeks.
- *Composition*: a story may be selected because it helps balance the other stories.
- *Reference to elite nations:* some places are covered more than others.
- *Reference to elite people:* events affecting famous people.
- *Reference to persons*: news that has a human focus.
- *Reference to something negative*: bad news usually contains more of the above criteria than good news (Niblock, 2005).

The first of these might seem obvious since news should be up-to-date. There is great value in boasting 'the latest news'. But some of these values could be seen to threaten the idea of events having intrinsic importance. For example, 'meaningfulness' basically refers to whether the story can be made easily recognizable to an audience. A story that already fits into an existing frame of reference will seem more naturally newsworthy. It will also be unchallenging and require less contextualization. However, this means that stories that fall outside of existing frames of reference will tend to be ignored. Alternatively, stories will be given an angle that makes them fit an existing frame. Therefore, for example, a hungry child in Africa is yet another hungry child in Africa irrespective of the political or economic process that brought this about. So the following story would sound strange to, say, a Northern European audience:

> Here is the national and international news. Today there was further violence as a legacy of European colonialism and map drawing in Africa. Is it time for these countries to take responsibility? We show links between corporate activity and the civil war.

Consonance is a build-up to an expected event. Studies of local news in the US have shown concern that there is too much reliance on official events, sporting events, political events. News organizations like these events, as they can plan resources and use established routines.

Composition is where news must have a variety of content. After all news is for the most part a product that needs to be sold. What if there were, and there often are, twenty wars happening across the planet? Does a news bulletin just cover them all? Editors normally like a balance of material that includes some lighter human interest stories. But how does this need to have a range of subjects tally with the idea of intrinsic newsworthiness?

There has been much criticism of the 'hook and hold' format of news bulletins. In this format, material is ordered to get our immediate attention but with a promise of something else later on. We will be reminded of what is to come at different points hopefully so that we stay tuned. So news must be chosen to have the right events to fill this template.

Reference to elite places and persons is where events that involved elite countries or famous people are more likely to be covered. Ordinary people are less interesting as are countries that are outside of the major economic powers. Imagine the following bulletin:

> Today in East Zharifan ten people were killed in a bus crash, the country's worst ever.

or

> A man from Southern Chile was today released after being held hostage for six months.

The 'news instinct' could be said to be the internalization of these values (Patterson and Wilkins, 1994: 26). Inexperienced journalists are often said by their seniors that they were not able to 'see the story'. What they mean is that they are not yet familiar with these 'unofficial' criteria that Galtung and Ruge sought to make explicit. All of these criteria mean that news is not neutrally about the world, not about the events that affect all people, but that the news world is driven by a specific set of values.

Since Galtung and Ruge published their criterions, a number of others have been added. Gans (1980) added things like 'surprise stories'. Bell (1991) added predictability – journalists prefer things that can be prescheduled, and prefabrication referring to the existence of ready-made texts, such as press releases. They also like scheduled events, such as sports, concerts, etc. Harcup and O'Neil (2001) include entertainment, picture opportunities and sex.

There are a number of other news frames that commentators have identified. These determine the ways that news events, once chosen will not only be presented but also indicate some of the qualities that events must possess if they are to be perceived as having news potential. The headings used here are drawn from Bennett (2005).

Personalization

Complex issues are downplayed to personalize them in terms of the individual faults, mistakes, gains, losses, etc. that lie on the surface. A famine caused by western politics and economics is understood in terms of the suffering of one child and the heroism of a pop star who is raising money. Osama bin Laden has come to represent a mythical global terror. Complex ideologies and ways of life and political viewpoints are all merged under his face. Often we learn little about actual policies and the detailed results of policies, only that there is a clash between certain politicians. In such cases, personalization can only lead to lack of understanding.

Dramatization

Only bits of news that can be dramatized are dealt with. More complex issues and sociological context cannot be so easily dramatized. Drama also puts characters at the centre. Drama also suggests easy resolution when problems may be much more complex and long lasting. News media, for example, often become impatient in wars when no resolution appears to happen, after the initial excitement. They quickly lose interest in famines. News likes crisis and resolution – even though actual problems still remain.

Fragmentation

The need for dramatization and personalization means that stories become fragmented from each other. Dramatization and personalization mean that broader socio-political contexts remain unmentioned, for example, in the war on terror, 'terrorist' activities are not linked to western foreign policy. Famines and conflict on Africa are not shown in the context of 100 years of western intervention and map drawing but as bursts of drama. The ongoing effects of globalization and third world debt are not routinely included as part of the reason that there are famines.

The authority-disorder bias

The news likes to frame things in terms of threats, such as to social order, to democracy, to our children, etc., even when these things themselves are part of complex social changes or political situations. The war on terror, which is a threat to our democracy, is one such simplification. A rise in gun crime in European cities is seen as simple breakdown of values rather than as part of larger processes of social change and the marginalization of large sections of the population in the global economy.

What all these different news values and frames allow us to understand is why a hurricane in the US is news whereas those that happen in Asia or Africa are not, unless they involve particularly horrific casualties. When they happen in the US, elite places and persons such as 'The White House' and 'The President' can be mentioned, as we saw in our IRN example. These values allow us to explain why the suspect in the Bali bombings was simply guilty where all ambiguity are removed. Finally, it supports the idea expressed by Machin and Jaworski (2006) that the image and film footage archives are not in themselves ideologically constructed but are designed in accordance with the existing news reality.

These frames help journalists to select events from the vast array of things going on in the world. They also provide a sense of public expectation that the news should fulfil. So, if these frames and values influence what becomes news – the stories we see, who they deal with, the images we see of them, more so than the events themselves – is it meaningful to think of such things as 'truth' or 'bias'? Importantly, we can also, as Machin and Jaworski suggest, see how this means that certain discourses about how the world works remain dominant and others excluded.

Here is an example of the stories chosen by the IRN team for Friday, 26 September 2003. These were selected from the day's agency feeds. We can think about how each of these fulfils one or more of the News Values.

- The aftermath of a major earthquake in Japan, which had happened the previous afternoon;
- Reports suggesting controversial injections into the brain of a victim of the human form of 'Mad Cow Disease' seem to have had an effect;
- Mortar attack on civilians in Iraq;
- Labour minister is warning Prime Minister Tony Blair about consequences of taking Britain into war with Iraq;
- Released Colombian hostage is due back in Britain tonight;
- A new film advertisement to be screened in cinemas warning women about the dangers of date rape;
- Scottish National Party conference underway;
- British conker championships this weekend – recent good weather mean poor-quality conkers;
- Three-quarters of drivers say prayers at the wheel, according to the Automobile Association.

The earthquake has scale, and will run depending on the number of deaths (magnitude) and especially if there are British citizens affected (elite nations). There will also be fragmentation as the story, if lacking qualities, which activate the other news values, will cease to be reported. There may be a follow-up, if say an elite person makes a comment on the event, if it turns out there were national citizens involved, or if there is a charity appeal involving celebrities, although here the attention will be on the personalities and not on the complexity of the events.

Mad cow disease is dramatic ('controversial') and will be included for continuity, as this will have been in the news over the proceeding weeks. There will be no full scientific report and it is unlikely that we will ever learn as to whether the procedure was successful.

The mortar attack on civilians in Iraq qualifies under continuity, order/disorder and dramatization. Overall this is typical of the fragmented way that we get information about such conflicts. We will have little idea neither about exactly who carried out the attack nor of their political aims. The attackers will be linguistically evaluated as 'insurgents', 'militia' or 'extremists'.

The story about Tony Blair qualifies for elite persons and places. Politicians are the source par excellence. Here there is also personalization of issues where the actual facts are subordinated to this being a disagreement between individuals. This often conceals the actual issues.

The Columbian hostage story is included, as it is about a British person. It also has a dramatic element and a threat to social order. Such countries are depicted as wild and uncivilized. There will also be the chance for a personal focus on the returnee for a human-interest angle.

The date-rape story is dramatic, has an order/disorder angle, involves sex and is negative. In the British news media, like stories about paedophiles and sex-related events are of automatic newsworthiness, especially at times where there is a shortage of other material.

The Scottish National Party is included due to the elite nature of domestic politics. The party political system is naturally newsworthy although we may never learn about actual policies. This will more often be characterized by personalization and fragmentation.

The British conker championships and the drivers who pray at the wheel are included for compositional reasons.

Of course, how all these stories are written up, the lexical choices that will be made, how the participants and places are described, the kinds of verbs and adjectives that are used will depend on the identified market-oriented target groups as we saw in the case of the IRN bulletins. But we can see that certain discourses will naturally be favoured. Elite politicians and nations will be favoured. National and international events will be reduced to unambiguous themes and tend to appear in a fragmented fashion. The visual resources for these dominant discourses are then readily available in image and film archives to be searched and downloaded. Such visual representation, as Barthes (1977) reminds us, serves as proof of the reality of the nature of the events even if this is symbolized rather than documented.

However, what these frames and values do not allow us to explain is why we regularly see and hear news that is derived itself from other bureaucratic organizations. Most of the news we see is sourced in courtrooms, police stations, council offices, political administration, etc. These organizations therefore have huge power over the definition of news events.

The reliance on bureaucratic organizations

When I discussed news values earlier in the chapter in respect to the ITN news footage archive, I emphasized the way that journalists and news are dependent on the definitions of reality of other bureaucratic organizations. What this means is that while journalists may write up their stories neutrally without bias, the reality that they transmit is already framed through the procedures and interests of those organizations. The reason that journalists have developed this dependency is quite simply that like other institutions, news organizations have to find a way to manage reality in a way that is predictable. News organizations have to produce a daily supply of news events of the kind that fulfil the above news values and which allows a variety of material suitable for a bulletin or the different sections of the newspaper.

In the best possible case, local news-gathering would happen something like this: the reporters would find out the most important, relevant events to the community. To do this, they would have regular everyday contact with that community. Once they had come across a story they would then identify the person who could best give further information about those events to enable them to be fully understood from every angle. For example, a reporter might find out from a local nurse, spoken to in a local cafe, that the epidemic of hospital-based infections on her ward can be directly connected to a decade of cutbacks in cleaning and hygiene. The journalist could then do background research, investigating the agencies that have been contracted to do the cleaning with untrained staff employed without contracts. They could research hospital expenditure and then interview nurses and doctors, gain access to the financial and staffing records to show changing patterns in cleaning. In the piece all points of view are covered. As a result the readers are informed about issues that deeply affect and shape the community around them. Instead, of course, what we would get as news in such a story would be an official statement citing statistics and probably a political comment stating that hospital managers should take responsibility.

In reality, this best possible case has never really happened at all. For newspapers there has always been the massive practical problem of needing to provide a regular, predictable, economically viable source of news events. For this reason journalists are simply not able to act out this best possible case.

Historically, journalists developed solutions to the problem of supplying steady predictable supplies of news stories by establishing *beats*. These beats would take them into regular contact with sources, such as the police, councils and other bureaucratic organizations. These organizations process the kinds of events that are newsworthy on a daily basis at a pace that is predictable. So, rather than digging around in the community, reporters can access files and reports produced by these organizations. Reporters cannot spend their days wandering the streets hoping to come across something newsworthy. Even if they did come up with something big, occasionally this would not be sufficient when a daily title would require at least say three pieces from each reporter before lunchtime to have enough copy to fill the newspaper. To provide a regular supply of copy that qualifies as newsworthy, the reporters follow a beat, which brings them into contact with organizations that produce such news events. Therefore, a beat is the routine path and set of locations that a reporter will visit each day.

However, since the events must qualify as newsworthy, these cannot just be any kind of place. They must be the kind that produces a regular supply of easily usable, legitimate, newsworthy events. Places that do just this are official institutions and bureaucratic organizations, such as government offices, law enforcement organizations, health authorities, the military, etc. So we might say that reporters do not find events. They do not detect them. What they do is put themselves into situations where they will be exposed to them.

Mark Fishman (1980) carried out an extensive study on the nature of news gathering at the provincial level. He gives the example of crime reporting. In any city there might be a number of areas where crime would not be too difficult to find. There might be an extensive drug subculture, a highly impoverished area where much crime takes place. But reporters cannot wait around on the streets until a crime takes place. Stories might come up, but not with the kind of frequency required to fill pages.

However, reporters can put themselves in places where crimes are regularly recorded. In a city there might be several law enforcement agencies, jails, and court systems where crimes are recorded, where a reporter can get hold of material that is easily convertible in to news copy. What they will do is visit the organizations that provide the best, predictable, easily usable events. For crime stories these are the courts and police sources.

There is a second reason that the reporter could not simply hang around an impoverished housing area waiting to find out about a crime. News requires official sources. Even though the people who live in the impoverished areas may be able to tell us more about crime, about what it is like to live on the margins of society, where there is mass unemployment and drug taking, where crime might seem the only way of life for many people, such voices are not official. They represent no official body. It would not do to have a news story that had its origins entirely in the words of John Smith, owner of the local café. The story about the lack of cleaning on the hospital ward could not be sources solely from a cleaner or a nurse. It would need a spokesperson or official. News stories must be seen to have their origins in official organizations.

Most importantly, the view of a bureaucratically structured society gives the journalists a list in advance of all of the relevant knowers for any topic of news happening. They will not necessarily be the experiencers of these events, such as the people in the disadvantaged housing scheme, where crime is rife. But they will be official knowers who will provide official-style information.

The dependency on official sources

We can see that this reliance on official sources itself has a gate-keeping nature. It means that news has a tendency to be heavily weighted towards certain kinds of events. The world as we find it in the news becomes a reflection of bureaucratically produced events. So we get an official definition of the world, or at least those events that are defined as relevant by official sources. In the case of crime we end up with an official view of crime events. Crime is defined by the records of the police and of law courts. This is presented without sociological and historical context. Of course it could be defined otherwise. In the 1930s, a team of researchers at Chicago University carried out studies into inner-city crime (Park and Burgess, 1927). They found that criminals were young men from marginalized social groups who shared the same social and moral values as young middle-class men. Crime was about bettering yourself, organization, leadership, individualism, pride. In short all the values prized by the wider society. The solution to 'crime', therefore, was to find a way to include these young men into mainstream society, rather than leave them in marginalized communities.

A reliance on official sources means that this kind of conclusion is less than likely. A news item gathered at a magistrates' court is more likely to hear that that the perpetrators were a menace to society, rather than the political policies that created the social situation in the first place. Clearly this process places power in the hands of those who already have institutional power to define the nature of the social world and the events in it.

This reliance on official sources can be seen through even a casual look at the daily newspaper or nightly television news bulletin. For the most part, news is devoted to the official action of government and elected officials where journalists have spent time in government offices or communicating with press officers. In a study of the *New York Times* and the *Washington Post*, Sigal (1973) found that government officials were the sources of at least three quarters of all hard news. Of course, the journalists may deal with these critically, but they are fundamentally about what politicians say and do. Meanwhile critical investigative reporting is sidelined (Bennett, 2005: 116).

The golden triangle of news beats in the US is the White House, the State Department and the Pentagon. Journalists will go there first for information. In other countries, it is their own political institutions. The press conferences and press releases produced by these institutions will be at the centre of news and defining the nature of events. On the one hand, journalists could argue that since these are elected by the people they write for them they should form the heart of reporting. But this means that their claims go unquestioned.

Bennett (2004) considered the reliance on official sources during the reporting of the Iraq invasion by the US and its allies. Before the invasion happened, there were reports that there was no link between Saddam Hussein and Al Quaida. It had also been reported that it was by no means certain that there were Weapons of Mass Destruction to be found in Iraq. But once the war was underway, there was 24-hour coverage from journalists in tanks and images of Saddam's statue being toppled. Few news stories continued to question connections between Saddam and 9/11. This is because, Bennett believes, the attention of journalists was firmly on official sources and political administration.

Bennett (2005: 2) argues that in these cases, such as crime, the healthcare system and Iraq, it is not that reporters are making up the facts. It is not that they are themselves distorting the truth. The problem is that news organizations are more likely to report accounts coming from official administrative sources over any possible contrary accounts from other sources.

This emphasis on official sources gives a huge advantage to those already in power for getting their issues on the political agenda. In the long term, clearly, we have a case where the kinds of problems and solutions presented in the news become limited to those defined by official sources. Bennett (2005: 118) shows concern for this. He worries that people will come to accept things like poverty, crime, war and political apathy as inevitable parts of the everyday world, rather than as the tragic results of the concentration of power and the nature of the way that we now run our societies.

We can use this discussion of journalism's dependency on bureaucratic organizations and official sources to understand more about the examples with which we began this chapter. The definition of the trial of the Bali bomber is simply a reproduction of a report from the court. Of course, in the IRN write-up this is obscured. But the public are so familiar with such official definitions of news events that this is not seen as problematic. When we read an article on events in the conflict in Afghanistan, we will find the comments of military representatives and foreign office officials. As such the events will routinely appear without sociological and historical context. The page editor will then be able to locate archive visual support, showing images or footage of suffering civilians and guerrilla fighters that match this theme. A search on the archives for visuals that match corporate crime or the illegal actions of states that manipulate whole economies or invade them in the name of their own interests will not be productive, simply because these are not established news frames and there are no official sources where such stories can be easily and conveniently be accessed by the journalist.

The commercialization of news

Finally, in order to understand the nature of the news reports and the visuals that support them with which we began this chapter, we need to understand the way that news organizations are financed.

Earlier, we described how society has expectations about the ideal role of the journalist – including that they should ensure that a diversity of views are heard. But this is problematic considering that news outlets are increasingly concentrated into fewer and fewer hands both at the local and global level, facilitated by successive changes in media regulation. These changes have allowed huge increases in the amounts of media outlets that can be owned by one organization, and have permitted owners to acquire cross-media interests. For example, in 2005 in the UK the Trinity Mirror group owned around 250 local titles. They were in a position where they had ownership of previously competing local titles such as in South Wales with the *Western Mail and South Wales Evening Post*. It also had shares in a number of radio stations and networks and shares in *Reuters*. In France, the Le Monde Group was controlling 43 different daily and weekly titles. In Spain, the bulk of newspapers were in the hands of four large groups, *Prisa, Correo, Zeta and Pearson*. Across Europe and the US most newspaper titles are part of such large media groups (European Journalism Centre Online, 2005).

For some theorists, studying the political economy of media, this increasing concentration of private ownership is at odds with the media being able to act as a watchdog for a democratic society. It is the fear that news outlets that are part of massive corporations will be unlikely to be critical of views that are favourable to corporate capitalism. In addition, it is argued that they will be unlikely to represent views that are critical of themselves, in other words, of large corporations. Such news media may be able to cover world poverty, for example, showing audiences heart-rending images of starving Africans. But the reporter is unlikely to connect this developing world crisis to its roots in global capitalism and the activities of global corporations and banking. We might find reports on anti-social behaviour in our cities, but little on the way that the associated poverty is related to economic policies and forms of social organization that are favourable to large corporations.

In the 1980s and 1990s, there were many big changes in the ownership and structure of news organizations. This was part of a more general bulking-up facilitated by changes in broadcasting regulation. The US Telecommunications Act 1996 was the catalyst for speeding up mergers and buyouts. The law encouraged competition, hence dragging down prices of news products. One school of thought to the right believed that the winners would be news consumers. Market logic meant that in the end there would be more choice and producers would seek to meet market requirements. But from another perspective, it meant that more could be owned and companies could get bigger. One advantage of increasing ownership of outlets for news journalism is that economy of scale means that if content is made centrally it can then be syndicated across the outlets. For example, the 1996 Act freed up how many radio stations could be held by one company. US-based Clear Channel soon had control over 1,200 stations (www.clearchannel.com). Similar cross-media groupings soon formed all over Europe, such as SER in Spain and EMAP in Britain.

Also challenging the idea of news organizations as neutral, media researchers point out that many of the major shareholders and investors in media corporations are investment banks and other large institutions that have interests across a range of other industries (Wasko, 1982; Herman and Chomsky, 1988). Some writers (Hollingsworth, 1986;

Herman and Chomsky, 1988; Kellner, 1990) see this as a process whereby media corporations will tend to support conservative policies, and will be uncritical of neo-capitalism, seeing it as a natural state of affairs. Herman and Chomsky give a number of examples of international atrocities, such as in Cambodia and East Timor, where the US government were directly involved, which were completely absent from the national press.

McChesney (2004: 21) shows that media corporations are among the biggest companies in the world. In 2002, McChesney shows, *Forbes* magazine calculated that over a third of the 50 wealthiest Americans generated the bulk of their fortunes through the media and related industries. He argues: 'our media, then, far from being on the sidelines of the capitalist system, are amongst its greatest beneficiaries' (ibid.: 2). These central players are able to lobby Congress and government sometimes with large amounts of cash, and other times in return for favours (Tunstall and Machin, 1999).

One of the effects of the deregulation of ownership has been the slimming down of the news production process to increase profits. Throughout the 1990s there were waves of redundancies in journalism. In print journalism, these waves were caused by developments in on-screen page make-up technology that made certain roles obsolete. Subeditors could now do the work of page compositors, for instance, while local reporters began to carry cameras instead of being accompanied by a photographer. Simultaneously, increases in commercial competition have enabled larger chains and conglomerates to use production cost-cutting as a way to maximize profits (Hallin, 1996; Bourdieu, 1998).

Combined with these commercial pressures have been the effects of news media. Bromley (1997) and Parker (1995) described changes in journalism where new recruits to broadcast stations were being trained in digital editing and script writing rather than traditional core investigative techniques that centred on producing well-substantiated news. The news we looked at in our IRN examples above, comes from one electronic newsroom, spliced together from news feeds and archive material. This will then be syndicated free to users, funded by advertising revenue (Niblock and Machin, 2007).

One major impact of commercial pressures and reduced staffing in the newsroom has been the increased reliance of news outlets on ready-made material. Many organizations, companies, councils, the government and advertisers, employ large numbers of people, many of them exjournalists to produce new copy that promotes their products, activities or broader interests. Of course such press releases will be written to fit in with established news values and news frames. In this way, they will be more likely to be used by office bound journalists who have few resources and little time for further investigation (Rampton and Stauber, 2000).

The influence of advertising

One of the arguments in favour of a commercial media is that market demand ensures diversity of output, which, in turn, is good for democracy. Given a free reign, the media, this argument goes, through the laws of supply and demand, will provide something for whatever market is out there. If audiences do not like something they will simply move on to something that they do. If we take the example of a newspaper, we could assume that if a title does not reflect the views of its readers then circulations will fall and eventually it will close, leaving behind competitors which give the market what it wants. However, political economy theories of media warn that this model of choice and diversity does not operate accordingly in the context of news journalism. This is because audiences and readers alone are not in all cases the primary source of income for news providers. Rather, for the main part, media get their income from advertising. Newspapers, for example, would run at a loss if they had to rely on cover price alone.

Curran and Seaton (1977) showed that newspapers have long relied heavily on advertising for their survival. In their book, *Power without Responsibility*, they show how the need to attract advertisers was crucial historically in the development of the press. Titles that were most attractive to advertisers could afford to spend more on content and appearance, and reduce their cover price to encourage mass appeal. Under market principles this suggests that readers are in a powerful position to demand content. However, we cannot assume that advertisers want to reach all kinds of people equally, and that they are indifferent to the content of the newspaper. Curran and Seaton show that if we go back to the mid-nineteenth century, when professional journalism was consolidating, advertisers were much less interested in newspapers that were read by the lower classes that had little expendable income. It was only after Second World War when there were paper shortages that advertisers supported the left-wing workers' press. Once paper shortages ended, advertisers boycotted left-wing newspapers in Britain. Curran and Seaton give the example of the *Daily Herald*, which had 4.7 million readers in its last year before closing, more than three times the number of the three 'upmarket' titles, the *Guardian, The Times* and the *Financial Times*. The *Herald* was still running at a loss on cover price alone. It had to close. Other well-read left-wing titles, they show, also closed due to lack of advertiser support, such as *News Chronicle* and *Sunday Citizen*. Gradually the only down-market newspapers that survived were those that were much more centrist in their politics. Therefore, through the loss of these newspapers, left-wing politics were denied any means of mass media support.

News values and advertising

In the case of our IRN radio news bulletin with which we started the chapter, the journalist had rewritten the story specifically for different market groups. This is because one of the major effects of the deregulation of the news media has been the pressure to increase revenues. This has meant being able to demonstrate to advertisers that particular kinds of consumers are being addressed. This does not mean that they have to be entertained, only that news must be tailored to speak to them. This will mean, for example, the lexical choices made to represent the participants will be chosen for the target group. It is common for linguists and discourse analysts to consider such choices but not for them to investigate the reasons behind these choices. Earlier we pointed to lexical changes in the 7 a.m. bulletin, we found words such as 'racing', 'forcing thousands', 'declared' and 'hit', connote action, drama and impending threat. This is not just about the 'bias' of the journalist but is systematic. Market research is able to indicate what kind of beliefs people hold, or what kinds of mood they wish to find expressed in the news at different times of the day.

We can see that by the 9 a.m. bulletin, the story was more humanized, allowing a different range of domestic – and female – voices to be used. Here the target audience is female and based at home during the day. Adverts will be heard between other content that are targeted to this specific group.

> A state of emergency's been declared in Washington, as Hurricane Isabel heads towards the east coast of the US. A hundred and thirty thousand people in North Carolina have also been told to leave their homes. The White House is preparing for the worst – boarding up doors and windows. But not everyone is on the move – Audrey Holloway lives in Hampton Village is staying put . . . (13 secs of woman talking)

Linguistically, the style is a mixture of the first two versions at 6 a.m. and 7 a.m. in terms of immediacy and specificity. Emphasis is placed on the experiences of women in this package, and the fact that people were reluctant to leave their homes. The pace of the vocabulary is less high-octane, less stereotypically 'male', which can be seen with the replacement of 'racing' with 'heads' to describe the movement of the hurricane. 'A hundred and thirty thousand people' have been included as the participants replacing 'businesses and schools' and the earlier sedated 6 a.m. bulletin where it was 'tens of thousands of people'. We also find a specific location is included, 'Washington', where it is assumed that the target listener would be aware of the meaning of this city. In other rewrites, only 'The White House' would be mentioned. We also find the inclusion of people being 'told to leave their homes' which is important for the target group. The bulletin ends with an interview with a woman braving the hurricane out. In fact, though less recognizable to British listeners, this is a typical US news frame or discourse where people stand up to such threats. In the British news, journalists would not tend to pursue this angle, preferring beleaguered, rather than brave citizens.

Critical Discourse Analysis of news texts

In this chapter, we have seen how we must understand the social and cultural goings-on that lie behind news to really understand the nature of the texts that we analysed linguistically at the beginning of the chapter. We must understand news not as the investigative activity of the truth-seeking reporter but as an institutional process. In the first place, we must give up the idea that we are dealing with simple journalistic bias or ideology in news texts. The analysis of the lexical choices of a text can reveal something of the broader discourses that are realized and therefore something of the ideology that is being communicated. But we cannot assume that this is down to the journalists themselves. They may, due to professional practice be neutrally reflecting the views and information that they have received from official sources, but this is nevertheless not the same as reporting the most important issues, investigation and corroboration which commercial changes have now made even less likely. We also need to be mindful of the way that what we see and hear as news is part of a commercially influenced process. Even public service news has budgets and resourcing constraints. So stories may be chosen or shaped primarily through the need to court advertisers. And finally, since news comes primarily from official sources and other bureaucratic organizations, news naturally tends to transmit the discourses of those sources. Crime, social problems, conflicts and international events all tend to reflect existing institutional concerns. Young journalists often begin their careers believing that they are indeed seekers of truth. But if they are to remain in the profession they must allow themselves to become institutionalized. Of course, they have the comfort of their professional ethic towards truth, although in practice most experienced journalists find little comfort in this. In terms of our textual analysis we should ourselves always be mindful of the massive influence of these institutional factors. We must also be aware of the massive amount of power that this gives to these institutions to define what becomes news.

5 News discourse II: Anti-racism and neo-liberalism in the British regional press

David Machin and Andrea Mayr

Introduction

In Chapter 4, we focused on news as institutional discourse and the increasing market-driven nature of news. One result of these commercial pressures has been a tendency in the press towards a more 'up-beat' coverage of lifestyle and consumer issues away from discussion of socio-economic problems. In this chapter, we turn to the analysis of a regional British paper, the *Leicester Mercury*, which through its positive coverage of ethnic minorities and the multicultural city, has been identified by the British government as a model regional newspaper and an example to be followed across the country. However, as we shall argue, this model of anti-racism and of 'multicultural cohesion' can be understood primarily as part of the role of the newspaper in promoting the healthy buzz of the city-as-brand in creating a positive vibe for advertisers and attracting investors. This commercial trend has to be understood within the wider context of ownership of newspapers and news organizations by a few powerful commercial corporations at the local and global level, and the resulting constraints on coverage that is critical of corporate capitalism. The *Leicester Mercury* itself is owned by the newspaper chain Daily Mail and General Trust plc, one of the UK's largest media holding companies, whose parent company, Northcliffe, runs about 100 newspapers in Britain.

The *Leicester Mercury* is based in the city of Leicester, which has a large ethnic minority population, soon to be over 50 per cent. Since the late 1990s, the newspaper has included the voices of ethnic minority community leaders, has criticized racist views, supported the multicultural policies of the local county council and has taken the decision to no longer cover 'sensitive' issues that might incite violence. It is not hard to see why from a government perspective this model is appealing, as it deflects responsibility away from the authorities, from broader social organization and economic issues to the individuals.

Research in media and critical discourse studies has detailed the nature of the open anti-immigration stance and racism of much of the British national press (Hartman and Husband, 1974; Murdock, 1984; Mclaughlin, 1999; van Dijk, 1999), where ethnic minorities were mainly represented in association with crime, violence, social welfare and problematic immigration.

It is probably safe to say that press coverage of open racism has become less prevalent and has been replaced by ethnic minorities being represented in a far more positive vein, such as through festivals and other 'exotica' (Cottle, 2000). Our own analysis of articles from the *Leicester Mercury* confirms this move away from anti-immigration and problem stories. At first glance, the Mercury appears to represent a much broader range of people, such as 'community leaders', 'ordinary people', academics and businesspeople. But a closer look at who is represented and how they are represented as doing and saying shows that there is no coverage of the structural inequalities that affect many ethnic minorities.

The approach taken by the *Leicester Mercury* is nothing but commendable, but its stance as an anti-racist newspaper is also framed by a commercial interest. Its editor and Leicester City Council (LCC) are aware that avoiding conflict and promoting harmony instead are crucial for attracting investors, businesses and advertisers and that a more buoyant coverage of events and people can only help in this process. In our analysis, we therefore ask serious questions of the ability of the commercialized press to address the social and economic issues affecting ethnic minorities and immigrants.

Methodology

Here we analyse three texts from a corpus of articles we collected from the *Leicester Mercury* in 2005. We conducted a lexis search, looking for articles containing the word 'multiculturalism', 'community', 'diversity', of which we found 32, and which we then looked up in the local library and photocopied, including the photographs. The texts we have chosen for analysis are representative of that sample. We also looked for evidence of articles with negative coverage of immigration and multiculturalism in the *Leicester Mercury*, but did not find any.

The method of analysis we adopt here is within the general framework of Critical Discourse Analysis (CDA), using a discourse-analytical/ multi-modal approach (van Leeuwen, 1993, 1996; Machin and van Leeuwen (2005). The multimodal approach is important, because it is not only the written language that contributes to the representation of multiculturalism in the paper but also the visual input. We combine this with a discourse-historical approach as outlined by van Leeuwen and Wodak (1999) and Wodak (2001). The discourse-historical approach seeks to integrate as many of the genres of discourse referring to a particular issue as possible, as well as the historical dimensions of that issue. Thus, in analysing linguistic representations of multiculturalism in the *Leicester Mercury*, we focused not just on the actual newspaper texts, but we also included, and drew evidence from, the historical context and background information of immigration to Leicester. In addition, we interviewed the editor of the *Leicester Mercury* and a policy officer from LCC to gain a better insight into the representation and practice of multiculturalism, in which the paper and the Council play such an important part. If we are to understand the discourses we find in the newspaper, we must locate them in the socio-political reality in which they are used.

So in investigating the construction of various discourses of 'multiculturalism' in the *Leicester Mercury* and in line with one of CDA's main tenets we are using an interdisciplinary approach, integrating linguistic, historical and socio-political perspectives. This interdisciplinary perspective enhances the purely discourse-analytical analysis of the corpus and sheds light on possible hidden agendas not visible at first sight.

In the following sections, we therefore provide an account of Leicester and its policy for multiculturalism, the role played by the *Leicester Mercury* in this and an overview of various models of multiculturalism and their associated discourses. We then move on to the actual linguistic analysis of texts.

Background

We now turn to the context for our observations. The city of Leicester, about 100 miles to the north of London, government figures predict, will soon be the first British city to have a non-white majority. In 2003, the ethnic population of Leicester was counted between 35 and 40 per cent, and it is estimated that by 2011 it will exceed 50 per cent (Singh, 2003: 42). There have been waves of immigration, especially in the 1950s from the West Indies, in the 1960s from India, Pakistan and Bangladesh, and then in the 1970s, when the former colonies evicted their Asian populations. During this last major wave, the ethnic minority population grew from 5 to 25 per cent. There was a surge in racial violence in the city along with support for the neo-Nazi National Front. But from the 1970s, unlike some other British cities with large ethnic minority populations, there were no major outbreaks of violence. In 2003, the government awarded Leicester 'Beacon City' status as confirmation of it being a model for others to follow.

However, not everyone has been so certain as to whether the lack of rioting in Leicester was connected specifically to the policies of the local council. According to Singh (2003), there are two distinctive features of immigration to Leicester that better explain the lack of rioting and tension. Our interview with Paul Winston, Policy Officer at the County Council, supported this analysis. First, waves of immigration were provided with an abundance of cheap inner-city accommodation, which meant there was no competition with white communities for social housing (Solomos and Singh, 1990). This also prevented groups from becoming neighbours, as is the case in the northern cities, where this has had a huge influence on racial conflict (Phillips, 1981).

Second, the biggest factor in preventing riots in Leicester was the kinds of immigrants that moved into the city. Many of those, who came from the former colonies, were 'twice immigrants' who brought with them a high level of professional competence, of education and entrepreneurial experience. In Leicester, there are over 10,000 registered Asian businesses (Singh, 2003). Even in a context of racism and discrimination, these people were more equipped to adapt to the local economy and to generate their own wealth (Vertovec, 1994). Winston observed that Leicester's prosperity is owed mainly to Indian business.

Leicester has therefore avoided some of the levels of inner-city deprivation and its associated problems that have been a feature of the northern cities. However, the centrality of poverty and socio-economic factors in racial conflict has been signposted by much sociological research (e.g. Dorling and Thomas, 2004; Simpson, 2004). Yet these factors have not been highlighted in government policy and guidelines for multiculturalism.

Singh (2003) warns of increasing levels of socio-economic deprivation in Leicester which spell out considerable dangers. He warns of the backlash in white communities where there is a feeling of 'colonialism from below' and where people become minorities in their 'own cities' (Singh, 2003: 45). In Leicester these communities, like those on the largely white estates, are unskilled and form part of a growing underclass. As Britain deindustrializes and manufacturing is moved to cheaper production areas around the globe, the role of these groups in society is not discussed. While LCC (2002) does acknowledge that not all groups share equally in the success of cultural diversity, this is not something that is covered in the *Leicester Mercury*.

In 2005, the Chairman of the Commission for Racial Equality, Trevor Phillips, in a speech described Leicester as one city that was sleepwalking into segregation. The newspaper texts analysed here were produced shortly after this speech and can be understood partly as a response to it. Concerned with its image of city-as-brand, The Council and the *Mercury* rallied to challenge this assessment of the situation in Leicester.

The *Leicester Mercury* and Multiculturalism

The *Leicester Mercury*, the city's daily local newspaper, has a circulation of around 90,000 daily. Editor Nick Carter has been active in local politics to promote diversity and understanding. When he became editor in the late 1990s, he inherited a right-wing newspaper in the model of its parent, the *Daily Mail*, still noted for its intolerance. The paper was producing an Asian version which he closed down, feeling that an integrated version was needed.

Prior to the 2001 general election, Carter was founder of the Leicester Multicultural Advisory Group (LMAG), made up of local media, the police, faith groups, head teachers, other community groups and academics, which meets each month to discuss integration and cohesion. Carter himself had been concerned about the period leading up to the elections, where the two main political parties were both pressing to appear toughest on anti-immigration, particularly of the effect that this would have on community relations in Leicester. Also it was during 2000 that government statistics predicted that Leicester would have a minority white population by 2011, which had been presented negatively in some national media. Carter felt that both these issues could heighten tension in the city. He told us that he decided either not to cover any issue that might fuel conflict, and, where possible, take a positive stance on others. This meant a change in what was perceived as the role of the local newspaper

> from being passively responsible on reporting, to being proactively responsible. We're now more sensitive about whether something should be covered or not. There have been incidents in a couple of neighbourhoods where tensions have resulted in violence or confrontations. We may have automatically written about this before, though now we're more aware of how such reporting would have an impact on the wider situation, with the potential to aggravate matters.
>
> (From Commission for Racial Equality, winter 2003, http://193.113.211.175/publs/connections/conn_03wi_united.html)

Carter told us that there are two reasons why this model makes sense for newspapers: moral and business. The moral reason is that a community will only welcome a newspaper that welcomes that community. The business reason is that large minority groups are important to advertisers and in a city like Leicester it is the Asian business sector that basically drives the local economy.

While undoubtedly Nick Carter has made a big difference to reporting racism and multiculturalism in Leicester, there are limitations to what the local newspaper, or any commercial news media, can cover for very simple economic reasons. The press, as we pointed out in Chapter 4, has always relied heavily on advertising. Many commentators have pointed out that since the 1990s there have been waves of commercialization that have had a massive influence over the way that newspapers are run. McManus (1994) and Underwood (1995) have both revealed the way that newsrooms have become run by marketing people.

It has also meant even greater attention to courting advertisers. Since the mid-1990s many newspapers, now part of large press chains, have been relaunched through processes of market-led rebranding to maximize advertising revenue. There can be no socio-economic commentary, particularly if it might offend leading advertisers such as the local councils.

It is in the context of all these factors that we take up our analysis of the newspaper's coverage. It is in this highly commercialized news context that we find models of multicultural cohesion being generated.

Discourses of multiculturalism in the *Leicester Mercury*

In this section, we look at discourses of multiculturalism in our sample texts. We wish to reveal the way that the newspaper's positive representation of multiculturalism does in fact conceal and gloss over important problems that are central to understanding these issues and therefore recontextualizes social practice (van Leeuwen, 1993), in this case the social practice of multiculturalism. This is done in a way that is favourable to the ideology of the city as a brand and in the context of the newspaper as a commercial instrument. In this way, we suggest, it can be seen as being recontextualized through the language of neo-liberalism and the new capitalism of New Labour (Fairclough, 2000, 2003). Actual causes of racial conflict and their solutions are recontextualized through liberal models of essential sameness and through 'sharing' and 'talking', rather than through addressing social deprivation.

Van Leeuwen and Wodak (1999) have shown that it is through discourse that social actors constitute knowledge, roles and identities. And we can say that these discourses represent a kind of knowledge about what goes on in a particular social practice, ideas about why it is the way it is. These are the 'scripts' contained in the *Mercury* articles as to how multiculturalism gets done and by what kinds of people. A 'script' is a portion of knowledge, often shared unconsciously 'within a group of people and drawn upon in making sense of the world' (Fowler, 1991: 43). And if we assume that discursive acts are socially constitutive, playing a role in the production and construction of social conditions, what are these in this particular case? Are they those that are in harmony with discourses of neo-liberalism?

Before the actual analysis of the texts, we summarize the different ideologically motivated models of multiculturalism as described by Maclaren (1994). These can be thought of as theories or discourses of multiculturalism that can be found separately or together in any one society. We use them as a point of reference to think about the discourses used in The *Leicester Mercury* (see Machin and Mayr, 2007).

Discourses of multiculturalism

Conservative: Here ethnic groups are seen as different, with some being superior to others. In societies organized on this basis there will be a common culture based on the superior model. This model involves assimilationism, where groups should take in the superior dominant values. Maclaren sees the US as being characterized by this model. There may be a right to surface difference with an insistence of shared values at the core. Differences such as festivals and religion are permitted, provided these do not interfere with the society of the dominant value system.

Liberal: According to this model, groups are essentially the same and equal. People share fundamental deeper values associated with family, hard work and pleasure. Cultural differences are simply the surface ways, the rainbow of colours that express these similarities. This is often referred to as the 'carnival' version of multiculturalism or 'disneyfication' of cultures (Ritzer and Liska, 1997). This model can be criticized for missing actual deeper differences between ethnic groups.

Left-liberal: In this model, there is both diversity and real difference. But this tends to lead to essentialism, where fixed groups exist and where there are authentic voices that represent them. Emphasis on equality smothers important cultural and other differences, such as class, gender, sexuality, etc. Like the liberal view, this model tends to exoticize otherness and creates a sense of reified cultural authenticity. There is an important role here of 'authentic experience'. This involves a person's proximity to the oppressed as giving them the authority to speak. The political is often 'reduced only to the personal' (Maclaren, 1994: 52).

Critical left: Here, there are no monolithic groups. Instead people are affected by a range of interests, such as race, gender, religion, social-class. Whereas left-liberal multiculturalism equates resistance with destabilizing dominant systems of representation, critical multiculturalism goes one step further by asserting that 'all representations are the result of social struggles over signifiers and their signifieds' (MacLaren, 1994: 57–8). This model aims to get rid of any totalizing language of the 'other'. Maclaren also says that 'People can be situated very differently in the *same totalizing structures of oppression*' (ibid.: 58–9; emphasis in original). So in this view, to address race riots, we might need to look at what makes everyone's life such that they do riot. Here we might examine capitalism, deprivation and running cities defined by commerce and business as contributing factors.

We have chosen three texts that allow us to characterize the discourses of multiculturalism found in The *Leicester Mercury*. These also allow us to discuss the different voices that are represented in the newspaper: 'ordinary' people who are for or against multiculturalism, officials and school children. The full texts are given in the Appendix.

Text 1: the 'racists'

Text 1 is titled *'Would I go to Highfields?' laughs one of the snooker team. 'Only in a tank'* (19 November 2005). Here the journalist goes into a pub in a white working-class area which was mentioned in the speech by the Chairman of the Commission for Racial Equality, Trevor Phillips, as one of the areas in danger of turning into 'ghettoes'. This text represents those who are not part of the multicultural fabric of the city. We find conservative discourses of multiculturalism. Drawing on these discourses the participants are shown to believe that the city is being overrun by immigrants who should be assimilated and not allowed their own culture.

Firstly, what discourses do the 'racists' in Text 1 use? The journalist quotes them as drawing on a number of familiar racist discourses, described by van Dijk (1991). They can be characterized through the following examples:

> 'Would I go to Highfields' laughs one of the snooker team incredulously. 'Only if I was in a tank. Would I go down Belgrave Road at night? Forget it.'
>
> 'Belgrave is a no-go zone, reasons the 48-year-old who's never lived more than 400 yards from this club.'
>
> 'They've got all the kids learning about Hindus and Muslims and all that,' he says. 'They should be learning our religion – not theirs. When in Rome, and all that.'
>
> 'Coloureds, whispers the 82-old. It used to be 3 in 10. It's 9 in 10 now.'

> 'We are getting fed up because the whites are getting overrun,' says Jocelyn.
>
> 'As far as I'm concerned it's our country not theirs.'

These speakers expect a conservative assimilationist model of multiculturalism. If immigrants come to Leicester, then they should adapt to local values and practices. The speakers feel that they have been let down and become second-class citizens in their own land. At the same time, these incomers have made the city dangerous. It is commendable that these kinds of views are shown negatively in the press.

However, in the context of the background we gave to multiculturalism in Leicester, there are problems with the way that these people and their discourses are represented. Should the journalist not have said something about poverty and marginalization? *Mercury* editor Nick Carter acknowledges that there are no real details or a contexualization regarding the views of such racists and why they blame minorities rather than the authorities. But he said that the *Leicester Mercury* was a tabloid newspaper and not the *Guardian*. So the implication is that readers would not attend to such levels of analysis. This reflects van Leeuwen's (1996) suggestion that tabloids legitimize what they say through authentication in the personal and in 'real' experiences rather than arguments.

Let us now move on to our second text, in which people are very positive about multiculturalism in Leicester. As we shall see, these also favour an assimilationist model of multiculturalism.

Text 2: the 'multiculturalists'

Text 2 is titled '*The people have changed. There's no such thing as a black and white table in here now*' (19 November 2005). Here the journalist enters a pub which previously had 'a reputation as the most racist pub on the most racist estate in Leicester', to speak with the owners and customers. Everyone is shown to be positive about multiculturalism and mixing in Leicester. This is seen as evidence that Trevor Phillips was wrong in his comment that the city was moving towards 'segregation'. In this text we find a mixture of conservative, liberal and left liberal discourses of multiculturalism.

> 'I've got a boy and a girl by a Portuguese Indian from Goa,' says a lady called Sharon, rummaging in her purse for pictures. 'And I've got another lad who's half-Indian'. 'They're grown up now,' she says, 'but I'll always remember a thing in Humberstone Park when my daughter was little. I was sitting on a bench and some kids started calling her a Paki. I hate that word and I said: 'Excuse me,

but do I look like a Paki?' 'They said no and I said: 'Well, I'm that girl's mother. A Pakistani is someone who comes from Pakistan. She comes from Leicester, like me. 'That was ignorance, that was all it was,' she shrugs. 'My kids never have any problems now. It's all changed. People are mixing. That old ignorance is disappearing.'

'I'm like the whites,' he smiles, 'I don't speak any of the lingo either. But I've never had a problem with anyone in Belgrave or Highfields.'

'They are just like all of us, she shrugs.'

'We are all mongrels, she smiles, but mongrels are the best aren't they?'

Here people express the view that they are assimilated and therefore like the whites. As in Text 1, a conservative view of assimilation dominates, which is expressed both as 'becoming like whites' and as a melting pot, where difference disappears. Alongside this, we find the liberal discourse of everyone being the same. It is this one that makes the melting pot possible.

Text 3: 'the practice of multicultural mixing'

This text has the title *'How do I look to you*?' (3 December 2005*)*. Here the journalist enters a classroom to watch a session of 'Swapping Cultures', a government initiative to encourage young people to exchange information about their different cultures, thereby seeking to encourage them to go beyond tolerance for other cultures towards an active celebration of diversity and difference. In the article, the journalist cites some of what the teacher and the young people say in the classroom discussion about living in a multicultural society. He writes:

'Multiculturalism isn't something you learn out of a book here . . . It's displayed in college fashion shows where students model the clothes of different cultures, it's experienced in sharing food and music, and it's celebrated by getting involved in one another's cultural and religious festivals.'

'Swapping Cultures is a good thing,' says Mustafa Saleh. 'if you don't know one another properly that's when conflicts break out.'

The journalist himself says:

'It's black, it's white, it's Muslim, it's Sikh, it's Somali and it's everything else in-between.'

'Children are the future of this city. We need to get them talking.'

There is the idea that cohesion and intercultural harmony can be established by talking and sharing. This is the discourse of how multiculturalism is actually done and does provide a hint at what might take place when people do mix. Here we can say that there is a 'script'. This script involves 'talking' and 'sharing' culture and festivals. The comments above draw on a left-liberal model of multiculturalism, where there are differences and we can speak as members of essentialized groups to give people access to this culture. They also express a liberal carnival view of multiculturalism. Here we can experience other cultures through festivals and exotica, such as food and clothes. Following this script will prevent racial conflict.

We also observed that the official view on multiculturalism, represented in the *Mercury* by community leaders and business people, emphasizes that people live where they do and behave the way they do through *choice*. It is emphasized that segregation might be about choice, thus recontextualizing it away from 'ghettoization'. As one Leicester business man, quoted in the *Mercury*, put it,

> People live in the areas they *choose* to because of important things such as places of worship, shops, food and other businesses. A lot of people are prospering now and *they move to new areas*, and so you will see plenty of BMWs and Mercedes parked outside terraced houses. (29 November 2005; emphasis added)

So the script also seems to be about people choosing to mix and talk and that it is their responsibility to do so.

Summary

In the three texts analysed here, multicultural society is defined through a combination of conservative models of assimilation and melting-pot with some elements of a liberal view where difference is superficial. There is no mention of socio-economic issues. In fact what characterizes these texts is the importance of talk in itself, the importance of communication.

This exemplifies one of the tendencies in late modern capitalist society: to treat what are often social problems as being caused by lack of communication and as resolvable through more and 'better' communication without major structural changes (Cameron, 2000). This fits well with a world-view in which people are basically equal and share the same interests, so that the source of conflict between them must be local rather than structural. This is not to disparage the importance of communication between the different communities in Leicester. But to suggest that conflicts are mainly or largely caused by lack of communication serves to gloss over deeper-seated problems. Neo-liberal rhetoric of choice and individual responsibility (Fairclough, 2000, 2003) replaces actual investment in social services and social welfare.

No text draws on the critical left model. Absent from the newspaper therefore are discourses which deal with two issues. One, there may indeed be differences that can not simply be reconciled by talking. A definition of multiculturalism as surface difference realized through cuisine and festival does not really allow for more profound differences between ethnic groups. Two, there are great differences across and within ethnic groups as regards access to resources, jobs education, opportunities. Research has shown that it is the groups most influenced by these factors who will tend to riot. Paul Winston of the LCC told us that this was precisely why he was concerned with levels of poverty and marginalization of people living in certain areas of the city. These included Bangladeshi and white, former working-class, areas.

There is no clear model of multiculturalism in these texts. The liberal view of carnival multiculturalism dominates. In fact, as we will now demonstrate, it is not so much what people say as how they are described, how the reader is encouraged to view speakers, that is, the true assessment of the discourses that they use.

We now move on to the analysis of the social actors represented in these three texts. How are those who appear in the texts described and what do they say and do?

News discourse as recontextualization of social practice: the representation of social actors in the *Leicester Mercury* texts

For our analysis of how participants or social actors are represented and evaluated in the three texts we have just looked at, we use van Leeuwen's (1996) social actor analysis and van Leeuwen and Wodak's (1999) recontextualization of social practice. As soon as there is a representation of a social practice, in this case the social practice of multiculturalism, there is recontextualization, by which is meant the transformation of social practices into *discourses* about social practices. Therefore, media texts are recontextualizations that not only represent social practices, but also explain and legitimize them (Caldas-Coulthard, 2003). One way of legitimizing representation is through the use of the voices of experts and officials, a strategy frequently used in media discourse. In our year's sample of texts from the *Mercury*, it was often 'community leaders' or other officials who were quoted on multiculturalism and integration of the various racial communities in Leicester. Another way of legitimizing, characteristic of tabloid newspapers, is personalization. This is the credibility of the ordinary and everyday as opposed to the official and remote. The texts analysed here use mostly personalization.

According to van Leeuwen and Wodak (1999), recontextualization usually contains the following elements:

Substitution: As they are represented, the elements of a social practice can be substituted for something else. Both the social actors themselves and the activities can be substituted. For example, social actors can be represented by types, through *functionalization*, that is, in terms of professional role or social activity, or through *identification*, that is, in terms of their physical characteristics. The details and complexities of activities can be substituted by generalizations or abstractions. The actual practices of resolving ethnic conflict can become substituted by simple acts of 'talking' and 'sharing'. Yet these are represented outside any concrete settings. Social actors can be represented in terms of who they are, through appearances and feelings, rather than what they actually do.

Addition: Recontextualization also involves adding elements. Addition involves legitimation and reactions (van Leeuwen and Wodak, 1999). Reactions in particular are a prominent feature of the texts analysed here as they represent actors' feelings, their worries, fears, problems, etc. The local community newspaper is especially interested in representing the feelings and opinions of people. This gives a sense that the community is present within the newspaper. In the representation of multiculturalism in the *Mercury* texts, the discourses may in fact be conservative and support neo-liberalism and business interests, yet we are encouraged to align with them on the basis of the feelings of the speakers.

Evaluation: Recontextualization always also involves evaluation of the social practice that is written about (van Leeuwen, 1993). Events and people in each recontextualization are represented according to the goals, values and priorities of the presenters. Hence, those who recontextualize and are in control of the media discourse they present to the public – journalists, editors, etc. – become quite powerful arbiters of social meaning. It has been stated above that the *Leicester Mercury* has a policy of upbeat coverage of the local (business) community and multiculturalism, so that the community must be represented positively and those who oppose multiculturalism are represented as 'other' and as a minority, whose concerns are delegitimated through a number of linguistic devices. As we will see, this process recontextualizes ethnic conflict into something that is not influenced by socio-economic factors, which sociological research, however, has shown to be central.

Representation of social actors in the texts

'Social actor' analysis (van Leeuwen, 1996) can help us to find out how people ('social actors') are identified, categorized and evaluated in texts. Social actor analysis, a set of 'socio-semantic' categories, can be conducted both linguistically and visually (Machin and van Leeuwen, 2005), as we shall demonstrate below. We focus on van Leeuwen's concepts of 'nomination', 'categorization' and 'classification', as these most clearly allow us to distinguish how the participants are represented in the texts.

Nomination: is typically realized by proper nouns, which can be formal (surname with or without honorific title, e.g. *Mr Phillips*), semi-formal (surname and first name) or informal (first name only).

Categorization: social actors can be categorized in two basic ways: *functionalization* and *identification*. When functionalized, social actors are categorized by their function in society (by their profession or social activity) as, for example, '*community relations expert*' or '*leader of the Muslim community*'. Identification means that social actors' identity is defined in terms not of what they do but what they 'more or less permanently, or unavoidably, are' (van Leeuwen, 1996: 54). There are three subtypes of identification: 'relational identification' (identification in terms of people's relationship to each other, for example, *aunt, my friend*, etc.), 'physical identification' (identification in terms of physical characteristics) and 'classification'. Of these, classification is particularly important in the texts analysed here:

Classification: social actors can be represented as classes or generic types, according to age, gender, class, race, ethnicity, religion, etc. It can be made clear that these are more or less unchangeable types, such as a '*a black person*' or '*a white person*'.

This level of analysis is important as it allows us to think about which kinds of social actor are individualized and humanized and which are positively or negatively evaluated. As we shall see, to some extent those people represented as good say very little in concrete terms and are represented as speaking largely through abstractions (van Leeuwen and Wodak, 1999). Yet we are encouraged to evaluate what they say on the basis of who they *are* not through what they say.

Representation of social actors in Text 1, the 'racists'

Here, as we said above, the journalist goes into a pub in a white working-class area which was mentioned in a speech by Trevor Phillips as one of the areas in danger of turning into 'ghettoes'. Here is how the social actors are represented.

> *Trevor Phillips*
> *The Chairman of the Commission for Racial Equality*

Language and Power

> Sir Trevor
> Steve Hill
> Coloureds
> The ethnics
> Steve
> The 48-year-old who's never lived more than 40 yards from his club
> One regular
> One of the snooker team
> A lady who wants to be known only as Mrs Smith
> The 7-year-old
> The Indians
> Smiley Ernest Lee
> Jocelyne Milsom
> The 82-year-old

Apart from one picture of a regular customer, Steve Hill (see Figure 5.4 on page 108), there are no visual representations.

Nomination

Trevor Phillips is both nominated semi-formally (*Trevor Phillips, Sir Trevor*) and functionalized, whereas some of the social actors are only nominated semi-formally (e.g. *Steve Hill*).

Categorization: functionalized (what they do), identified (what they are)

Trevor Phillips is functionalized in terms of occupation *(the Chairman of the Commission for Racial Equality)*. Others are identified as typical old time pub goers, through age (*the 48-year-old . . ., the 79-year-old*, etc.) and through smiling (*Smiley* Ernest Lee).

Classification: groups of people

As we just said above, there are specific social actors who are nominated, as in '*Steve Hill*', but also generic types, as '*coloureds*', '*the ethnics*', '*one regular*' and '*one of the snooker team*'. We would however argue that in this text all are made generic through the introduction to the piece. The journalist positions this as a place that belongs in the past: '*It's telling, perhaps, that the main concessions to technology are the colour TV on the wall and the electronic security system on the front door*'. Therefore 82-year-old '*Smiley Ernest Lee*', while nominated, is represented as part of this.

In these cases, we are not taken close to any of the social actors through longer nominal groups. Evaluative terms emphasize only age, apart from 'smiley'. Most of the participants remain remote. The evaluations do not represent these people as violent or aggressive racists, only as from the past. The use of 'smiley' indicates that they are not evil, and may even be approachable. It is also telling perhaps that there is no pictorial representation of these actors.

The journalist also classifies these participants through 'othering'. The strategies for othering that he uses are 'pejoration' and minoritization' (Bishop and Jaworski, 2003). Pejoration is achieved mainly through word selection and there are examples of the journalist evaluating the people in the club in subtle, yet quite negative terms, as in '*the 48-year-old who's never lived more than 400 yards from this club*', implying an inward-looking perspective. Through minoritization, actors can be represented as visible, but not as representative of the white population in Leicester, as the journalist points out ('. . . *it might be completely unrepresentative of the way most white people in Westcotes (and everywhere else) view this city, but it's how they see it*'). These are therefore a generic group of people who are not like the majority. They remain distant, generic, dull, anti-immigrants, but approachable.

What participants are represented as doing

Van Leeuwen (1996) has discussed the way that participants can be evaluated according to the language that is used to describe their actions. The selection of words, 'whether formal or informal, seemingly neutral or emotionally loaded, signals the speaker's or writer's attitudes about the other group' (van Dijk et al., 1997: 171). Stylistic features are among the major means of communicating opinions, and play a significant role in the overall strategies of positive self-presentation and negative other-presentation. A lexis search of verbs to describe what the participants do reveals the following:

> *say*
> *grumble*
> *have a different view*
> *drum their fingers on the table*
> *getting fed up*
> *laugh incredulously*
> *are not happy*
> *whisper*
> *confide quietly*

Clearly, the participants' utterances are evaluated negatively as 'grumbles'. They are 'not happy' and 'drum fingers on the table'. There is laughter, but it is 'incredulous'. They 'whisper' and they 'confide quietly'; after all, what they say is construed as racist. As will become clear as we go along, in a typical tabloid move, we are encouraged to evaluate personalities, not issues. It is these evaluations that allow the substitution of a concrete, detailed argument for abstractions of 'talking', 'sharing' and 'mixing', that are the staple of multicultural cohesion according to the *Mercury*, therefore concealing socio-economic issues.

Representation of social actors in Text 2, the 'multiculturalists'

Here we move on to the representation of participants who are represented as being involved in multiculturalism and therefore as non-racist. The participants are represented as follows:

>community relations expert Trevor Phillips
>the landlady with a welcoming smile
>a wiry little woman half-swallowed by her voluminous pink jumper
>the jumper
>a black or brown person
>the natives
>the cheery Asian face
>Harj Bhandal
>Arif Khan, a hyperactive talker who runs the Cob shop next door
>Anil Keshwala, owner of the neighbouring Nisa Today's store
>Sarah Allan, 42
>mother-of-four Anita Patel
>Steve Farmer
>54-year-old Steve
>the 28-year-old Sikh
>Mr Phillips, chairman of the Commission for Racial Equality
>a lady called Sharon

There are three images in this text: (1) A group of named Asian women sit around a table smiling and touching glasses (Figure 5.1). The caption is 'Pal's act: Anita Lad, Raksha Chauhan, Dharmi Soni and Vanessa Singh enjoy an evening at Tiranga Café Bar'. (2) A shopkeeper smiling and the back of a customer's head. The caption is 'Anil Keshwala, owner of 3KS Nisa supermarket, in Hastings Road', enjoys some banter with a customer (Figure 5.2). (3) Head and upper body of Cob shop owner smiles slightly but thoughtfully at viewer. The caption is 'It's in the mix: Arif Khan, part Irish part Indian Cob Shop owner in Hastings Road (Figure 5.3). All are medium close shots. The images are 'demand' images (Kress and van Leeuwen, 1996/2006), where the participants look out engaging the viewer, rather than 'offer' images,

News Discourse II

Figure 5.1 'Pal's act: Anita Lad, Raksha Chauhan, Dharmi Soni and Vanessa Singh enjoy an evening at Tiranga Café Bar'.

Figure 5.2 'Anil Keshwala, owner of 3KS Nisa supermarket, in Hastings Road, enjoys some banter with a customer'.

107

Figure 5.3 'It's in the mix: Arif Khan, part Irish part Indian Cob Shop owner in Hastings Road'.

Figure 5.4 'Regular customer: Steve Hill enjoys a drink at Westcotes Constitutional Club'.

which place viewers at the side as voyeurs looking on at an exhibit. The café, shop owner and regular customer are all shown as individuals in medium close up and are named. The group of women are Asian women in a café yet they are also named.

Nomination

We can see that, with the exception of Trevor Phillips, all actors nominated in the texts are lay people. Through nomination, we are taken closer to them. Some actors, such as Arif Khan and Anil Keshwala are both nominated and functionalized by their occupation.

Classification: groups of people

Linguistically there are generic types, such as *'a black or brown person'*, *'a cheery Asian face'* and *'the natives'*. But for the most part, unlike the previous text, there is extensive individualization. This is done through descriptive terms. We learn about tiny details. These evaluate the actors positively.

Categorization: functionalized (what they do), identified (what they are)

Trevor Phillips is again functionalized as '*community relations expert* Trevor Phillips' and 'the *chairman* of the Commission for Racial Equality'. We learn nothing of his look or gestures. This allows him to stay a somewhat faceless professional expert in community relations. Then there is the *landlady*, there is Anil Keshwala, '*owner of the neighbouring Nisa Today's store*' and Arif Khan who '*runs the Cob shop next door*'. Apart from this functionalization, these actors are also described in terms of what they are, down to idiosyncratic gestures: the landlady has a *welcoming smile*, Anif Khan is a *hyperactive* talker and a *wiry little woman* wears notable clothing, a *pink jumper*. She is then even referred to as 'the jumper'. It is important that in this instance, 'the landlady with a welcoming smile' contrasts with the unqualified 'smiley Ernest Lee' in the previous text, whose smile is open to interpretation by the reader. Notable also is that the 'racist' regular in the previous text was simply a 'regular', while the 'non-racist' is a 'regular customer'. At the heart of the newspaper is its role in harmonizing the construction of 'the community', the 'us', with the city as a centre of business and commerce. Customers, rather than simply 'regulars', are part of this kind of construction of community. This is how we earn valued citizenship in the discourse of neo-liberalism.

Visually, there is both functionalization of the shopkeeper and the Cob shop owner and identification in terms of these people as ethnic minorities and in terms of them being warm, smiling and offering open invitations to interaction through the way they engage with the viewer.

This is very different from the first example, where the participants remain remote. This remoteness is even reinforced by the absence of any visual representation of the actors. It is through evaluation, linguistic and visual, that the writer demonstrates the positive attitude of the paper with regard to multiculturalism. Intimacy is created through the longer nominal groups and representing actors through physical identification as in 'a *wiry little* woman *half-swallowed by her voluminous pink jumper*'; 'the landlady with a *welcoming smile*'; '*a cheery Asian face*'. This is reinforced by the things they say:

> 'We get a brilliant crowd in here', says Harj Bhandal. 'Most nights it's half Indians and half-white.'
>
> 'When we took this place over, it had been derelict for years. No one wanted it. Now everyone mixes fine.'
>
> 'Black, white, Indian, West Indian, whatever – everyone mixes together – and it's brilliant.'

This attention to detail through identification is a characteristic that van Leeuwen (1996) has associated with tabloid news styles. This is part of the way the newspaper aligns itself alongside ordinary people and the community. Official views are reported more 'coldly', with the journalist showing that the actors have access to and understanding of these views, which may have value. Both of these techniques work to legitimize the discourses that are realized in the text.

When we look at what the participants are described as doing in this text, we find the following:

> *shout*
> *ask*
> *mix*
> *chat*
> *sniff*
> *get restless*
> *nod sagely*
> *explain*
> *shrug*
> *smile*
> *chuckle*

This is a much more positive evaluation of the actors than in the previous text. Terms such as 'shout' in combination with 'mix' and above all 'ask', 'smile' and 'chuckle', add up to give a positive vibrant evaluation, especially when considered in the context of the broader linguistic and visual representation. But when we analyse the discourses produced by these people, we find they have little in concrete to say and some of what they say might be considered as equally disturbing as those produced by the 'racists' (e.g. 'I'm like the whites, he smiles, I don't speak any of the lingo either.'

Representation of social actors in Text 3, 'the practice of multicultural mixing'

In this text, the journalist attends a session of 'Swapping Cultures' in a Leicester school. The social actors are:

> *Swapping Cultures director Adam Newman Turner*
> *Sam Nwanuforo*
> *Tutor*
> *Sam*
> *Hindus*
> *Muslims*
> *Blacks*
> *Whites*
> *A Chinese girl*
> *Hasseb Malik*
> *Gita*
> *Leon Mattis*
> *Paddy Ayres*
> *Saphire*
> *Mustafa Saleh*

Visually, there is one large photograph where a white boy and a black girl face each other in close shot (Figure 5.5). The viewer sees the scene from the side. The boy on the left looks down, while the girl looks at him, smiling. This is the visualization of the headline 'How do I look to you?' Since the white boy is to the left, we might interpret this through Kress and van Leeuwen's (1996) principle of Given-New compositions. The boy, white, looking down, the Given, whereas the black girl, now confronting him, is the New.

As in Text 2, the participants are positively evaluated – a girl 'smiles shyly', another 'giggles nervously'. The teacher, Sam Nwanuforo, is 'chirpier than the dawn chorus' and is described as 'setting his ever-present smile to full beam'. In this last case, we might question whether the same observation would have been made of a white teacher. There is extensive individualization through nomination as most of the

Language and Power

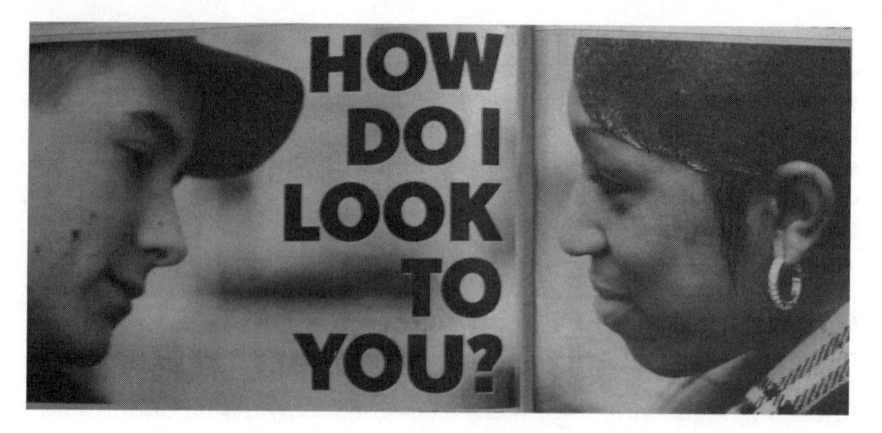

Figure 5.5 'Boy and girl at 'Swapping Cultures' session'.

young people are named. But all those who speak, represent monolithic essentialized ethnic groups. This is enhanced visually by the photographs.

Nomination

Most social actors are nominated semi-formally (*Paddy Ayres*) or informally (*Gita*). This serves to humanize them.

Classification: groups of people

There are four groups: Hindus, Muslims, Blacks and Whites. The young people are nominated, but are also represented clearly as representatives of ethnic types. They are not shown looking at the viewer, so we do not engage with them. The equal frame sizes and postures also suggest sameness and genericity.

Categorization: functionalized (what they do), identified (what they are)

The tutor and the Swapping Cultures director are functionalized. The tutor is nominated both formally ('*Sam Nwanuforo*') and informally ('*Sam*'). He is also identified through his gestures, which further evaluate him positively. He has 'a beaming smile'. This is the only time an official is dealt with in this way. The children are all represented in a way that identifies them as members and representatives of ethnic groups. Participants are described as doing the following things:

    scuff trainers
    discuss multiculturalism

rub shoulders
sit next to
fingers knotted
designer-label cuffs are gnawed anxiously
worry
be chirpy
giggle nervously
avoid gaze
shrug
smile bashfully
be bubbly
trot out comments
set his ever-present smile to full beam

Most of these actions are both positive evaluations and humanize the participants. This is done by showing them as shy and slightly hesitant. These are not generic youth that might intimidate you in a shopping centre but are thoughtful and vulnerable. They are basically positive ('*bubbly*', '*chirpy*'). This is also realized visually where the (white) boy on the left looks down bashfully, while the (black) girl on the right smiles at him.

Summary

In the three texts analysed here, those who are 'racist' are represented as being quite rare and as living in the past. The journalist 'others' these people by saying that they do not represent what most white people in Leicester think about multiculturalism. These people are not represented visually. On the other hand, the anti-racist community is represented intimately with descriptions of clothing and gestures. These people are bubbly, lively and smiley. Visually, we see them smiling and engaging warmly and confidently with the viewer.

Conclusion

As we stated at the beginning, our analysis raises questions about the role of the local press, here in the case of the British government's best model of practice, as regards multiculturalism. On the one hand there are positives. We move away from overt racism, hostility to immigrants and association of ethnic minorities with crime and social problems. And we might even say that here is an instance where capitalism and market logic can bring about antiracism. To a certain extent, positive representation of immigration and of ethnic groups, even if it is to court advertisers and to attract business, is certainly beneficial to the community. But there are two problems. First, if newspapers decide not to report 'sensitive issues', does this not challenge their role as eyes and ears of the public? Can a newspaper not be anti-racist and still provide responsible coverage of difficult issues? In this last case we believe lies the problem of the local newspaper as a commercial instrument.

The *Leicester Mercury* can be commended for positioning itself as pro-immigration and not reporting ethnic minorities solely or largely in the context of crime or social problems. But our critical analysis has demonstrated that the commercial nature of a local newspaper, such as the *Leicester Mercury*, and the need to attract advertisers and represent a positive buzz about the city as a business and investment centre means that multiculturalism becomes recontextualized in a form that is disconnected from the socio-economic problems that lie behind marginalization, frustration and conflict. Stripped of this important level of detail, what is presented is abstracted and as such speakers tend not to give concrete instances of actual mixing, except in the commercial environments of shopping and consumption. This is all very much a part of the discourses of neo-liberalism promoted over the last decade by New Labour and before that by the Conservative government. These discourses remove governmental roles in social welfare and merge healthcare, education, and multiculturalism with discourses of consumer choice with the addition of individual responsibility (Fairclough, 2003).

The critical discourse and multimodal social actor analysis of discourses in the *Leicester Mercury* has demonstrated that its model of multiculturalism and its definition and assessment of social actors backgrounds highly important factors in the causes of racial conflict in Britain. We have argued that these are excluded since they do not sit well with the ideology of an advertiser-driven newspaper which must create a positive buzz of business and commerce. What we have seen is that in the city-as-brand model of multiculturalism there is no room for poverty and marginalization. In this model, cohesion and harmony is about individual choice and talking.

6 Defence discourse I: the visual institutionalization of discourses in war monuments

Gill Abousnnouga and David Machin

Introduction

This chapter is concerned with the power of institutions to control discourse and to (re)contextualize social practice, through visual texts, or *multimodally*. Specifically, the chapter considers the way that the British authorities were able to shape the way that people came to see the First World War, and subsequent wars, through the visual discourses signified by carefully designed war monuments. These visual discourses were a crucial part of justifying the deaths of millions of young men around Europe in the interests of the ruling elite of the colonial powers when there was growing unrest among the working classes.

In your city or town centre, if you live in the US or certain parts of Europe, there will be a monument dedicated to the soldiers of First World War where some of the several millions of soldiers who died during the conflict will be commemorated by a statue, obelisk or cross constructed during and after the war. These memorials form part of the institutionalized rituals of commemoration and mourning for young men who died in combat zones of wounds, disease or drowning in the mud as they took and lost mere inches of land. These monuments are generally viewed by some historians (Winter, 1995; King, 1998) as a formalized system of mourning, helping families and communities deal with their losses. These are mundane everyday reminders legitimizing national identity and the idea of collective national interest in the manner described by Billig (1995). Yet behind this 'banal nationalism' is a clear case of ideological manipulation.

Written on the monument, sometimes along with the names of young men who died, will be an inscription. It will read something like: '*To the Glory of God and in memory of these men who sacrificed their lives for King and Country*'. This language, through its lexical choices of 'sacrifice', 'glory' and 'country', signifies a particular discourse about the deaths of the young men – a discourse that includes kinds of participants, values and sequences of events. Therefore, these inscriptions tell us about the meaning of the war in which they died and the kind of people that fought. This was a war where God supported the cause and therefore one which was noble and good. It was a war where young men willingly offered their lives, where there was a great honour to die for a nation state.

Of course other linguistic choices could be made on the inscriptions, such as 'madness', 'abuse' and 'victims'. During the time of the war and afterwards, there were many other discourses representing the war and what the deaths of these young men meant. Novels written by former front-line soldiers (e.g. Remarque, 1926) reveal a very different account of confused, frightened and angry men seeing themselves as abused by the ruling classes of either side. Historians write of young men feigning madness and self mutilating rather than go to war once conscription began – practices that increased as the war progressed causing problems for conscription numbers (Bourke, 1996). When the monuments were unveiled they were often treated with resentment by the working-class population.

The messages written on the monuments, therefore promote one particular model of war's place and meaning in our societies. They represent an official, institutional discourse of the meaning of war and the loss of life and serve as a powerful device for legitimation (Michalski, 1998).

While the inscriptions communicate discourses about the meaning of war and death linguistically the monuments also communicate visually. In this case rather than lexical choices designers and planners made deliberate choices of visual semiotic resources. Why are statues placed on pedestals or against obelisks in the style of ancient Egypt? Could they have been placed at eye-level perhaps? Why are the figures not entirely realistic representations of men? Why is there only one rather than many men depicted? And why do many of the soldiers carry, rather than wear their helmets? All these are choices that also connote discourses.

The visual designs of these monuments are easy to take for granted as they are a common part of our landscape. But just as there could have been alternative lexical choices on the inscriptions, there could also have been alternative choices of visual semiotic resources. Common during the time of monument building were drawings and cartoons depicting young men in military uniform crucified surrounded by fat, gloating, obscene ruling classes. What if this image had become the model for statues around Europe and the US?

This chapter provides a multimodal analysis of British war monuments built to commemorate the deaths of the young men in First World War. These monuments are still used today as part of annual ceremonies

Defence Discourse I

Figure 6.1 Arthur Stadler cartoon 1927.

and often the names of the 'fallen' from subsequent wars have been added to them. While to some extent the discourses have changed, much remains the same. Crucially the origins of these discourses, their deliberate institutional design, has been largely forgotten. These discourses are communicated both linguistically and visually, or *multimodally,* by the monuments.

Multimodal Discourse Analysis

More recently in CDA, there has been a visual turn, inspired mainly through the work of Kress and van Leeuwen (1996/2006) and O'Toole (1994) which has lead to a more systematic approach to analysing the way that visual semiotic resources create meaning. Kress and van Leeuwen showed that much communication is 'multimodal' rather than 'monomodal'. Therefore discourses, along with their values, participants, actions settings, etc. can be signified by both linguistic and visual semiotic choices. Prior to this discourse analysts had focused mainly on the way that discourses were realized, that meaning was created, through the linguistic mode. But many of the texts analysed, such as advertisements, newspapers, official documents, etc. also communicate at a visual level. So, for example, a study of an advertisement might reveal the use of linguistic devices such as directives (commands) and neologisms (rhyming), which are used to sell products to address the viewer and help them to remember slogans. But what if the advert, as they usually do, also carries images? How do features of the composition such as the gaze of the model, also serve to communicate a form of address such as a demand? How does the arrangement of the elements in the composition help to create rhythm on the page such as in the case of coordination of colours in the clothing worn by the model and the colour of the product? If we only consider the linguistic choices evident in the text we therefore miss meaning created visually. In the case of the monuments we wish to understand in this chapter, what would we miss if we only analysed the inscriptions and not the statues or obelisks themselves?

Importantly, Iedema (2003) points out that once discourses become dominant and realized in different modes of communication, they take on a greater quality of truth. A particular discourse of war once established in the language of political speeches, newspapers, war monuments and stories of glory and an evil enemy found in movies and video-computer games, can lead to new sets of practices. Authorities legitimize war not only through language but through images and monuments. The discourses can then more easily appear as common sense and as value neutral.

Kress and van Leeuwen draw on Halliday's systemic functional linguistics (Halliday, 1978, 1985), to propose a systematic approach to describing and analysing visual language. Hence, multimodal Discourse Analysis analyses both language and images to establish what kinds of discourses and power relations are realized. Just as monomodal CDA would consider lexical choices in linguistic texts so multimodal CDA can systematically analyse the visual semiotic choices. As in the case of the lexical choices in language these give the analyst access to the connoted discourses. So if a monument depicts a soldier walking purposefully forward through no-man's land, as in many of the US First World War cases designed by Ernst Moore Viquesney, what kinds of participants, behaviours, goals and values are connoted? What kinds of sequences of action are being suggested? Certainly this is not a sequence of events where terrified, vulnerable young men are forced into muddy trenches, untrained, where they will soon meet death through disease or drowning if not the bombardment of artillery.

One crucial point made in other chapters in this book is the importance of understanding the context of production of texts. It is not sufficient to simply read texts. We must place them in the context of decisions made in their construction. As Fairclough (1995a: 57) argues, it is crucial that our analysis identifies 'the social and cultural goings-on' of which the text is a part. In other words to carry out a 'Critical' analysis rather than just a textual analysis of monuments we need to know something of why they were build and the context in which they were built. Wodak has put this argument another way, insisting that we should use a 'discourse-historical' method. This means that we should provide context to reveal the origins of discourses in a society. Being critical, Wodak (2001: 2) claims, involves the practical linking of social and political engagement with a socially constructed society. To understand the monuments as multimodal texts we need to know something of the context of when they were built and the decisions made in their design.

Historical Context

The First World War from 1914–1918 saw deaths of conscripted soldiers in unprecedented numbers as the big European colonial powers struggled over access to territories and resources particularly in Africa and the Middle East: an estimated 723,000 died in the United Kingdom alone, with over 2 million wounded (Quinlan, 2005), and over 8 million in the war as a whole. Ninety per cent of the UK dead were working-class men (Bond, 2002: 24) who were sent off to kill their German working-class counterparts. As news of the deaths of soldiers began to reach their communities, people began to erect small monuments, or 'shrines', to those who had enlisted from their street, workplace or organization to which they belonged. These would be a record of all the names of the volunteers from a particular community. But these were also seen by the authorities as a way of celebrating the act of volunteering and as a way of promoting the war effort and contributing to war propaganda (Winter, 1995; King, 1998). As the death toll escalated, and the end of the war was in sight, the call for more permanent war memorials in central civic spaces throughout the country was promoted by newspapers and political figures (King, 1998). This call resulted in '. . . the largest public arts project ever undertaken in Britain . . .' (Moriarty, 1995: 8).

In each location, war memorial committees, consisting of representatives from public officials, religious figures and 'lay' people – generally influential people in the community – decided on the plans for the location and form of the monument to be erected. The cost of commissioning and erecting a war memorial, at least in the provincial towns and villages, did not depend on central government funds but was to be financed through public donations. Plans for the war memorials were considered by the committees not only for their perceived representation of both grief and gratitude, but also on the basis of costs. Many plans had to be revised in terms of a change of material or size of the intended monument due to lack of funds (Winter, 1995; Quinlan, 2005). In fact much of the impetus for the monuments came at an official level as general public interest was weak and often antagonistic. Attendance at public meetings and contributions was sometimes low (King, 1998).

The committees themselves had their own agenda for the meaning of the monuments. In her discussion of the memorial at Llandudno, Bourke (1996) tells of how the committee wished '. . . no suggestion of callousness or brutality associated with war . . .' (Book of Remembrance, Colwyn Bay War Memorial 1914–1918, (Colwyn Bay, 1922), cited in Bourke, 1996: 228).

Political jostling was commonplace as the various groups argued over the form that the memorials were to take. One example is the case of the 'national' war memorial in Cathays Park in Cardiff. This was constructed as a national Welsh monument pushed particularly by the Cardiff based newspaper the *Western Mail*, owned by a wealthy businessman. Appealing to its readers to rally together as one, under a single national identity, they started a subscription fund with their own donation of a hundred pounds (*Western Mail*, 24 October 1919, in Gaffney, 1998: 53). Gaffney proposes that the *Western Mail* had its own reasons for pushing the nationalist case citing the immergence of socialism within many local authorities, which was challenging the Liberal stronghold (Gaffney, 1998: 54–5). Nationalism was seen as one way to prevent the working classes seeing the ruling classes as the enemy, especially when there was rising cynicism as regards the reasons for the war (Hobsbawm, 1983).

It is in this climate of a rising Socialist trend, not only in Britain, but spreading from Russia throughout Europe, that the memorials were constructed. The fear of this trend is well documented by historians. According to Mosse (1990), the construction of the Cenotaph in London was first proposed during peace celebrations in July 1919 under a concern to promote national unity. Arnot (1967) refers to the effect on British Parliamentary decisions following the revolution of 1917. Strikes, mutinies and opposition to the war all increased in the year following the Bolshevik revolution. Events in Russia were certainly in the minds of the early Labour movement in Britain and influenced their early decisions in party policy (McKibbin, 1974; Laybourn, 1997).

The fear of Bolshevism was also uppermost in the thinking of Winston Churchill at the time, who was intent on '... strangling near to birth the Bolshevik regime in Russia.' (Jenkins, 2002: 350). The role of the building of the war monuments was one way of speaking to communities who had lost all their young men and also to the men who returned from the front. Hobsbawm (1983) points to the fact that just how close Britain was to a working-class uprising is largely whitewashed from popular history. He sees the construction of monuments around Britain as core part of the deliberate attempt by the authorities to consolidate the idea of nationhood in the face of the communist threat.

In his description of how, during this period, a revolutionary spirit was spreading throughout Britain, Arnot quotes Lloyd George, from a confidential memorandum, who said that the whole of Europe was:

> ... filled with the spirit of revolution ... there is a deep sense not only of discontent, but of anger and revolt, amongst the workmen against the war conditions. The whole existing order in its political, social and economic aspects is questioned by the masses of the population from one end of Europe to the other. (Lloyd George, quoted in Arnot, 1967: 150)

According to Arnot, this spirit of revolution also existed in the British army at the time; the mutinies of January, and the demonstration by police and prison officers in Hyde Park in June 1919 can be attributed to this revolutionary spirit.

There is evidence that the establishment was also concerned about the attitude of returning soldiers. We see this clearly in an essay by Rudy (1918), published in the *Contemporary Review*, which states that he was often asked his opinion by 'officers' and 'ministers of the Church' about what 'Tommy' may be thinking after his war experiences. Writing while the war was drawing to a close, Rudy spoke of the contrast of the real soldiers on the front and the idealized representations of them at home, warning that the reality conflicts with the idealized versions. He spoke of the 'dangers' which might face the 'homeland' (Britain) and 'its empire' when the soldiers returned from the war, fearing that they would either go to '... to the extremist camp or he will help form some powerful organisation of his own' (Rudy, 1918: 551). He spoke of the enormous profits being made by businessmen who were involved in the manufacturing of goods for the war while living in the safety and comfort of home. The realization of the inequalities of society had, Rudy informs, dawned on 'Tommy' and was made even more evident through the war process.

As Moriarty (1997: 130) points out, the monuments supported official interpretations of the war. In her description of the unveiling ceremonies, she acknowledges their role as emotional events, but also highlights the role of officials. In the '. . . carefully orchestrated . . .' unveiling ceremonies where they took the opportunity to tell the crowd how to interpret the memorial, for example, by carefully explaining the meaning of any religious iconography.

Some historians recount the public hostility at some of the unveiling ceremonies of the statues, where there would be heckling and members of the crowd would jeer ironically if anyone wanted a medal, pointing to their worthlessness (Quinlan, 2005). The alignment of the deaths of these working-class men for King, God and country was seen as an additional insult. In 1921, during the silence of a remembrance ceremony at Dundee, some started singing The Red Flag, a riot broke out and police had to disperse the crowd (Quinlan, 2005).

There were left-wing calls to build pacifist monuments that failed due to lack of funding and official support. Bruno Taut proposed a glass reading room for pacifist literature in Magdeburg, Germany, which was never realized. Nor was Käthe Kollwitz's design for a statue of kneeling grief-stricken parents in Belgium. Perhaps the only example is Bernard Bleeker's expressionistic monument in Knappe, Munich, where soldiers advancing are reflected on the opposite side by crosses which mimic the same patterns of their movement (Michalski, 1998: 96).

It is in this context that we must place our multimodal analysis of the war monuments. These monuments are a taken-for-granted part of the landscapes of our villages, towns and cities, just as we take for granted their central roles in the ceremonies where we listen to prayers of mourning and gratitude, hear solemn military music and see senior members of our institutions carrying solemn expressions, their heads bowed slightly, contemporary soldiers marching by grand in their ceremonials. In these commemorations there will often be national flags and soldiers who have fallen in more recent or ongoing wars will be mentioned. The monuments still do their work after nearly a century and still serve to legitimize the wars that are fought in the name of profit. In the terms of Billig (1995), deeply politicized issues such as war can be reconstituted through mundane background accepted attitudes and perceived realities.

Methodology

In the analysis that follows we are interested in the way the monuments represent visually rather than linguistically. We carry out the analysis using two theoretical tools 'metaphorical association' and 'iconography'.

In the first case much of the methodology offered by Kress and van Leeuwen (2003) and van Leeuwen (2005, 2006) in particular is based on the way that we tend to understand visual signs through association. In the second case, we think about the way that visual signs work (Barthes, 1973) and how their meaning can become established over time where the origins of the meaning may even be concealed (Panofsky, 1972).

Metaphorical association

Much of the meaning potential in visual communication comes from metaphorical association (Kress and van Leeuwen, 2001, 2006; van Leeuwen, 2005, 2006). A simple example is that red can mean danger. This can have its association in fire or in blood and the idea of wounding. There are many things that are red that are not dangerous of course, and these might lead to other associations. In combination with other visual signs, red can have the potential to mean love and sensuality, through association with the heart and lips, for example. These different meanings are all part of the meaning potential of red that comes through experiential association. Of course in different cultures different associations might dominate due to specific cultural shared experiences.

Kress and van Leeuwen (2001, 2006) show how there are many other features of colours that have their meaning potential on the basis of association. Saturated, rather than diluted, colours are associated with emotional intensity and excitement as opposed to moderation. Pure, rather than impure colours are associated with certainty as opposed to ambiguity.

The same experiential association can be found in gestures. For example, when a person says 'I am this far from telling him what I think', and emphasizes a small distance between their thumb and forefinger, a metaphorical association is made between physical distance and emotional feeling. Art Psychologist Rudolf Arnheim (1997: 117) notes that we use the same gesture for a clash of opinions as we do for a crash of cars, the same for a big surprise as for a big fish. He suggests that 'human beings are naturally aware of the structural resemblance uniting physical and non physical objects' (ibid.: 118). Therefore, he says, we often draw on these resemblances when representing the world. Such resemblances can then become established in their own right so that the origins become obscured.

Lakoff and Johnson (1980) see metaphor as a fundamental feature in the way that humans organize their experiences. They believe that we understand metaphors on the basis of our concrete experiences. So we all share certain physical experiences of being upright, lying down, of certain kinds of movement just as walking or of feelings, such as tiredness. We can then transfer these to understand and explain more abstract ideas. For example, since we are used to eating food that is easy or difficult to chew and swallow we can use the same principle to think about ideas. We might think about moods in terms of being up or down. This might have the physical association of having energy and being up or being without energy and lying around.

Van Leeuwen (2005: 30) says that the essence of metaphor is transference. So there is a transference from one domain to another due to some perceived association. So qualities of a crash between two cars can be transported into representing a clash of opinions. The size of physical objects such as fish can be transported to the size of a big surprise, the redness of blood can mean danger.

This idea of metaphorical association is extremely useful for thinking about the semiotic choices in visual and physical designs. For example, if we make a statue pedestal thick and heavy it can offer associations of strength. Alternatively a slim pedestal might mean sophistication. This will depend on other semiotic choices.

Iconography and iconology: the meaning of visual signs

The semiotician Roland Barthes (1977) was interested in the way that signs and their meanings are shared by people in a culture. He was interested in the way that signs come to be attributed arbitrary but shared meanings. So the word 'lion' has come to mean the animal we associate with that term. There is no reason for this to be the case; it has simply become established that way. Barthes shows how visual signs can be thought about in the same way, as having arbitrary symbolic meanings. So flowers can be a sign for romance; green can be a sign for all environmental issues.

We can use some of Barthes ideas to think about the ideas and values or discourses that the people, the places and the objects that we find in visual communication stand for – what are the kind of associations that signs carry. This is what we will call iconography.

Denotation

Barthes described two levels of meaning in images or visual communication. The first is denotation. We can think about this in terms of what the image documents. It can show *particular* events, *particular* people, places and things. A photograph of a family member or a house can be said to simply document or denote these things. In the image, we see them as they were at the moment the photograph was taken. A news photograph might denote or document a political meeting or a riot. So asking what an image denotes is asking: who and/or what is depicted here? So a monument might denote a soldier from First World War.

Of course we never really see any image in this kind of innocent way. Images usually mean something to us and they can never be neutral representations. Even photographs may be taken to dramatize a moment, or may choose to capture participants who will make a story appear more newsworthy. An enemy militia soldier might be photographed close up to make them appear intimidating. Children can be photographed from above to make them appear vulnerable. You may even take a photograph of your house from the best possible angle to make it appear more flattering. So there is no neutral documentation. But denotation, for Barthes (1977), is one way to think about the first level of meaning.

Connotation

We can also ask what ideas and values are communicated through what is represented, and through the way in which it is represented. This is Barthes' second layer of meaning. While a monument might denote a soldier from First World War we can ask what ideas and values about that soldier it connotes.

When analysing an image or design at this level we can look for elements that transport meanings from other domains. We can think about the kinds of metaphorical associations that are at play. It is these associations that connote particular discourses, models of the world, scripts of likely sequences of activity.

Barthes (1973), in *Mythologies*, called connotative meanings 'myths'. Myth is the concept used to express the dense associations of what is represented in an image or a sign. For example, a British flag could be used to connote all the myths surrounding Britishness. Some might use the flag to call upon myths of resilience of character, and patriotism, for example. In fact flags tend to all be used to connote very similar sets of myths, as do national anthems: loyalty, glory, landscape, etc. Of course such myths are very important to mobilize people and to legitimize certain kinds of social organization.

In fact what Barthes calls myth can be thought of simply as a discourse. And in the tradition of Critical Discourse Analysis we can look for the way that connotative meanings are used to promote particular discourses that reflect particular power interests.

Barthes emphasized that any kind of sign can have this connotative power. People, clothing, postures, settings, objects, colours can all be used to activate particular discourses. We can usefully carry this model to our analysis of monuments.

Iconographic Symbolism

Visual elements can also mean, not so much by transport of meaning from another domain, such red being used to connote danger or sensuality, but because they have come themselves to represent particular ideas or concepts. This is particularly important in the analysis of monuments.

The study of iconographic symbolism was used by Panofsky (1970: 54) to analyse the meanings in paintings. He realized that objects, animals, persons and even postures, were used to symbolize particular people, values and behaviours. These had become conventions, established over time. He points out that

> a male figure with a knife resembles St Bartholomew . . . a female figure with a peach in her hand is a personification of veracity . . . two figures fighting each other in a certain way represent the Combat of Vice and Virtue.

But it wasn't only people that could be symbolized in this way but also abstract shapes such as the Christian cross. Product logos can similarly come to represent ideas and values as can certain architectural styles. Here we can see that rather than metaphoric association, as in the case of thick lines, or saturated colour, these signs connote because of arbitrarily assigned meanings. The study of iconographic symbolism means that we look for the way that features, such as persons, objects, poses, gestures or other elements in a composition, represent persons, values or ideas.

For Panofsky it is possible to trace the origins of all such symbolism. In the case of monuments we should be able to explain choices of objects, shapes, persons and postures through looking at their history.

Panofsky believed that this symbolism could be found not just in objects, persons and abstract shapes but also in the very form of layout and choice of materials. These could 'reveal the basic attitude of nation, a period, a class, a religious or philosophical persuasion' (1970: 7). All compositions, what they contain, how they are realized, he says, 'are a symptom of something else' (ibid.: 8). Why would a sculpture use bronze rather than stone or plastic? Why would a person be depicted in a particular posture? Why would they carry a particular object rather than another?

Monument Analysis

In this section we analyse features of the monuments which we can understand through metaphorical association, connotations and iconographic symbolism. Just as in texts we can look at the way lexical choices connote certain discourses, we can do the same for these visual semiotic choices. While our analysis was carried out on 100 monuments, including obelisks, statues and crosses we choose a number of examples in this chapter to illustrate our points, although here we are primarily interested in statues. The analysis follows under headings of design features.

Height

To begin with, the pedestal is very important in monuments where there are statues. Here we have the meaning potential of height which has both metaphorical and connotative meaning. Jewitt and Oyama (2000) and Machin (2007) discuss the way that angles in photographs can connote particular relationships between the subject of the photograph and the viewer. If the camera angle appears to look down at the subject, onto the subject, there is a sense that they are less powerful. This is often seen in news photographs of children to emphasize their vulnerability. If the camera angle looks up at them they appear more powerful. In the case of a photograph of children this would make them appear threatening. This meaning potential comes from our everyday experience of feeling powerful or vulnerable in terms of height. As children looking up at the world gives a feeling of vulnerability. Dog trainers often tell owners to kneel down to stroke young dogs because of the intimidating nature of height. This same kind of meaning potential operates in the case of statues that are placed on pedestals (see Figure 6.2). They are meant to convey power, awe and respect. They are meant to convey strength. Imagine if they were to be placed in a hole in the ground, or even at the same height, at eye-level. Clearly, we are not to regard them as equals, nor as below us. How would it appear if a statue of a soldier peered up at us?

There is further meaning potential in height. Van Leeuwen (2005) speaks of the metaphorical associations of height. In our societies we generally associate height with status, as in 'upper class', and we make ourselves lower by kneeling before royalty. But we also associate height with loftiness of ideals. This can extend to the association of fantasy, as in when we say someone's head is in the clouds. The opposite of this is someone being grounded or down to earth. These meanings combine to convey higher status and loftiness of ideals.

Of course the statue could not be too high on its pedestal either. On the one hand it must fit with local town planning, as was important at the time. Imagine a statue to the unnamed soldier in a small town placed on a pedestal of the likes of London's Nelson's column. But this

Language and Power

Figure 6.2 Tunbridge Wells statue.

would also be inappropriate for other reasons. The ordinary soldier should not be placed too high. Such things are reserved for specific individuals and normally those from history who have an epic role in the nation's real or imagined history, such as Nelson.

It is also significant that the pedestals on these monuments are broader rather than slim. We could imagine a monument supported by a slender iron bar. This would be sturdy but not connote the same level of strength and weight of significance. Much of the meaning of the monuments lies in the metaphorical association of weight and durability transferred to mean weight of respect, importance of the act in which the soldiers were a part and the act of sacrifice itself. And of course to connote the stability of the endurance in our society's memory.

Size

The figures in war monuments are slightly bigger than real life people, but normally only by about 1 foot in height. So the soldiers are normally about 7 foot tall. This makes them literally larger than life, although not to the extent that they appear outsized or like a giant. We can imagine the meaning potential of a very small soldier, about the size of a doll, or alternatively of a very large one of about 30-foot soldier. Here we clearly have associations of size with significance. In the last case this would be too much and would seem to excessively represent the soldier. Vastly larger than life statues are generally found often in cases of dictators where the idea is to create an imposing image. We see this in the plywood figure of Saddam Hussein fixed to the Ishtar Gate in Baghdad in the 1980s and the Victory Arch which represented his forearms holding swords that were made from the metal of fallen Iraqi soldiers. Michalski (1998: 197) describes this as 'as unabashed but symbolically multifaceted ruler's cult'. Such outsized monuments are pure militarism. Another example is the Stalin monument in Budapest destroyed in 1956. Here the intention is to represent the person as more than just a person but as the very nation itself. In the First World War monuments the soldier statues are to represent simply strong and significant soldiers.

Size is a different matter as regards the size of architectural structures. National monuments, such as in London and in Cardiff, and County monuments such as in Lincolnshire, must be sufficiently large to connote a broader area of commemoration. This is particularly important in the context of the architectural styles that are used that we will come on to shortly.

Figure 6.3 Cardiff National monument.

Style and design

From 1914 to the mid-1920s, when most of the First World War monuments were built there was a fashion in Art Deco and in classicism which had been common in public buildings and monuments from the latter half of the nineteenth century. Art Deco itself was highly influenced by the design styles of ancient Egypt. Post-war there was a desire, realized in architecture, to return to a time which connoted ideas of strength and power, high ideals and thinking. Egypt, Greece and Rome have long been much idealized in Northern European thought.

In the Cardiff monument, we see all of the features that were classic to this style. We find columns that form a colonnade, as we might see on the Acropolis. In fact, some memorials such as at Lincoln closely resemble the Acropolis. Other monuments use pilasters which are the columns that project slightly out of walls but are false and serve decorative rather than supportive functions. These are often found on block style monuments on either side of inscriptions. Monuments also have pediments, which are the triangular sections at the end of the roof which often themselves contain figures or animals. There are architraves, which are beams that connect sections yet appear to have only decorative function. Columns are often used to create a portico which is sort of an entrance porch. We see this on the Cardiff example. We also find 'crepidoma', which are the layers of construction making the base step-like. Such monuments reflecting the classical style also have complete symmetry to give a sense of balance and elegance. Monument designers wrote of the connotations of such architectural styles being primarily civilizing. Troost (1942: 7) wrote of the importance of Greek style monuments built by the third Reich 'how German order has tamed the chaotic forces of the Eastern Steppes' (quoted in Michalski, 1998: 104). Through these designs then this squalid war and abuse of working-class lives becomes connoted not only through sacrifice to nation but also through themes of classical civilization with high ideals. Since these civilizations are themselves generally familiar to us through monuments and sculptures, beautiful white marble and structure, it is a simple step to make the dead young men a part of this world.

Another important design feature of war monuments is the obelisk. Again this reflects the Egyptian influence on the Art Deco that was fashionable at the time. The needle shaped obelisk was used to represent a sun ray and the sun god Ra in Egyptian symbolism. While the obelisk would have been in keeping with the local designs of the times it was also a further way to connote the magnificence of empire and history and the eternity.

Defence Discourse I

Figure 6.4 Greek God soldier.

The majority of war monuments in villages across Britain took the form of the cross. This was used to symbolize sacrifice. King (1998: 129) suggests that this image became to refer 'in most people's minds' to the sacrifice of the soldier likened to the Christian belief that Jesus had sacrificed his life for mankind. This idea transferred easily into the: 'supposedly willing and generous laying down of their lives by soldiers in defence of their country and their ideals' (ibid.).

The figures of the soldiers themselves are clearly inspired by Greek statues (Moriarty, 1997). We can see this in the chiselled features and perfectly formed bodies of the Tunbridge Wells, Cardiff and Edinburgh examples (see Figures 6.2, 6.3 and 6.4).

The young boys who died become represented as Greek Gods, bursting with vitality and beauty, idealized. This style itself also connotes the magnificence of these former empires with their power, strength, fineness of art and thought and general sophistication. How would a statue that represented a working-class 17-year-old, thin from poor diet and disease in the trenches have appeared?

Such Godlike characteristics were also common in the comic strips of the 1920s and 1930s where superheroes defeated supervillains.

These angular faced heroes were also significant in Soviet propaganda art and Nazi Arian imagery, such as in the statue of the Berlin Torchbearer.

There are a number of ways that we can think about these representations. To begin with, we can use the concept of 'modality'. Kress and van Leeuwen (1996/2006) discuss the way that language provides us with resources for expressing and assessing levels of truth in language. As we saw in Chapter 4, these are modal verbs such as 'may', 'will' and 'must' and adjectives such as 'possible', 'probable', or 'certain', which are used to express different levels of certainty. So 'I will be there' is more certain, and therefore of higher modality, than 'I may be there'. Kress and van Leeuwen believe that there are also resources in visual communication for expressing levels of modality. As in language, these can be used to hedge and distance from certainty. They produce a list of eight visual modality scales. One in particular is useful for us here. This is the scale that describes the articulation of detail on the subject. This is a scale that runs from maximum articulation of detail to minimum articulation of detail. For example, we might compare a detailed drawing of a person with a cartoon (see Figure 6.1). In the first of these there is greater articulation of detail than the second. It is therefore of higher modality. On the statues of the soldiers we can ask where detail has been removed, and where therefore modality and certainty are lower. Machin and Thornborrow (2003) argue that removing certain aspects of reality allows different rules to apply. They give the example of fairytales. In reduced modality worlds, children often become more powerful than they could in everyday life. They show how advertisers also reduce modality in certain ways to give the impression that products will allow purchases to connote certain values and lifestyles. To some extent these statues are of lower modality. The soldiers have clean skin and no finer details. Where modality is lowered, Kress and van Leeuwen argue, there tends to be higher levels of symbolism. The lowered modality of the figures helps the viewer therefore to imagine different realms of possibility for agency, worlds where we can act with complete nobility perhaps.

On the other hand, certain features on the statues are exaggerated. Van Leeuwen (1996) refers to this exaggeration of certain features as 'overdetermination'. In this case where certain features are exaggerated, such as in Barbie dolls and Action Man figures, the symbolic quality of the representation is increased.

We can draw out the choice of semiotic resources in terms of representation of the soldiers by considering the Will Lambert project for the Revensbrück Concentration Camp Memorial. Here the camp victims were represented in slight abstraction where faces and shapes were only vaguely discernable and where lines of the figures and pedestal were rough as if done in sketch with a thick pencil, almost as if seen through fog. In contrast our soldier statue is clean and vivid and beautiful to connote an idealized body belonging to a Greek God.

Materials

The main materials for the statues are bronze, and the pedestals and building structures are granite or fine stone. Here we have connotations and metaphorical associations. Durability in the rock connotes durability in memory. Granite and marble can also be polished to create a crystalline glossy surface and give clean sharp edges. This in itself can connote high-standard craftwork but is important in the classical architectural style. We can imagine the opposite connotations realized by the messier lines and unevenness of rough sandstone. This does not connote the same kind of regality or magnificence. Bronze was used partly not only because it is easy to mould but it also has connotations of weight, value and shine. Would it be the same were a statue made of tin or iron? Would it be possible to commemorate the deaths of millions of soldiers with a plastic statue?

Gaze

Kress and van Leeuwen (1996/2006) were interested in the way that images can be thought of as fulfilling the speech acts as described for language by Halliday (1985). When we speak, we can do one of four basic things. We can offer information; offer services or goods; demand information; demand goods and services. In each case there is an expected or an alternative response possible. Kress and van Leeuwen didn't think that images could realize all of these, but believed that there were two kinds of image acts: 'offer' and 'demand'.

In demand images the subject looks at the viewer who is therefore addressed. This is a visual form of address. The viewer's presence is acknowledged and, just as when someone addresses us in social interaction, some kind of response is required. In real life if someone smiles at us we are required to smile back, although of course the image will never know if we do not comply. Of course the kind of demand that is made will depend on other factors such as facial expression, posture and setting, for example. The subject may demand that we feel pity.

In offer images the subject does not look at the viewer. There is no interaction and the viewer remains unacknowledged. Here the viewer is encouraged to look at the scene or individual solely as an onlooker or as a voyeur. So in this case the viewer is offered the scene as an information available for scrutiny.

We can use these ideas to think about the way statues of soldiers engage viewers as they do not look at the viewer. They do not engage with the viewer nor demand a response through gaze. We can see this in the Cardiff and Tunbridge Wells examples. Rather they tend to look upwards, forwards to the horizon, or downwards in mourning. So we can think of these as offers. We can of course ask why this is? Why do they not look at us? The simple answer is that this would simply have been too much and creates a whole different meaning. How could the survivors have dealt with being looked at? If the soldiers, the dead, whose lives had been thrown away looked at us a response would be demanded, rather than us simply being offered a scene as information. Do we want to see the dead, who were sent to this awful fate, to die a lice-ridden death, staring right at us? What kind of response could we feel compelled to give? Such a choice would have been disastrous in the context of wanting the public to see the soldiers as part of a different world, one of the glory of God and magnificence of classical civilization.

Poses

It is clear from the decisions of committees and designers that there was to be no obvious aggression, fear or suffering in the monuments. Poses and facial expressions connote calmness. The Tunbridge Wells statue is typical of soldiers who are depicted as waiting, ready to defend but with a calm peace and certainly not displaying aggression or fear. Around Britain we find these Greek gods waiting calmly without fear, ready for sacrifice.

Other soldiers are depicted as striding confidently. This is odd considering that many of them died, machine gunned in no-man's land, as they were ordered to march slowly towards enemy lines as the Generals did not think them capable of following more complex orders. We can see this in the Abertillery monument (see Figure 6.5) where the soldier walks forward, hat raised, gun held by his side. This monument resembles the American 'Doughboy' memorial designed by E. M. Viquesney, of which there are over one hundred around the US. Viquesney himself documented that he wanted to portray the soldier striding confidently and purposefully through no-man's land. This was meant to show the determination to defend what was right but certainly not aggression. The Cambridge monument is one further example of a soldier striding forward merrily and purposefully.

In the case of the Tunbridge Wells, Abertillery and Cambridge monuments we see that the soldiers have bare heads. In Christian art, the bare

Figure 6.5 A soldier marching forward in victory.

head has had the symbolic meaning of revealing oneself to the power of God. This is why a man should not pray with his head covered, although also why in some cases it is important to have the head covered. But revealing the head this way requires considerable purity, which of course the soldier who sacrifices his life for the love of King, God and county does have. The origins of this symbolism can be found in Corinthians (1,11: 7). Of course, the removal of hats also connotes an individual spirit, a lack of regimentation and control. In the Tunbridge Wells case it indicates a sense of invulnerability, perhaps since the soldier is now immortalized.

In the Cardiff memorial we find the soldiers in Olympian pose, reaching upwards with their offerings, but in energetic and graceful stretch as if in an act of athleticism. The symbolism of the wreaths themselves date back to ancient Greece, adopted into Christianity as a symbol of the victory of the redemption – laurels used to denote military victory. In this case the wreaths are held up in offering to the dolphins and the winged figure. The dolphins themselves are symbolic in Christian art of the resurrection (Ferguson, 1942) and the winged figures holding swords of victory (Quinlan, 2005). Quinlan (2005: 59) describes the designer, Sir Ninian Comper, as '. . . the outstanding church architect and ecclesiastical designer'. This explains the intense religious symbolism included in the memorial. As well as other war memorials, Sir Comper had a long list of church designs to his name.

We also find soldiers waiting calmly, guarding, or even with head hung in mourning. We can see one example of this in the Hyde Park Royal Artillery monument.

In this case (Figure 6.6) we find the artillery man standing confidently upright, legs apart and confident. His posture connotes that he is trustworthy and certain of his deeds. This is emphasized by his stockiness which brings the associations of strength and immovability. He looks off to the horizon which is often used to connote looking to the future or to greater things. He is clearly certain and comfortable in his vision.

Summary

The war monuments that we find around Britain recontextualize the brutal, squalid practice of war and the cruel disregard for the lives of young working-class men. The monuments do this linguistically through inscriptions which refer to 'sacrifice', 'glory', 'God' and

Figure 6.6 The soldier protecting at Hyde Park London.

'country'. And they also do this visually. Statues often depict soldiers as calm, willing and certain and they carry religious symbolism. The soldiers are big strong, handsome and healthy – also evidence of what fine young men they were. But visually quite different discourses are also realized where monuments and statues connote the magnificence, sophistication, beauty and eternity of the empires of Egypt, Greece and Rome. The statues often depict the soldiers as Greek Gods. This is not realized linguistically but only visually. This is important because what can be depicted visually rather than through language follows different rules since it can always be claimed that the visual is a matter of interpretation. So, for example, in news photographs we can always find generic Muslims depicted, even though linguistically we could not write 'all Muslims are the same'. It would seem unreasonable to say something like 'Our dead young men are as Greek Gods immortalized through a civilized war of high ideals' given the reality of the situation.

Conclusion

These monuments are a taken-for-granted part of the landscapes of our villages, towns and cities, just as we take for granted their central roles in the ceremonies where those gathered listen to prayers of mourning and thanks, hear military music and see senior members of our institutions carrying solemn expressions, their heads bowed slightly. Most importantly we take for granted the language that these monuments have helped to institutionalize allowing the millions of deaths of young working-class men as the ruling classes of the colonial powers squabbled over territory in Africa and the Middle East to be recontextualized through a language of 'bravery', 'God', 'country' and 'sacrifice' and the connotations of magnificent classical civilizations. This is despite the fact that many of the young men who died would have had little idea of the meaning of the nations for whom they fought and at a time when there was much criticism of the war. Throughout Western Europe there were signs that the working classes were willing to mobilize against the government and establishment. Yet these aspects of the war are more easily erased when glorious bronze monuments of gentle Greek God soldiers stand around in our towns, strong and certain enforcing institutionally contrived discourses of war. But what if there had been some way to institutionalize statues of the crucified soldier depicted by Arthur Stadler? How would this have influenced the way we now think of war? Would we so easily be so passive while our governments wage wars in the Middle East, where their corporations have vested economic interests, in the name of Democracy and Freedom?

7 Defence discourse II: A corpus perspective on routine and rhetoric in defence discourse

Tony Bastow

Introduction

One of the main aims of this book is to show how institutions *construct* a representation of the world, rather than reflect an objective reality. Institutions do this because it is in their strategic interests. To retain the power they hold, they will draw upon an established repertoire of linguistic patterns and phrases which their consumers will expect, but which others may seek to resist.

Members of institutions, therefore, are predisposed to talk about themselves in certain ways. Even casual listeners may become aware of some of these phrases through their repetition in the media. When government officials are heard using phrases such as 'spreading democracy' and 'winning hearts and minds', we can get a sense of not only how particular speakers are predisposed to think of themselves in certain ways (or represent institutions in certain ways), but also of how such processes may be less than apparently benign.

One means by which we can empirically investigate an institution's 'repertoire of preferred expressions' is through corpus methodology. I use this methodology to show how certain prominent linguistic features in a 'special' corpus (or collection) of geopolitical US defence speeches can be compared with linguistic features in the language overall, as evidenced in what is known as a 'reference' (or general) corpus. This is a similar collection, but of language used in a general way. In other words, this kind of analysis involves a comparison of what is the 'normal', habitual, routine use of language in everyday English with that which characterizes the language produced by a particular institution. What is distinctive will 'stand out' from what is normal in the language as a whole. These differences in lexical and grammatical features will allow us, as has been shown in previous chapters, to think about what kinds of discourses are connoted by particular institutions.

In turn we can use these observations to think about how these institutions, in this case the US military, seek to maintain their power and influence.

Corpus Linguistics

While corpus analysis allows us to make some of the same kinds of observations of the discourses produced by institutions, it is a different approach than we generally find in Critical Discourse Analysis (CDA). Corpus Linguistics (CL) is an empirical approach to natural language which is generally used to show the frequency of items and patterns in texts associated with particular contexts of use. 'Corpora' (singular 'corpus') are large, principled collections of texts stored in machine-readable form. The term 'principled' means that the texts are sampled, either according to a predetermined external criterion or an internal criterion. In the case of this chapter, the texts were chosen according to the external 'geopolitical criterion' that each should deal in some way with America's relations with other countries around the world. This means that we can measure and examine the lexical choices found in this sample to understand the discourses promoted by the US military.

In this respect corpus linguistics is somewhat different from the other approaches discussed in this book, where, on the whole, an individual text, or small set of similar texts, are analysed within a particular framework, such as Systemic Functional Linguistics (SFL), and claims are made about those texts.

It is because it uses a large sample which is accessed systematically that corpus analysis is able to guard against some of the criticisms that are often made of CDA, whereby documents are chosen specifically on the basis of the interests of the analyst. O'Halloran and Coffin (2004) and O'Halloran (2007) refer to this as 'over-interpretation', whereby an overstrong claim is made by an analyst who might have a vested interest in making such a claim (see also Widdowson, 1995, 2000, 2004). In other words, corpus methodology can be used to uncover recurrent language patterns over a range of similar texts, which a conventional CDA analysis concentrating on a single or limited range of texts may overprivilege.

Importantly, corpus analysis facilitates comparison. It allows the chosen sample to be compared with language in everyday language use. So if we find a disproportionate usage of certain items or phrases in a special corpus, such as of US military speeches, when compared to the reference corpus, this may be an evidence of ideological bias, and may be a way in which particular values are reinforced and sustained. As Stubbs (1996: 158) states, while

> such recurrent ways of talking do not *determine* thought . . . they [do nevertheless] provide familiar and conventional representations of people and events, by filtering and crystallizing ideas, and by providing pre-fabricated means by which ideas can be easily conveyed and grasped. (emphasis added)

It is these recurrences, along with their collocational preferences, that tell us about how an institution's values and beliefs are presented as taken-for-granted, routine and common sense. In other words, in the context of the terminology used in previous chapters, it leads us to ask what models of the world, kinds of participants, values and identities are fostered by the discourses produced by an institution?

Corpus Linguistics and CDA

If we accept the idea that much CDA research is based on 'partial description and political commitment rather than on rigorous analysis and open minded enquiry' (Tyrwhitt-Drake, 1999: 1082), corpus methodology may be a means of placing the discipline on a firmer footing. In fact, a number of studies have already been undertaken which use corpus methodology for CDA.

Fairclough (2000: 12), for example, used a corpus comprised mainly of speeches by Tony Blair to show that New Labour 'sets out to achieve consent not through political dialogue but through managerial methods of promotion . . . treating the public as its consumers rather than as citizens'. Using clause and process analysis as his principal methodology, Fairclough attempts to show that 'social exclusion' is 'an outcome rather than a process – it is a condition people are in, not something that is done to them' (ibid.: 54).

Fairclough makes his case by showing the overrepresentation of a number of key words in his corpus, such as *we, Britain, welfare, partnership, new, schools, people, crime, reform, deliver, promote, business, deal, tough and young*. From this observation he is able to say something about the discourses that are signified lexically.

However, this approach, compared to a more corpus-centred approach, is limited. For example, his New Labour corpus is not contrasted with a comparative corpus of former Conservative government speeches (certain features of which, Fairclough claims, New Labour has inherited). This means that some of his claims remain unsubstantiated. For example, he notes that of the 64 instances of *values* in his New Labour corpus, 29 of them occur 'in contexts of change, modernization, or more specifically applying traditional values to the modern world' (ibid.: 47).

However, without a Conservative government corpus to compare against, claims regarding the similarities and differences between the two remain speculative and intuitive (although Fairclough does make reference to certain individual speeches).

Other corpus studies in CDA have been Flowerdew's (1997) study of lexical and grammatical features in the speeches of the last British Governor of Hong Kong, Chris Patten. Flowerdew's purpose was to expose the myth that Hong Kong's way of life had always been characterized by western liberal values of the free market, freedom of the individual, the rule of law and democracy, and to show that it was a myth Patten was concerned to develop about Britain's legacy to Hong Kong (ibid.: 458). Although again there is no comparative corpus in which it is possible to claim that the grammatical and lexical features are indeed different.

What we can see from these two cases is while corpus methodology has been useful in enhancing critical approaches to discourse, greater use could be made of comparative data, either in the form of a reference corpus (the benchmark to what is 'normal' in the language) or another special corpus (see Baker and McEnery, 2005; Orpin, 2005; Partington, 2003 for some good examples of this).

Corpora used in this chapter

As just stated, corpora can be general or specialized. An example of a general (or 'reference') corpus (which was used in this study) is the Collins Cobuild 'Bank of English' (BoE), which contains over 500 million words of written and spoken English of various genres, divided into 11 subcorpora, including British broadsheet newspapers, Australian newspapers, UK speech and US books. This corpus can be used as a basis for comparison to show what is unusual or particular in a special corpus. An example of a special corpus is the one used in this study, namely, the specially created one-million word Department of Defense (DoD) corpus, comprising 269 geopolitical speeches between the years 1995 and 2001 given by senior defence officials (mostly secretaries of defence and chiefs of staff). These were downloaded from the Department's official website at www.defenselink.mil/speeches.

It should now be clear as to the advantages of comparing a special corpus against a reference corpus. First, we can discover what items are particularly prominent in a special corpus by comparing relative frequencies *between* the corpora. It does not matter that corpora are of different sizes, since it is *relative* frequency which corpus linguists are interested in, usually expressed in number of occurrences per one million words. Secondly, once we have discovered the items that are unusually prominent in a special corpus in comparison to a reference corpus, we can then go on to examine the lexical, grammatical and discourse features associated with those items. In other words, this is an excellent way, it is claimed, to establish a more systematic basis for identifying the discourses produced by a particular institution. Rather than simply choosing a text that allows the analyst to make a case, actual frequencies of words and features can be compared to everyday language use.

The following sections explore three topics in the DoD corpus to draw out its discursive practices – pronouns, binomials and metaphor. In the case of certain pronouns and binomials, these were shown to be unusually frequent in the special corpus giving some clues about the institutional world view and strategies for maintaining power. A discussion of metaphor is also included in this chapter, as it is well-known as a persuasive voice. In all three areas – pronouns, binomials and metaphor – we are not just interested in frequency, but also in textual environment.

Pronouns: consensual *we*

Goodin (1980: 105) has remarked that

> an important aspect of appealing to audience prejudices is the orator's claim to share their perspective . . . The 'language of participation' in general, and the word *we* in particular, figures importantly in this process. Use of the first person plural implies a unity between the speaker and his audience that is typically a fraud.

While the term 'fraud' may be too strong a claim, it may certainly be argued that pronouns not only play a role in the manufacture of solidarity and consensus within a particular discourse community, but that they influence – albeit covertly – the audience. We can illustrate this with examples from the DoD corpus shortly to show how the military establishment attempts to persuade its audience that they share common interests as regards international affairs.

Looking first at the frequencies of personal pronouns per one million words found in both the DoD corpus and the 'Bank of English' (my reference corpus), we can see in Table 7.1 that the total occurrences of *we, us* and *our* in the DoD corpus amounts to 27,601 per one million words, compared to only 6,069 times in the Bank of English, a four and a half fold difference. In the DoD corpus, also, the frequency of *we/us/our* (14,536) significantly exceeds the *combined* frequency of *I/me/my* (5,395), they/them/their (3,510) and *you/your* (3,104).

Table 7.1 Frequency of pronouns in the DoD and Bank of English corpora (instances per 1 million words)

DoD corpus		Bank of English	
we	15,355	*it*	10,423
our	10,109	*you*	8,091
I	7,629	*he*	6,978
it	6,335	*they*	4,772
you	5,073	*his*	4,324
they	3,225	*we*	4,185
their	2,286	*she*	2,756
us	2,137	*her*	2,435
them	1,400	*your*	1,818
he	1,373	*my*	1,708
its	1,362	*them*	1,632
your	1,172	*him*	1,556
my	1,151	*me*	1,411
me	1,072	*our*	1,162
his	859	*its*	1,152
him	231	*us*	722
her	100	*I*	571

To draw out the meaning of this we should first note that *we* may function 'exclusively' or 'inclusively'. An example of inclusive *we* might be: 'Shall *we* go to the cinema tonight?', where *we* refers to both speaker and addressee, while an example of exclusive *we* might be found in the rejection letter to a job applicant: '*We* regret to inform you ...', where *we* refers to the institution only, not the addressee.

In the Bank of English, from a random sample of 200, 148 instances of *we* were found to be *exclusive*, with the pronoun often referring to institutions, companies or political parties, such as in the following example:

> *We* are committed to providing you with the best service possible and throughout 1995 we will be striving to do this. So that you have an idea of how we performed in 1994 ...

In the case of political discourse, it is the *inclusive* 'we', however, which often predominates, although this is not always a straightforward concept. Beard (2000: 45) adds that 'the advantage of the plural pronoun forms is that they help share the responsibility, especially when the decisions are tricky, when the news is uncertain. In their broadest reference they can show the politician in touch with all of the country, even all of the world'.

Language and Power

It is not difficult to see how useful the inclusive first person plural pronoun might be, then, if a government needs to persuade a nation to go to war or to accept an unpopular policy. As Wales (1996: 62) expresses it:

> The politician-speaker [frequently] uses *we* with the double inference and presumption that he or she is not only speaking on behalf of the party or government, but also on behalf of the audience ... the rhetorical implication is that the audience or readership must therefore share the government's views as being the only correct views.

Margaret Thatcher exploited the strategy after the Falklands War, when she declared at a Conservative Party rally: '*We* are entitled to be proud ... *this nation* had the resolution to do what it knew had to be done – to do what it knew was right' (quoted in Billig, 1995: 89). The 'we' is conflated with 'this nation', moving the pronoun away from its exclusive reference to the Conservative Party.

An example of this consensual, inclusive 'we' from the everyday English (the BoE) is:

> I want to keep *the government* out of the business because *we've* got the best health-care quality in the entire world.

Again, 'we' seems to stretch beyond 'the government' to everyone in the nation.

In the DoD corpus, the ambiguous scope of inclusive *we* is exploited for clearly rhetorical purposes. In the following examples, no right-minded person would *not* want 'peace' and 'democracy', or would *not* want to disassociate themselves from 'agents of terror':

> ... that *we* always pay tribute to the people who are protecting *us* and serving *us* and building a better life for all of *us*. As a result of their service and sacrifice ... *we* can enjoy greater prosperity, and *we* can continue this effort to spread peace, democracy, free enterprise, all across the globe.
>
> As President Bush said this month in his defense policy speech at the Citadel, 'Every nation knows that *we* cannot accept, and will not accept, states that harbor, finance, train or equip the agents of terror.
>
> Today all can see that the spirit of our nation is strong. And the heroes? *We* don't have to look far to find them. On September 11th, they were here and in New York, pulling friends and strangers out of the fire and the rubble.
>
> (DoD data)

Because we all want peace, prosperity, democracy, etc. it is only natural that 'we' (i.e. all of us) should support service personnel and 'heroes'

Table 7.2 Functions of *we* in the DoD corpus

Dept of Defense *we* (exclusive)	83
US Government *we* (exclusive)	21
US + another country/countries (inclusive)	8
US *we* (inclusive)	74
Indeterminable	14
TOTAL	200

who are implicitly responsible for preserving these values. Of course this connection between the two things, the wanting peace and supporting soldiers is not a necessary one. Yet the military is able to use this to claim to speak on behalf of a collective 'us', of common sense.

In what follows I define the scope of a random sample of 200 instances of *we* in the DoD corpus by looking at the wider discourse (i.e. several lines around the item's occurrence). This helps us to see how the military often obscure the difference between 'we' and 'you' for strategic purposes. The findings from the corpus are given in Table 7.2.

We can see that while just over half (104) of all instances of *we* would seem to be exclusive, referring to either the Department of Defense or the US government, at least 82 instances are interpretable as inclusive. Compare this to the BoE cited earlier, where, from 200 instances, 148 occurrences of *we* were exclusive. One explanation for this is that, while in other contexts, asymmetries between discourse participants are more usually expressed through the exclusive 'we' (e.g. 'we', your bank speaking to 'you', our customer), defence spokespersons seem to be deliberately obscuring the boundaries between 'we' and 'you' for rhetorical reasons.

This can be illustrated by the following extracts, in which *our forces* may be interpreted exclusively as the Department of Defense's (the employer's) forces, or inclusively as the speaker's and hearers' forces (i.e. the military institution as a whole), or wider still, as the American people's forces (the secondary 'audience', given the dissemination of these speeches on the internet):

> Thanks to investments made during the Cold War, *our* forces are still capable; and they are doing *us* proud in Afghanistan today. But if *we* are to maintain the necessary military force, it will require significant increases in defense spending; both to make up for current shortfalls, and also to acquire the revolutionary new capabilities *we* need to meet the threats of tomorrow.
>
> The experiences of September 11th remind us that enemies of freedom seem always with us. And if *we* are to defend freedom, *we*

must remain constantly on guard; ready for surprises; ready to fight today's wars even as we prepare to defend our people and our way of life from new and different and unexpected threats.

What this shows is the way the military are deliberately ambiguous about exclusions and inclusions. This means that actual acts and who is responsible and on whose behalf they are done can be obscured. Nevertheless the DoD clearly uses the language of inclusion to legitimize its actions, speaking from a collective position of 'we' and 'us', relying on semiotic ambiguity for persuasive ends.

If we move away now from considering the function of *we* in the DoD corpus to looking at the pronoun's cotext, the data show that it is often associated with moral obligation to act or resist, with the most frequent right collocates being modal or semi-modal auxiliaries such as *must* (846 instances), *need to* (502 instances), *have* to (377 instances) and *cannot* (171 instances):

ur warfighting capability –	we *cannot afford* to sit idle.
have strategic implications,	we *cannot afford* the risk of our
g and field time. Similarly,	we *cannot allow* such a maintenance
ything that must be done, so	we *have to assume risks*. When I te . . .
lations with China. It's why	we *have to keep reaching out* to Ch . . .
r greatest success story and	we *must vigilantly guard* the quality of
rd, and Reserve – approach.	We *must be ready to*: 'Shape' the . . .
Century capabilities!	We *must do better* than this or equipment
deal with future challenges.	We *must continue to modernize* th . . .
ritical readiness challenge,	we *need your continued support* for . . .
e that we have the equipment	we *need to train and execute* our
the force needed to meet it.	We *need your help* to get there. Yo . . .
ets the highest standards!	We *need to reinforce* our recruiters' suc

Again, attempting to 'fix' the first person plural pronoun on an inclusive/exclusive scale is difficult, subject to hearer interpretation. While exclusivity is apparent in *we need your help to get there* [where 'we' = Department of Defense], *we cannot afford to sit idle* may be interpreted as either inclusive or exclusive, depending on the hearer. Whatever interpretation, one thing that is apparent is the association of *we* with modal auxiliaries, reflecting the need for preparedness. The pronoun's function in this corpus, then, is inherently persuasive.

In the majority of cases where *we* collocates with *have*, however, they occur not as part of the modal *have to*, but as the auxiliary in Present Perfect structures – 'we' here are projecting 'ourselves' as agents of

Defence Discourse II

positive change and achievement. In all of the examples that follows, *we* is exclusive (the DoD or the US government), but the effect is still to persuade the audience of the rightness of its determined efforts:

ries. For example, in Africa	we have *instituted* a program called the
en off more than a year ago.	We have *fundamentally strengthened* our s
three of the four examples,	we have *already exceeded* them. Our
aircraft. In each instance,	we have *met or exceeded* the aircra . . .
s not haphazard. As Marines,	we have *long prided ourselves* on f . . .
of all of the NATO members.	We have *reinforced* the bonds of tr . . .
d to expand NATO's security.	We have *reversed the aggression* and slau
t of our funding shortfalls.	We have *implemented* improved business pr
nted out in September, while	we have *consistently defined* a requireme
ed. [Laughter.] But it's why	we have *supported* establishing Pe
during the past three years,	we have *been able to procure* seven . . .
ortcoming. As in past years,	we have *resourced* training to

Positive self-representation is also evident in relational (attributive) processes (Halliday, 1994: 119) in which qualities of steadfastness and commitment are attributed to 'us':

challenging market. Although	we are presently *successful* in our
ss' into the new millennium.	We are ever *mindful* that it has be . . .
bout the superpower paradox.	We are *supreme* in every way, in ev . . .
point today. Quite simply,	we are *ready* today because of your
s position vis-a-vis Taiwan.	We are *committed* to supplying Taiw . . .
e advantage of the fact that	we are presently *unchallenged* by a
The bottom line remains that	we are *ready* today, but our readiness

Linked also to the imperative of 'what we need to do' is the present tense of current situations, including what *we face* in the future (130 instances) and what we *need* now:

America illustrated well why	we *continue to need* trained and re . . .
d – the enduring challenges	we *face* in taking care of people, whil
egy for the uncertain future	we *face*. This strategy, however, does
y major kind of conflict. So	we *face* these threats. If we're compl
and finance ministries that	we *face* real dangers that demand real re
represent the kind of world	we *face* today. They demonstrate th . . .
d at Taiwan. Taiwan will say	we *need* more defensive equipment. . . .
y a powerful reminder *of* why	we *need* land forces, but they

147

Freedom and democracy cannot be taken for granted, it seems, and if we wish to preserve them, we 'inclusively' must assume responsibility – this is implicitly the case, even when the first person plural pronoun is only textually exclusive.

To sum up, I have focused on the use of *we* in a special corpus, the DoD corpus. It was chosen not only because it is inordinately frequent, but because it functions differently from the norm, as evidenced in a general corpus. I have demonstrated that, by looking at *we*'s collocates and the wider cotext, the pronoun 'can become an ambiguous term, indicating both the particularity of 'we' the nation, and the universality of 'we', the universally reasonable world. In this way, 'our' interests – those of party, government, nation and world – can appear to coincide rhetorically, so long as 'we' do not specify what 'we' mean by 'we', but, instead, allow the first person plural to suggest a harmony of interests and identities' (Billig, 1995: 90). This 'harmony of interests' is what successful politicians are good at 'manufacturing'.

Binomials

My next level of analysis deals with what are known as binomial phrases. These have a powerful rhetorical function in persuasive discourse. Hatzidaki (1999: 136), who carried out the first, large-scale, corpus-driven study of binomial phrases defines the 'binomial' as follows: 'The formula WORD1 *and* WORD2 is a binomial if its members are syntactically symmetrical, i.e. they belong to the same word class and have the same syntactic function.' Examples include *hearts and minds, tough but necessary*, and *attract and retain*. The first of these is a nominal binomial, the second an adjectival binomial, and the third a verbal binomial.

Before continuing, let me explain why I chose binomials for examination in this case. Investigating 3- and 4-word n-grams (contiguous word sequences or 'clusters'), the analysis of the corpus revealed (Table 7.3) that among clusters foregrounding elite persons and places, such as *Secretary of Defense* and *the United States*, the sequence of *men and women* was very frequent.

Indeed, the most frequent nominal binomial in the DoD corpus is *men and women,* with 426 examples (or tokens). As Table 7.4 below shows, the word *men* rarely coordinates with any other word:

The binomial *men and women* is also frequent in the Bank of English – Hatzidaki (1999: 391–9), for example, found it to be the most frequent binomial in both the BBC and British Books subcorpora of the Bank of English – but it is the difference in *co-text* which is perhaps the most telling, as we will see later.

Table 7.3 Three- and four-word clusters in the DoD corpus

Three-word clusters		Four-word clusters	
the United States	1539	weapons of mass destruction	335
the Cold War	501	the Department of Defense	229
we have to	445	the United States and	221
men and women	426	of the cold war	215
Secretary of Defense	365	of the United States	197
of mass destruction	352	in the United States	193
in the world	349	the end of the	193
one of the	348	at the same time	185
that we have	343	thank you very much	181
weapons of mass	337	**men and women** in	143
going to be	318	to be able to	143
we need to	304	I would like to	136
be able to	302	our **men and women**	129
the end of	297	and **women** in uniform	121
the Department of	295	*the* **men and women**	**119**

Table 7.4 Binomials with *men* in the DoD corpus

Types	Tokens
men and women	426
leaders and men	2
men and boys	1
men and material	1

If we consider the collocates of this binomial (Table 7.5), first of all, we will note the presence of *our* in 1st left, 2nd left and 2nd right position, as well as *uniform* in 2nd right position, with 75 instances of *our men and women* being followed by *in uniform*. The software used for this kind of analysis displays the collocates of the search term ranked in terms of frequency. The collocation data is organized in four columns, where there is one column for each position surrounding the keyword: 2nd left, 1st left, 1st right and 2nd right. So, for example, the 1st left refers to the word before the search term and 1st right refers to the word following the search term. The columns we see below show the collocates in descending order of frequency.

Table 7.5 Collocates of *men and women* in the DoD corpus

2nd left		1st left		1st right		2nd right	
58	of	107	**our**	120	in	101	**uniform**
33	to	99	the	86	who	44	the
22	the	23	**young**	59	of	36	are
19	**our**	16	military	7	to	17	**our**
15	for	10	of	5	have	15	**serve**
13	and	10	The	5	and	7	have

A closer look at the corpus reveals that 75 instances of *our men and women* are followed by *in uniform* (note that Table 7.5 above cannot be read in linear, left-to-right fashion: the preposition *in* at 1st right position after *men and women* might govern a different noun phrase, such as *the Balkans*).

As we will see from a representative sample of concordance lines below, the complete noun phrase *our men and women in uniform* is associated with a number of rhetorical items. First, the determiner *our* invites the listener to share in the actions, duties and responsibilities of the soldiers. *Our* here would seem to be maximally inclusive – it includes the American people (see previous section). Secondly, *men and women* is rhetorically resonant in a way, I would suggest, that a denotationally equivalent phrase (e.g. *US armed forces*) may not be. Unlike *forces*, the phrase *men and women* is vivid and imaginable. The institution, in other words, is 'personalized'. This is important, if we consider the spokesperson's desire to involve and persuade his/her listeners. In using the phrase *men and women in uniform* the speaker is perhaps better able to appeal to the hearers' sense of loyalty and indebtedness towards service personnel, while at the same time mitigating perceptions of the military as a dehumanized, or dehumanizing, world; they are, in other words, 'men and women' like us.

The rhetorical phrase *our men and women in uniform* is also surrounded by highly evaluative words – they are under *strain*, under *burden* for their *service and sacrifice* – therefore as civilians we must show our *commitment* and *support* for their *welfare* and *security*:

which help *ease the burden on*   our men and women in uniform.
his *resolve and commitment to*   our men and women in uniform.
this *job weighs heavily upon*   our men and women in uniform.

the *safety and security* of	our men and women in uniform.
o are managing the *welfare* of	our men and women in uniform.
verything possible to *support*	our men and women in uniform.
fety and *physical security* of	our men and women in uniform and their
obligation we owe not only to	our men and women in uniform,
he *magnificent performance* of	our men and women in uniform. But this
the *service and sacrifice* of	our men and women in uniform.
gratitude on behalf of all of	our men and women in uniform for all th
the *biggest single strain* on	our men and women in uniform is the

It will be noted above that *our men and women in uniform* tends to be preceded by *of* and other noun phrases such as *magnificent performance (of)* and *service and sacrifice (of)*, and that it usually occurs in clause-final position (over half the lines), perhaps inviting applause (Atkinson, 1984). On this latter point, only in a handful of cases does *men and women* occur in subject position:

> *Our men and women in uniform* put up with a lot of sacrifice. One of the biggest sacrifices is constant . . .
>
> *Our men and women in uniform* need the support of their leaders in Washington—and they have it!

As far as the adjectival premodifiers of *men and women* are concerned, the most frequent are *young* and *military*. In the case of *young*, this is frequently preceded by other evaluative adjectives such as *bright*, *capable* and *outstanding*. It seems that if you are 'young' in this discourse you must also be 'superb' and 'impressive':

to continue recrcuiting *bright*	*young* men and women of character from
to meet with the *very capable*	*young* men and women that are serving. G
ountry, and for the *dedicated*	*young* men and women who are serving in
men in uniform are the *finest*	*young* men and women that our country ca
rld. It attracts *high–quality*	*young* men and women, it trains them to
llenge. They're the *finest of*	*young* men and women. I looked in
ctivity, you find *outstanding*	*young* men and women serving the nation
cial-*gifted, serious- minded*	*young* men and women who were prepared
ing commitment to the *superb*	*young* men and women who serve in its
excellent choice for *talented*	*young* men and women. For fiscal year 1
s. And as *impressive* as those	*young* men and women are, what is even
t produces fit, *well-adjusted*	*young* men and women who have strong v

151

In the Bank of English, statistically significant collocates of *men* and *women* include *between* and *both*. In a representative sample of lines from the BoE, *men and women*, as complement of the preposition *between*, are seen less as a composite body with a common objective than as discrete entities, in which contrasts of lifestyle, temperament and sexuality are emphasized:

and *emotional differences*	*between* men and women which are ignored
re were *frequent disputes*	*between* men and women, between young
the *essential differences*	*between* men and women? <p> Had Dr
f the *biggest differences*	*between* men and women. <p> If you are
st 50 years *the relations*	*between* men and women, and between
ose days *the relationship*	*between* men and women was <ZF1> ver

In summary, while the collocates of the binomial *men and women* in the Bank of English emphasize individualism and difference, *men and women* in the DoD corpus are construed as a cooperative composite. Any differences that may exist are simply absent in the discourse. Reality, as has been emphasized before in this book, is never an objective reality – it is what an institution *constructs* as real.

The third most frequent binomial in the DoD corpus is *friends and allies*, with 67 instances. Unlike the majority of binomials, it is reversible: *allies and friends* also occurs, with 47 occurrences.

Both *allies* and *friends* refer to countries which accord with US policies; as such, the two coordinates of the binomial may incline us to categorizing the binomial as 'synonymous' (Gustafsson, 1975). Rhetorically speaking, *friends and allies* may have an intensifying function, similar to 'echoic' binomials (where WORD1 is identical to WORD2), such as *more and more* and *stronger and stronger*.

Although *our* is the most frequent 1st left collocate in both *friends and allies* and *allies and friends,* proportionately this determiner collocates more frequently with *friends and allies* (66 per cent) than with *allies and friends* (38 per cent). It also tends to collocate with items such as *cooperation, interoperability,* and *engagement*:

ed States seeks *cooperation with its*	friends and allies for political
ancing our *interoperability with our*	friends and allies, maintaining
ay military *engagement with our*	friends and allies through a
of active *partnerships with our*	friends and allies. It means car
Armaments *cooperation with our*	friends and allies will help us
ve authority to *work closer with our*	friends and allies across a whol
. y power; *working in concert with*	friends and allies; helps contri
r greater armaments *cooperation with*	friends and allies. Deploying

Allies and friends, on the other hand, appear to be in a more asymmetrical relationship with respect to the US than *friends and allies*. Whereas the latter are construed as more or less cooperative partners in a joint enterprise of some kind, *allies and friends* are seen as discrete entities, of lower status, and frequently in need of *reassurance and support*:

   eployment and use: assuring   allies and friends *of the United States;*
   ust be able to *reassure our*   allies and friends *– to work with the eme*
   to be able to *reassure our*   allies and friends, *and deter and defeat*
   nited States to support our   allies and friends *from NATO to Israel, t*
   . is to be able to reassure   allies and friends, *and to deter and def*
   . interests, and reassuring   allies and friends. *As stated in the NATO*

The second significant difference is that *allies and friends* are frequently geographically specified as *European*, *German* or simply *regional*, which is not the case with *friends and allies*; that is, *friends and allies* are vaguer, more indeterminate than *allies and friends*. The effect is to suggest that *our friends and allies* are so well known that the need to identify them overtly is unnecessary. *Allies and friends*, on the other hand, require qualification:

   w the United States and our allies and friends *in Europe* are moving t
   indeed all of our *European*   allies and friends, is somewhat similar
   chauble; and all our *German* allies and friends; ladies and gentlemen.
   ns America and our *regional* allies and friends in recognizing the com
   es, along with our *regional*   allies and friends, has yielded results
   relationships with *regional*   allies and friends. For example, the

This is interesting from a rhetorical point of view. As noted, the binomial *friends and allies* occurs 67 times in the corpus, or 77 per cent as a proportion of *all* binomials and coordinate structures with friends as WORD1. Other simple binomials with *friends* (such as *friends and colleagues*) accounted for only 7 per cent, while other non-binomial coordinate structures (*friends and potential enemies*) accounted for another 7 per cent. Compound binomials (*friends and coalition partners*) comprised 4 per cent, while the remaining 12 per cent consisted of phrases such as *our friends and our allies* (where a determiner, rather than a modifier, before WORD2 excludes them from the category of binomial).

In contrast, the simple binomial *allies and friends* only constituted 45 per cent of the total. Other simple binomials with *allies* as WORD1 (*allies and partners, allies and forces*, etc.) accounted for 7.2 per cent, while compound binomials (*allies and coalition partners*) made up

23.7 per cent of the total. Non-binomials constituted 24.1 per cent. This information is illustrated in tables 7.6 and 7.7 below.

Thus, not only does *friends and allies* occur more often than *allies and friends*, the former's rhetorical force, I would suggest, appears to be enhanced by the relative *absence* of other binomial types or coordinate structures in the discourse. Conversely, the relative frequency of *allies and* modified WORD2, in contrast to the simple binomial *allies and friends*, as well as the frequency of other simple and compound binomials with *allies* as WORD1, tends to *mitigate* the taken-for-granted rhetoric of the simple binomial where it *does* occur. *Friends and allies* becomes a familiar but conveniently vague phrase, easily passing us by, if we do not stop to think who these 'friends and allies' might be.

Shapiro, commenting on Shakespeare's language in *Hamlet*, draws particular attention to the fact that binomials may cause a blurring

Table 7.6 Coordinate structures with *friends* as WORD1

Binomial	Percentage
friends and allies (binomial)	77%
Other binomials (e.g. *friends and foes*)	7%
Compound binomials (e.g. *friends and coalition partners*)	4%
Other coordinate structures (non-binomial) (e.g. *our friends and our allies*)	12%

Table 7.7 Coordinate structures with *allies* as WORD1

Binomial	Percentage
allies and friends (binomial)	45%
Other binomials (e.g. *allies and partners*)	7.2%
Compound binomials (e.g. *allies and US forces*)	23.7%
Other coordinate structures (non-binomial) (e.g. *our allies and the Russians*)	24.1%

of distinctions. This blurring may, of course, be politically expedient, in discourse that seeks to downplay differences between men and women, that equates 'friends with allies'. If the single item 'friends' is 'deeply misleading' in international relations (Fairclough, 2000: 153), how much more misleading might it be to conjoin it with 'allies'?

In summary, the *absence* in the discourse of 'differences between' men and women, I would suggest, leads to a downplaying that any difference might exist, while the conjoining of 'friends' with 'allies' suggests the two concepts are more or less the same, where in other discourses they may be quite separate.

Metaphor

This final section examines how corpus methodology may be used to explore the power of metaphor in persuasive texts. As Charteris-Black (2004: 7) maintains: 'Metaphor is a figure of speech that is typically used in persuasion; this is because it represents a novel way of viewing the world that offers some fresh insight.' In this respect, metaphors may be seen as reflecting an evaluation on the part of the speaker, and a reflection of the values of the community on whose behalf he or she speaks. Those evaluations, if repeated often enough, may eventually become 'naturalized', part of the mental framework of its producers and consumers.

First, let us consider what we mean by metaphor. Metaphor has been defined as 'the use of language to refer to something other than what it was originally applied to, or what it "literally" means, in order to suggest some resemblance or make a connection between the two things' (Knowles and Moon, 2006: 3). Elsewhere, it has been described as 'a word or expression that is used to talk about an entity or quality other than that referred to by its core, or most basic meaning' (Deignan, 2005: 34). Thus, the 'core' meaning of 'flood' might be 'overflow of a large amount of water beyond its normal limits' (*Oxford Dictionary of English*), while its transferred, 'non-core' meaning might be 'arrive in overwhelming amounts or quantities' (ibid.), as in 'flood of refugees'.

The concepts of 'literalness' and 'coreness' are not as straightforward as they are sometimes presented, however. What is deemed literal and psychologically core may be partially dependent on what the discourse participants of a particular community *consider* to be literal and core. For example, in the sentence taken from the DoD corpus:

> We seek a steady and sustained *engagement* in our bilateral relationship

Is political engagement more or less 'core' than a marriage engagement (assuming that both are to be understood as metaphors in the first place)? If there is a core, 'literal' sense of 'engagement' outside these two specific senses, what sense might that be?

For the purposes of this chapter, I will be considering items as metaphoric in the DoD corpus where they would appear to be more 'core' in the language as a whole. In this chapter, the analysis is restricted to 'natural environment' metaphors, specifically the items *landscape, sea, wind* and *flood*. I have chosen these, as they are perhaps the most 'novel' amongst a set of fairly conventional metaphors in the corpus, and have more usual (core) usages in the Bank of English. Being fairly striking, they may act to influence, to persuade, in more powerful ways than the more conventional (possibly dead) metaphors such as *engagement*.

Landscape

If we look at the Bank of English, we will find that the majority of 'landscapes' are literal (as in landscape painting). Where they are metaphorical, they tend to be *political, economic* and *business*, with the notion of 'change' being important:

Bubb says the *business* landscape has been radically *changed* by the
vestigate the *changing* landscape of the society it draws its
ur legal and *community* landscape, that it will *transform* the way
Australian *corporate* landscape. Not surprisingly, Hadid i
revolution *changed* the landscape and the way of life of the indig
he country's *cultural* landscape with numerous books and political
eature of the *economic* landscape. No doubt, the Government should t
how much the *political* landscape had *changed* since the time when
n sight, the *political* landscape is *changing*. In tomorrow's world
of Moscow's *political* landscape is murky at best, with no clear
nsformed the *political* landscape of Britain. The DAILY MIRROR

However, there are a significant number of metaphorical instances where *landscape* reflects a psychological reality:

defines her *emotional* landscape by connection with Kim. I did not
l, where the *emotional* landscape had turned like a kaleidoscopic vi
part of our *fictional* landscape, impeccable prose is not the only

m the *emotionally flat* landscape of her robotlike existence in her
to the imposed *mental* landscape of the new orthodoxy, then affect
e kind of *metaphysical* landscape or something <F0X> Oh yes I
tions about our *moral* landscape; and which, for its evocation of
f New York's *psychotic* landscape in search of a sly and elusive pa
teriors' are about the   landscape *within*. It's a place that's never
ist can detect how the   landscape *of inner emotion* contributes to th

An examination of 20 instances of *landscape* in the DoD corpus shows a similar association with change and psychological reality, where *threats* and *challenges* need to be *faced*:

> Today, those men and women in uniform *face a landscape of new and diverse threats.*
>
> We're now in the midst of molding our military to this *ever-changing landscape of threats* . . .
>
> Your efforts have become even more critical as our men and women in uniform *face a landscape of different and diverse challenges* . . .

Fear of the unknown would often seem to be metaphorized as natural phenomena here. Lee (1992: 9), for example, argues that the following sentence represents the people of Soweto (from a white perspective) as an uncontrollable force: *(they) had been simmering with unrest and then erupted, and later swept through a roadblock like a river.* Similarly, perceptions of geopolitical instability or threats are often encoded in terms of uncontainable natural forces (such as fire) in the DoD corpus:

> Yet the region remains a *tinderbox*, with potential *flash points* from Korea to the Taiwan Straits and beyond, that, if *ignited*, would have *scorching effects* on the security and economies in Asia, North America and around the globe.

These extended metaphorical images are comparatively rare in the corpus, but items such as *sea* and *winds* do occur with some frequency in their metaphorical sense, and I will consider these next.

Sea

As one would expect, the vast majority of 'seas' in the BoE are literal (e.g. Mediterranean Sea). The same can be said of the DoD corpus. Of the total number of occurrences of *sea* (195), only 13 were metaphorical. Metaphorical *sea* often serves as noun premodifier of *change* to form the lexical item *sea change* (first used by Shakespeare), meaning 'radical change':

sphere that has undergone a	*sea change* of epic proportions. Al
wn. Today, we've achieved a	*sea change* in our financial affair
dergoing *three* fundamental	'*sea changes*' with which we must de
you. In fact, that *second*	'*sea change*' – global economic int
the past will recognize the	*sea change* presented by this new c
few words about that *third*	'*sea change*': the accelerating pace

This is in contrast to the Bank of English, where most occurrences of metaphorical *sea* are qualified by prepositional phrases such as *of faces, of red,* etc. (metaphorical *sea,* therefore, being semantically associated, for the most part, with people and colours). This gives a sense of confusing or unquantifiable mass:

sity to what has been a	sea of *blue* suits and red ties.
the ball high into the	sea of *blue and red* behind Alan King
to see, so huge was the	sea of *bodies*. He said: `This is the w
ked eye could see was a	sea of Brazilian *yellow* with a dash of
gure become part of the	sea of *color* and form. But now he reali
ght not be moved by the	sea of *excited faces* in the auditorium
e prospect of viewing a	sea of *faces* turned expectantly towards
eroes are marooned in a	sea of *fans* as 50,000 jubilant support

There are also a significant number of instances in the BoE in which *negative* psychological states are invoked with *sea*:

ng for the truth amid a	sea of *confusion* or your being left on
them over into an angry	sea of *debt*. Making your fortune by investin
feel tossed about in a	sea of *dejection, bafflement, loss and despa*
olly wrong. Afloat on a	sea of *delusions*, the Americans seem to enjo
hope flashes up, then a	sea of *despair* rages, and always leaves one f
or she would sink in a	sea of *misery*. Klara had a business appointme
ive Are you living in a	sea of *negation*, always saying `No, I can't

Metaphorical *sea*, as previously mentioned, does not have this association with confusion or negativity in the DoD corpus. Defence spokespersons will understandably invoke the positive and the challenging in the lexical item *sea change* and avoid the negative associations of metaphorical *sea* apparent in the general corpus.

Wind(s)

Of the 32 examples of *wind* or *winds* in the DoD corpus, and their derivations such as *windswept*, 18 were literal, the remaining 14 metaphorical, of which a representative sample is given below:

help us endure the *gale force winds of change in the region*. And a
vide protection when the *gale winds* blow and tremors strike. A sec
d we are witnessing *hurricane winds* shaking virtually everything i
en in the so-called *hurricane winds of change* – our culture, our
simply react to the *hurricane winds of change in the world*. And we
that we're going to have the *winds of change sweep across our conti*
erything being *shaken in this wind*. And how technology had really m

The phrase *winds of change* is a reference to the former British Prime Minister Harold Macmillan's address to the South African Parliament in 1960, in which he said that 'the *wind of change* is blowing through this continent (i.e. Africa). As can be seen from the above concordance lines from the DoD corpus, *wind(s) of change* similarly collocates with *continent, region* and sometimes *world*.

In 7 instances, *hurricane* collocates with *wind(s) of change*, while *gale* collocates with *winds* twice. This natural force is construed as potentially devastating, one apparently affecting the core of the American way of life. Although powerful to the outsider, Charteris-Black (2004: 108–9) suggests that physical environment metaphors reflect different cultural and historical experiences between Britain and America: 'For the majority of English people nature is conceived as something to be controlled within a domestic space, whereas for Americans the powers of nature are seen as larger and more elemental.' Although evidence in the DoD corpus does seem to support this observation, the powerful emotive impact of metaphors which draw upon these elemental forces is undeniable.

Flood(s)

Of the 34 instances of *flood* or *floods* in the DoD corpus, 21 were metaphorical, as opposed to 13 which were literal. The *literal* senses of the lexeme in the corpus tend to function as premodifiers, or occur in paratactically coordinated noun phrases:

p assistance to West Coast *flood victims*. When fires raged out of co
r we're responding to help *flood victims* in Germany or Georgia when
al, military medical care, *flood control and environmental cle*

battled snow, rain, wind,	*floods and mud* to bridge the Sava
elief operations following	*floods and hurricanes*, battled against
They fight wild fires and	*floods and hurricanes*. They do everythi

while metaphorical senses tend to be followed by prepositional phrases (e.g. *flood of words*). In addition, three instances of *flood(s)* collocate with *refugees, suggesting* that they are 'constructed as a 'natural disaster' like a flood, which is difficult to control as it has no sense of its own agency' (Baker and McEnery, 2005: 203). In addition, verb forms such as *flooding, flooded*, and so on, are often metaphorical:

power in its history, and the	*flood of refugees* to our shores
t Auden called 'the dangerous	*flood of history.*' I would suggest t
Here comes the orator, with a	*flood of words* and a drop of r
d's relief organizations, the	*floods of refugees* from wars and
hreat - that Soviet WMD would	*flood the global black market* an
ll kinds of stories that were	*flooding the newspapers* at that time
of these terrible wrongs have	*flooded our living rooms* all oves we
best way to attack us was to	*flood our Department of Defense with*

To sum up this section on metaphor, we have seen that *landscape* typically collocates with *threats*, *winds* with *change*, while *flood* frequently collocates with *refugees*. Implicit in all these metaphors is the fear that if America does not adequately prepare itself (e.g. by spending more money on its military), then its values, way of life, even its survival may be under threat. Recurrence of particular metaphors in a particular domain show that 'evaluative meanings are not merely personal and idiosyncratic, but widely shared in a discourse community' (Stubbs, 2001: 215), and it is these evaluations which are aimed at creating a change of consciousness in the listener. It could be said that what perhaps underpins all the metaphors in the DoD corpus is the implicit notion of threat, whether real or imagined. It is what the DoD is good at 'manufacturing'. Creating fear is one way of persuading people their taxes are being well spent.

The following two (very similar) extracts, which incorporate some of the metaphors discussed above encapsulate this notion, seeming to have the rhetorical force of psychologically preparing its audience for an uncertain future:

> Given the high stakes involved, security *architectures*, even more than financial *architectures*, must be built on a solid *foundation*, not *shifting sands*, if they are to provide protection when the *gale winds blow* and *tremors strike*.

> Given the high stakes involved, the security *structures*, no less than financial *structures*, have to be built on solid *foundation* and not on *shifting sands*. And it's these *cornerstones* – our engagement, the bilateral relations, the multilateral channels – these are going to help us endure the *gale force winds of change* in the region.

It is, of course, easy to read too much into metaphor, and we should, once again, avoid overinterpretation. Lee's argument – mentioned earlier – that *erupted* and *swept* are associated with volcanoes and rivers, for example, has been challenged by O'Halloran (2007), who found that, in hard news stories, such items are, in fact, associated more with *human* phenomena. If *regular* readers of hard news stories are used to reading that '*fighting* erupted', then 'erupted' 'could well be understood . . . in terms of violence, conflict, etc. . . . rather than volcanoes' (ibid.: 13). The items *erupted* and *swept* have become so delexicalized in this register, he suggests, that they are barely recognized as anything greatly out of the ordinary.

However, what I have been arguing here is that for readers *outside* a particular register, outside the defence establishment in this case, the situation may be different. *Landscapes, seas, winds* and *floods* in the DoD corpus, in their metaphorical usages, *do* retain their potency for outsiders, because as outsiders we usually encounter them in quite different (often literal) contexts. The outsider encountering 'landscapes of threats' and 'hurricane winds of change' may indeed be affected by their relative novelty, given the differences in the collocational environments of such items in a general corpus.

Conclusion

This chapter has considered a number of ways in which corpus methodology can be used to explore features of rhetoric and persuasion in the defence world. One application of corpus methodology is its ability to reveal the preference an institution has for particular items and phrases, as well as the common patterns these items and phrases may enter into. Indeed, it is these oft-repeated linguistic routines that may precisely characterize the community under investigation, and be part of its everyday rhetoric.

While CDA's mainly qualitative analyses have provided interesting insights into the use of language by institutions, these can be corroborated with quantitative methods, which corpus methodology can provide.

In the case of the Department of Defense, I have shown that not only is inclusive *we* very common (beyond the 'norm', if we accept our reference corpus as representing the norm), but also that it is typically associated with deontic modals of obligation. We have also seen, through an analysis of contiguous 3- and 4-word sequences, that the binomial phrase *men and women* is also very common. While we have found that the same binomial is also frequent in our reference corpus, the textual environments are very different. We have also seen that *friends and allies* is, to all intents and purposes, a single unit of meaning, 'friends' being synonymous with 'allies'. Its reverse, on the other hand, *allies and friends*, on account of its different collocational preferences, is a binomial whose two lexical items are not yet fused into a single, 'naturalized', unit of meaning.

Finally, we have considered metaphors, which through the connotative meanings that they engender are used to promote the interests and concerns of the institution under discussion. In particular, we have seen that 'natural environment' metaphors are predominantly used by defence spokespersons to persuade listeners of the threat posed by its enemies. Threats imply the need for preparedness, and preparedness is only possible if the public is willing to pay for it.

In conclusion, as we have stressed throughout this book, institutions never present an objective 'truth'. Rather they are engaged in a construction of reality through discourse which appears natural and commonsensical. It is 'natural' because it is routine and ubiquitous, and because it repeats well-trodden themes. Corpus methodology is therefore a useful tool in revealing what is linguistically routine and ubiquitous in an institution, though not necessarily so in the world at large. As Sornig (1989: 95) maintains: 'The selection and arrangement of stylistic resources and devices . . . may serve to bring a certain perspective to the fore, to 'talk' somebody over to one's own point of view.'

8 Conclusion: Researching institutional discourse

Andrea Mayr with Tony Bastow

Introduction

The aim of this chapter is to help you with designing and conducting a research project of your own involving written, spoken and/or visual institutional discourse. It includes information on planning and designing a study, a discussion of the practicalities and ethical issues of data collection and transcription and the writing-up stage. The advice given here is mainly intended for students who will be doing a dissertation as part of their undergraduate or post-graduate degree programmes. Some advice given here may be useful for Ph.D. students, although for a project of that scale requirements are usually more complex and exacting.

Choosing and refining a suitable research project

The suggestions made here are made to help you choose a topic similar to those dealt in the previous chapters of this book: written, spoken and visual multimodal discourse characteristic of a particular institutional setting or situation. Depending on the content of your course of study, one of your aims will be a close linguistic analysis of certain features of the language of the institutional situation, while you may also want to attempt a description of the situational and larger cultural context, particularly if you approach your analysis from a critical discourse perspective.

There are many ways of studying language in context and the sheer number of possibilities can be daunting, especially for first-time researchers. One useful approach suggested by Delin (2000) is therefore to limit yourself to certain linguistic features of particular types of institutional discourse. You may want to:

- Select a discourse type, for example, doctor-patient interactions, classroom or workplace discourse, welfare aid literature, etc. and analyse their linguistic features and the wider institutional contexts in which they are produced;
- Select a particular linguistic feature, such as the use of discourse markers (*oh, mmmh, right, I see*), attitudinal/evaluative lexis, and

analyse the meaning and/or frequency of these features in one or several genres (e.g. newspaper articles);
- Select a more general feature, such as politeness, turn-taking, interactional control features and analyse the linguistic features to express these, again either in one text, genre or across a range of genres.

Reading relevant literature

To come up with 'good' ideas for research topics, reading up on previous research in the area is a necessity. That way you will get a much better idea of the research area, what the arguments and questions are and what the current state of knowledge in the areas is. It is important to do some of that reading before you embark on the actual collection and transcription of data, since what you read can help you design these stages of your research project. For example, you may want to analyse patterns of turn-taking and interruptions in the classroom. To do a careful and accurate transcription of these interactions, it is very useful to familiarize yourself with how previous researchers have dealt with the practicalities and ethical issues involved in recording and transcribing spoken data (More about these below). By looking at previous literature you may also notice gaps in the knowledge about a subject (e.g. there is not a lot of literature on workplace discourse that has dealt with the linguistic constraints increasingly imposed on employees in the service sector), disagree with certain research findings (e.g. in the area of language and gender) or come up with additional research questions (e.g. how do employees resist or acquiesce in these impositions and how do they do that linguistically?).

The ability to find relevant references is an important research skill in itself and will improve the quality of your research project. You should start building up your bibliography right from the beginning, citing clearly and correctly, bearing in mind the form required by your institution. While this may sound like a rather trivial suggestion, it helps you to keep track of your's and other people's research and you won't have to track down elusive references at the end of your project.

Reading critically

Your search of the library catalogue, of electronic databases and the world wide web will bring up what can be a bewildering array of sources and you will have to decide which sources are of immediate use to you. It is important that you develop the ability to think critically about your work: ask yourself what exactly you are trying to find out about your topic.

Using print and electronic devices

You will use these resources to acquire a sound grasp of your topic, gain knowledge of how previous research in your area has been conducted and the strengths and weaknesses of various methodologies.

Increasingly, libraries offer electronic resources, such as catalogues and databases, which can be accessed via the web and are therefore retrievable from computers located anywhere. Often books and journals are no longer held in the libraries themselves, but can be retrieved through electronic delivery.

The advantage of library catalogues and databases is that they store collections of systematically collected and evaluated information, which are organized by author's name, title, place and date of publication. When searching the catalogue, you can do that completely at random and you should allow for serendipity, although it is much more productive to be systematic in your search procedures and record keeping. Keep records of all your searches, including the key words you have used, so you won't repeat work already done for previous searches.

Searching the internet

The internet has become a very useful tool for research, and can be helpful for building your literature review. Unlike library catalogues, where information is indexed into separate fields and presented consistently, with the internet it is search engines that provide this service. The internet will not help you in obtaining a systematic overview of a field, but it is very useful for initial exploration of a topic early on in the research and when you are looking for a specific document, author or institutions you already have some details about.

A word of warning about websites: many websites do not conform to academic conventions as these are still being developed. You may not find all the information needed for an academic citation, such as the name of an individual author, in which case you should at least name the organization which provided the site. Providing only the URL is too general. You should always include the date on which you visited the site, especially if the site is undated. The domain at which you found a site can help you locate the publisher of the website: for example, domains such as '.com', '.edu' or '.org' indicate a commercial or educational site or an institution. Online journals usually do provide citation details which adhere to academic conventions. Like print journals and books, they have also usually been peer-reviewed, that is, evaluated by experts in the field before publication. For the vast majority of internet sites, however, this does not apply, but they can still be of value. Bertrand and Hughes (2005), for example, point out that even if certain websites are polemical and do no not present a thorough academic argument, they may still be useful in demonstrating certain strands of public opinion on certain topics, particularly media-related ones.

Conducting the research project

Once you have decided upon a research topic, there are several common ways of conducting a research project. Cameron (2001: 182–5) sums these up as *replicating, comparing and contrasting, taking issue with a previous claim,* and *describing something new.*

If you replicate a previous study, you use the same or similar question(s) and methods a previous researcher has used, but you collect your own data. Students often worry that this approach lacks 'originality', but they should bear in mind that a small-scale dissertation project is more a research training exercise than a truly original piece of work. Besides, finding out if certain patterns found in previous studies are replicated in your own research is one way of making reliable generalizations about their occurrence. On the other hand, things may have changed over time. If you think of racism in the press, a valid research question would be if negative representations of ethnic groups are less overt than they were maybe 10 or 15 years ago.

Comparing and contrasting involves comparing two different kinds of written or spoken discourse. You could build a corpus on tabloids and broadsheets and analyse how they differ in reporting on important events, for example, crimes. You may want to broaden this into an ethnographic study interviewing readers and taping conversations they may have about certain events reported in the news.

If you *take issue with a previous claim*, you would start from a claim you feel is based on people's prejudices or preconceptions and attempt to demonstrate why these are wrong or misguided. For example, you may want to take issue with stereotypes of why people watch soaps by interviewing them and taping them as they watch soaps to find out what particular discourses they use to describe their reasons for watching soaps.

If you *describe something new*, you focus on data that have not been analysed before and describe its discourse characteristics. The research on prison discourse reported in Chapter 3 would be an example of that. Although there were already many linguistic studies on classroom discourse at the time the research was conducted, there was no linguistic study of classroom interaction in a prison, as far as the researcher could tell. Nor was there much in the way of studies that had systematically applied some of the analytical categories developed in SFL and CDA to the analysis of classroom interaction.

Cameron (2001) points to the importance of previous research for analysing something new. First, it is important to find out if there are published studies on the chosen genre. In the case of prison research, there is a large body of sociological and criminological literature that describes the prison as a social system and which makes occasional reference to its institutional discourses including prison slang. There are also a number of prison classroom ethnographies written by social scientists and educationalists who have taught in prison. This literature provided an essential basis for framing the researcher's own research questions and research design. Second, previous literature may prove significant for investigating something new, applying a previously used linguistic model to it. Some of the linguistic categories developed and employed by Systemic Functional Linguistics (SFL) (e.g. Eggins and Slade, 1997) and by critical discourse analysts (e.g. Fairclough, 1989/2001, 1992) turned out to be very useful for the analysis of prison classroom discourse (see also Mayr, 2004).

Data collection

Once you have decided on your topic of study, the obvious next step is to consider the collection of your data. If you are going to undertake a close linguistic analysis of the details of spoken interaction, you will want to either take field notes of your chosen situation, or, preferably, audio- or even videotape the interactions.

Gathering spoken data

There are many theoretical and practical pitfalls in collecting and transcribing data, so some of the literature that has dealt with the biases that may creep in through recording and transcribing will be reviewed here. One particular problem concerns the presence of the researcher in the research setting s/he wishes to hold constant.

Before you start, looking at the methodologies of previously published work will give you important clues on conducting your own data collection, for example, information on numbers of speakers to include, amount of data, design of different questionnaire types, sampling and interviewing techniques, etc. The question of 'how much data' is just as much a concern of students as 'what type of data'. It is impossible to provide strict guidelines for how much data you should collect as this depends very much on your time and the type of your project. As a rule of thumb, transcribing five minutes of conversation can take up to one hour or longer, particularly if you transcribe multi-party conversation. Classroom or workplace conversations may be very long; so one way of dealing with them would be to focus on examples for transcription, while still using the entire conversations for your observations and interpretation. Another way of cutting down on a very long transcription task is to focus on certain key elements of talk such as openings and closing, false starts, interactional control and resistance strategies or certain topics of discussion.

In general, for projects involving interactions in institutional settings (schools, universities, call centres, offices, police stations, media organizations, etc.) you will need to obtain the close cooperation of others. Some factors might help you achieve a successful data collection experience. According to Delin (2000: 159), you should, if possible, choose

- A familiar situation: knowledge of the institution (maybe your own university, some of its teachers and student friends; your own workplace) will help you greatly in avoiding time-consuming steps such as gaining access to an institution and establishing rapport with its members;
- An inside contact: someone connected to the institution, either yourself, a friend or colleague, or better still, somebody in authority who is able to grant you permission for conducting your research; and
- Control over time: how soon you can obtain your recorded data is vital given that you often only have a few months to finish a project at MA level; but also for a Ph.D. the sooner you can gather your data the better.

Always bear in mind that because your project may be seen as an intrusion you could be denied access to the institution, hence the importance of a sympathetic inside contact. One possible way out of this problem is to convince people who represent institutions of the significance of your research and the possible benefits they might derive from it, although this probably applies more to large-scale Ph.D. projects. For example, Wodak (1996) conducted a participant observation study in an out-patient clinic in Vienna, the findings of which were then used for suggesting guidelines for improved staff-patient interaction.

Whatever project you envisage, the most important thing is to get the permission of those directly affected by it, that is, those involved in the interactions (e.g. students and teachers; colleagues at work) and their superiors. You may have to gain written permission from your subjects and their superiors, and a written letter from your tutor may help to establish your credentials. If you do research in schools, you will have to get the permission of parents for interviewing/tape-recording children. Bear in mind that these can be time-consuming steps.

Maybe the biggest problem with recording naturally occurring talk is how the researcher's presence may affect the (linguistic) behaviour of speakers, what the sociolinguist William Labov (1972a, b) has called the 'observer's paradox': researchers want to observe speakers as if they were not observed. As Vidich (1955) says, the researcher, by joining a social situation, disturbs a scene which he or she would like to hold constant. One way of reducing the paradox is that you do not actually sit in on a tape-recorded conversation, but only ask for permission to use the recorded tapes afterwards. This will not get rid of the observer's paradox completely, because people will still be aware of the recording equipment, but it will reduce it to a degree. On the other hand, you will lose out on the dynamics of the interaction, non-verbal behaviour and body language, unless you are allowed to video-tape interactions. It has to be said though, that most interactants become less self-conscious after being observed for a while, particularly if the researcher is present in the research setting for a longer period of time as a participant-observer.

Participant observation

Research that involves the active collaboration of the researcher in the field has been called 'participant-observation'. Participant observation changes the focus from objectivity and quantification to 'empathetic understanding', that is, understanding from the inside and taking in the perspective of its members. In practice, however, participant observation is very often not a single method, but is backed up with more 'objective' techniques, including survey techniques and statistics.

Unlike quantitative methods, such as questionnaires, participant observation exploits the interchange between researchers and the field. Observers become familiar enough with the setting they observe to experience it to some degree themselves. The strength of participant observation lies in the quality of knowledge you are able to attain through your involvement with the field.

For linguists, the main advantage of participant observation is its capacity to countervail the 'observer's paradox' (Labov) to a degree. Many linguists (e.g. Labov, 1972a, b; L. Milroy, 1980; Cheshire, 1982) have opted for a participant observation research method, not least because of its efficacy in making people less aware of the long-term presence of the researcher. Participant observation is a viable method for learning about people's lives as well as their speech patterns as it involves immersing yourself into a culture.

One difficulty concerns the social role of the fieldworker. Linguists have commented on problems fieldworkers might encounter on the basis of their age, sex, and social class (L. Milroy, 1987). Using an 'insider' to conduct the linguistic fieldwork, that is, one socially matching the subjects, may not necessarily be the best solution. The role of 'outsider' can be of advantage because people may be willing to share important information precisely because one is a 'neutral' outsider (see, for example, Edwards, 1986; Genders and Player, 1995).

Much has been said about the ethical problems surrounding participant observation. For the fieldworker, participant observation is extremely demanding not only in tact, but also in emotional involvement. Depending on the institution, one can feel a constant dilemma of being concerned with the people's personal situation while pursuing interests vital to the research. The field researcher has therefore a moral debt to those who made the research possible. This can range from carrying out small favours for them to leaving them a written copy of the finished piece of work.

Finally, the method is very time-consuming and somewhat wasteful. You may tape more hours of speech than you can ultimately analyse. Some recordings may turn out to be very difficult to transcribe and analyse, as the technical quality of participation observation data can be poor, especially when recording multi-party conversations.

Yet another problem concerns the question of whether one should enter the setting using a methodology of some sort or develop one as one goes along. Becker (1958: 653; emphasis in original) states that fieldworkers 'assume they do not know enough about [an area] *a priori* to identify relevant problems and hypotheses and that they must discover these in the course of the research'. Polsky (1969: 124–5) goes even further suggesting that entering the field with a prepared methodology is an obstacle. The argument is that understanding comes from *exploring* society, not by creating carefully prepared schemes and hypotheses. Although this is a valid point, it may work only for experienced researchers, not for students undertaking their first research project.

To summarize, participant observation is a method which is particularly conducive to analysing a social world, because it entails the more or less active collaboration of the researcher. It is probably safe to assume that one can have no complete appreciation of people's (linguistic) behaviour by exclusively relying on survey methods or formal interviews. This is not to suggest that by immersing oneself in a group's environment one can ever fully grasp it. As Wolff (1964: 127; emphasis in original), put it, the participant observer is '*in* but not entirely of the culture'. Nevertheless, through participant observation one can gain a far better insight into a social world than one does through quantitative methods, such as surveys or interviews.

Interviewing

Interviewing is clearly related to participant observation, as it is often used to complement it. Interviews can be done individually or in groups and in a structured, semi-structured and unstructured form. The advantages of interviewing as opposed to questionnaires are that spoken answers tend to be more complex and are often more revealing than written answers.

Like participant observation, the interview is never totally neutral as the interviewer is part of the interviewing process and an observer of it. Another common problem is that the respondents may misinterpret a question, may lie to protect themselves or give answers they think the interviewer wants to hear. This is a particular risk in cultures where it is impolite to disagree openly with a person or in more coercive settings, such as prisons.

Audio-taping is the most commonly used interview recording medium. It records everything, allowing you to transcribe what you need. Here is a list of things you need to be particularly aware of when you conduct audio-taped interviews:

- Make the interviewee(s) feel comfortable and listen carefully but without judgement.
- If you audio- or videotape the interview, always double-check the equipment is working.
- Always check with the interviewees beforehand if it is acceptable for them to be taped and be ready to switch the recorder off on demand. In this case, written notes is the best alternative.
- Always identify name of the person to be interviewed, the date and the place of the interview.

Transcribing spoken data

Without a written representation, talk is very difficult to analyse systematically. In this section we will therefore discuss several aspects of transcription.

Roberts (1997: 167) remarks that '[i]f talk is a social act, then so is transcription'. As one transcribes data, one relies on one's own social evaluations of speech in deciding how to put it down on paper. In other words, all transcription is representation and cannot be neutral. Therefore, transcribers should use or develop a system that can best represent the interactions they have recorded, and this means finding a balance between accuracy, readability, and what Mehan (1993) has called the 'politics of representation'. Transcription systems that make transcriptions increasingly accurate and readable have been developed (e.g. Edwards, 1992), but the categories worked out do not tackle the ideological issues of representation. How can the voices of informants be heard in the way they wish them to be heard? How can informants convey their identity through transcription? The representation of linguistic varieties has been discussed by sociolinguists and ethnographers (e.g. Preston, 1982; Tedlock, 1983). These authors have been particularly concerned with the stigmatization – the social evaluation the reader makes of the informant – when non-standard orthography is used to represent certain linguistic varieties, and they argue that it should best be avoided.

Which transcription conventions you use depends on your research purpose. Whereas some (e.g. Edwards, 1992: 368–70; Preston, 1982) suggest that words should be transcribed in standard orthography as 'writing cannot hope to capture the quality of speech' (Preston, 1982: 320), others, such as Roberts (1997) have raised the question about how researchers can transcribe the 'whole social person' (Bourdieu, 1991), to convey the speaker's identity. Ochs (1979), who was perhaps the first researcher to tackle the politics of representation, maintains that strictly standard orthography should be avoided, arguing that a modified orthography, such as that adopted by Sacks et al. (1974) should be employed, as it captures the way in which a word is pronounced versus the way it is written. Modified orthography includes items such as *gonna, wanna, ye know*, and the like. Bearing the objections against non-standard written representations of spoken discourse in mind, a 'moderate' system of non-standard orthography is advisable.

To sum up, in dealing with transcription, the researcher is confronted with ethical issues as well as accuracy and consistency. The challenge for the transcriber to best represent the speakers' interactions and identities through transcription is all the more an ethical question if s/he closely works with them and is thus implicated in aspects of their lives. Expressive as it often is, informants' non-standard language could lose much of its character if presented in standard orthography.

Another very important point is the confidentiality of the recorded material, and this is especially relevant if you intend to record speakers in institutional interactions. These interactions may be fairly banal and innocuous, but they may reveal names and other personal details. In this case, it is best to tell your informants/speakers that their names will be changed on the transcript. You may also want to return your tapes to the respective institution and its members after your research is finished and offer them a copy of your finished project. People offer you their time and you should always reciprocate by returning this favour in some way. Cameron (2001) also suggests offering people to delete parts of recorded data if they feel uncomfortable with certain parts of their talk being transcribed and used for research purposes.

Broadcast-spoken language

There are of course types of spoken (institutional) data to which these concerns do not apply because they are produced for a mass audience anyway: talk that is broadcast on radio or television. Much of the discourse in these is planned in terms of timing and topic, but it is not scripted, and should therefore contain features of spontaneous speech. So, ruling out the 'scripted' forms of broadcast talk (e.g. news broadcasts, soaps, TV dramas, radio plays), these types include 'fly on the wall' documentaries, live interviews on television and radio, radio phone-ins and talk shows.

A rich source of spoken data can be found in electronic form in computer corpora, which will be discussed later in this chapter. You can search for features you are interested in a quick and easy way, as there will be many examples of well-defined features in texts, such as discourse markers, overlaps, etc. One obvious disadvantage is that you can obtain only a written transcript, but there is also a big advantage in having a large amount of data which you do not need to record and transcribe first.

Collecting written data

In one way, collecting written data is easier than collecting spoken data, because you do not have to worry about the practical and ethical issues of recording and transcribing. On the other hand, you have to deal with the issue of copyright, as all published written texts of any kind belong to authors until 70 years after their death (at least in the UK). If your written research project is going to be published you have to clear copyright for any of the written texts you have used. This means contacting the original publisher and getting their permission.

If you intend an analysis of certain linguistic features in newspapers, many libraries hold back editions of newspapers or receive newspaper editions on CD-ROM, which can then be searched by date and keyword. You can save texts onto disc or print them off.

If you need written materials from certain institutions and/or companies, such as (teacher) training/workplace communication manuals, educational policy documents, bureaucratic forms, self-help and advice literature, etc. you may have to contact the relevant institution. Many of these materials are in the public domain though and therefore easily accessible. Even if your ultimate goal is to gain spoken data from an institution, you still should attempt to get your hand on written materials, because much of the spoken discourse that is produced in institutional interactions is often influenced, if not to say prescribed by, written documents or manuals (see, for example, Cameron (2000) on written regulations for spoken workplace discourse and Mayr (2004) on written instructions for teaching in the prison classroom).

Questionnaires

As we pointed out in the previous section, questionnaires are often used to complement more qualitative ways of data collection as they offer collection of data in the same, replicable way from a large number of respondents. Linguists (e.g. L. Milroy, 1987) have argued for using questionnaires in conjunction with other ways of eliciting data, because sometimes a better insight can be gained if you approach data from different angles. You may think that questionnaires are a way of circumventing the rather 'messy' process of spoken data collection and transcription, but they should be seen more as a complement to transcription and analysis, not as a substitute for it. From a discourse analytical point of view, talking in depth to a sample of people, listening not merely to *what* they say but also to *how* they say things, can provide almost a more 'accurate' picture of the way they perceive and interpret their social reality. What is more, designing a reliable and unambiguous questionnaire is far from easy, so it cannot be regarded as an easy option out of a difficult data collection process.

Designing a questionnaire

Before designing a questionnaire yourself, you may want to think about questionnaires you yourself had to answer in the past: Were they clear? Why? Why not? Were the questions too personal/difficult, etc? Questions should be as simple and as unambiguous as possible. This means avoiding leading questions, where the way a question is worded can subtly influence the way it is answered by the respondent, who may consciously or subconsciously detect an expectation or bias on your part. You need a clear idea what information is necessary for you so you do not end up with either too many or too few questions. Questionnaires are best started with some easy questions. If there are time-consuming questions, space them out or let the respondents know that there are questions which will take up a bit more time.

It is always useful to include one or two cross-referencing questions in which you ask in different words for the same information as in a previous question. This allows you to check the reliability of answers. You also have to think whether to ask closed or open questions or a mixture of both. Open questions do not require a one-word or curtailed answer. For example, with questions such as *Describe how you feel about . . .* speakers have more freedom to express their views. On the other hand, respondents may start to digress and you could end up with a large amount of data that is of little use to you. Open questions are also difficult to word unambiguously, difficult to process and more difficult to answer for respondents in that they take more time and effort from them. If there are many open-ended questions, there is the danger that respondents lose interest and answer them in a cursory way.

Closed questions (also yes-no questions) obviously steer respondents in the direction you want them to take; they are generally easier to answer, easier to process, but also rather limiting. Open questions are therefore more conducive to exploring social reality and revealing issues you may not even have thought about.

Bertrand and Hughes (2005: 71) recommend some interviewing before devising a questionnaire, so that ideas or concepts that come up in interviews can be incorporated into the questionnaire, rather than being based entirely on the researcher's preconceptions.

Finally, it is important to pilot your questionnaire on a group of people (maybe your student friends) to identify and correct flaws in the questioning and design.

Presenting questionnaires

Questionnaires can be presented and completed orally or in written form or a mixture of both by administering the questionnaire in writing and then let the respondents record their answers on audio or video cassette.

You can be either present or absent; if you are present you will need a lot of time, but you are guaranteed a higher completion rate and if anyone finds a question unclear, you can clarify things for them. In institutional settings such as classrooms or the workplace, questionnaires can be administered to a complete group of people. Although this saves time, you have no control over respondents some of whom may give inaccurate or incomplete answers.

If you send out questionnaires you can reach a larger number of people, but you will probably get a lower number of returns. You also have to make your questions very clear and unambiguous to avoid misunderstandings.

Corpus building and analysis

If you are interested in undertaking a corpus study, perhaps similar to the one described in Chapter 7, then there are various options open to you. You could choose an already existing corpus, such as the British National Corpus (BNC) or the Bank of English (BoE). The BoE consists of over 500 million words of spoken and written English of different genres, mostly British English, but with 25 per cent American English. The BoE is divided into a number of subcorpora, including the *Sun* newspaper (10.2 per cent), *The Times* newspaper (9.9 per cent), US National Public Radio broadcasts (5.5 per cent) and the BBC World Service broadcasts (4.5 per cent), all of which could be used for a research project on institutional discourse. Apart from these general 'reference' corpora with their genre-specific subcorpora, there are also pre-existing specialised corpora, such as the Corpus of Professional English (CPE) or the Louvain Corpus of Native English Essays (LOCNESS).

It may be the case, however, that the particular genre or variety you are interested in cannot be found in pre-existing sources. In this case, you may need to build your own specialized corpus. For this you will need to choose texts which satisfy some pre-defined external criterion. In Chapter 7 we looked at the rhetorical features in a corpus of geo-political US defence speeches which were downloaded from the DoD website, but your project might involve something quite different – perhaps you are interested in emails in the workplace or the language of university prospectuses. To establish that your data do meet your criteria, you will need to do some prior investigation of the texts – quick, skim-reading is usually sufficient. By doing this, you will get a feel for the characteristics of your chosen genre and perhaps form some hypotheses which you will subsequently test.

For concordancing you will need concordancing software, such as Mike Scott's *Wordsmith Tools* (available at www.lexically.net/wordsmith/). For the software to work successfully, you will need to download (or transcribe) and store your data as *plain text* files.

A frequent question is: how large should my corpus be? There is no real answer to this question. Investigations have been done on quite small corpora of just a few thousand words, while other researchers have created corpora of several million words. Our advice is that you should collect what you can (you may be restricted as to how much is available for you to collect). One thing that you should always bear in mind is that *quality* of data is generally more important than *quantity*.

Another consideration when building your own corpus is whether you need to seek permission from authors/publishers. If your material is non-copyrighted and freely available in the public domain (such as the speeches reported on in Chapter 7), then permission is not required. If, however, your material is copyrighted (e.g. from a book or manual), then normally you will need to obtain permission from the author(s), although in practice, publishers may vary in their attitude towards permissions, particularly if the material is merely being used for a student project.

By the time you have collected your data, you should already have in mind what your *research question* will be. Chapter 7, for example, discusses certain linguistic features in a special corpus by comparing them against those in a reference corpus. A reference corpus may act as a useful benchmark for what is 'normal' in the language as a whole. Alternatively, if you are interested in gender differences in institutional talk, you may want to compare two specialized corpora, a corpus of 'male' utterances and a corpus of 'female' utterances. Partington (2003), for example, because he was interested in contrasting rhetorical strategies, created two specialized corpora of White House press briefings, one containing the utterances of journalists, the other the contributions of White House spokespersons.

By way of concluding this section, it is worth bearing in mind what Baker (2006: 175) says about corpus-based discourse analysis:

> It is not simply a quantitative procedure but one which involves a great deal of human choice at every stage: forming research questions, designing and building corpora, deciding which techniques to use, interpreting the results and framing explanations for them.

Your research, therefore, will only be as good as the data you have at your disposal and the analysis you bring to bear on that data.

Conclusion

In this chapter, we have attempted to give useful advice to students who want to undertake small-scale research projects in the area of institutional discourse, dealing with the issues of defining research questions, qualitative and quantitative methods of data collection and transcription of spoken data. Ultimately, how you organize your research project will depend on the topic under investigation and your own judgement. But we hope that we have given you a clearer understanding of what is involved in the task of planning and exercising a research project and, in particular, some of the issues that need to be borne in mind when analysing the discourse of institutions and its members.

Appendix

Text I

Leicester Mercury
19 November 2005, Saturday
Section: p. 10
Length: 1205 words

1. 'The people have changed. There's no such thing as a black table or a white table in here now.'
2. Is Leicester a city of ghettoes, as community relations expert Trevor Phillips has suggested? Or are the different races mixing well? Adam Wakelin went to three very different parts of the city to find out.
3. A dozen heads rotate slowly, each following the rush of escaping fag smoke towards the pub door. The door clatters shut. Then, it all goes ominously quiet. Cigarettes stay clamped between pursed lips, conversations hang unfinished and eyes peer suspiciously over pint glasses at the new face.
4. 'What can I get you?' asks the landlady with a welcoming smile. 'Errr, I'm from the Mercury', I say. I was hoping for a chat about how people here get along and how they mix.
5. 'It's all right, he's from the Mercury', announces a wiry little woman half-swallowed by her voluminous pink jumper.
6. 'We saw the suit', shouts the jumper by way of an explanation, 'and we thought you were the police or the taxman or summat.'
7. A few years ago, The Hastings (then the Fox Runner) in Northfields had a reputation as the most racist pub on the most racist estate in Leicester. Everyone here says so.
8. If a black or brown person dared to come in there was a strong possibility they'd leave through the window. Few took the risk.
9. These days, the natives get restless over a collar and tie, rather than skin colour.
10. Northfields is in the electoral ward of Charnwood – on paper, the most ethnically mixed in Leicester.
11. A 53 per cent white to 47 per cent black and Asian, it seems the perfect place to visit to get an insight into the state of race *relations in this city.*
12. Except, as we all know, people don't live on paper.

13 In the real world, Charnwood is a ward of two distinct halves. At one end is the, mainly, Asian Green Lane Road. On the other sits Northfields, for so long a virtual no-go area to most of those from the Highfields end of town.
14 The Hastings is more or less in the middle. It's still not exactly the United Colors of Benetton, but things have obviously changed – the cheery Asian face which greeted me from behind the bar shows that.
15 'We get a brilliant crowd in here', says Harj Bhandal. 'Most nights it's half Indians and half whites'.
16 'When we took this place over it had been derelict for years. No-one wanted it. Now everyone mixes fine.'
17 How did that happen? 'The people have changed', says Arif Khan, a hyperactive talker who runs the Cob Shop next door. 'All the idiots have either left or been locked up. There's no such thing as a black table or a white table in here now.'
18 Anil Keshwala, owner of the neighbouring Nisa Today's store, tells you the same thing.
19 'We've been here three years and we've never had a problem', he says. 'Well, there was a bit of trouble with kids at the beginning, but that's sorted now.' People get on OK, says Anil. He sees it across the counter, particularly after school when gaggles of mums gather outside while the kids come in for sweets.
20 'It's not Asians and whites or blacks and whites', he says. 'It's everyone together, standing there having a chit-chat.'
21 Sarah Allen, 42, has lived in Northfields for 16 years.
22 The council asked her if she wanted to move once. So, she did – about 30 feet.
23 'Down', she chuckles. 'I got a flat on the ground floor. Why would I want to move? I like it here. The people make it.'
24 It used to be nearly all whites when Sarah came here. Now, there's Asians, West Indians, Kosovans, Albanians, Iranians, 'everyone really'.
25 'They're just like all of us', she shrugs. 'You move into a new area and it takes you a while to suss it out. You start speaking to them and they're lovely.'
26 You do hear the odd bit of bellyaching about the Kosovans and Albanians, says Arif. That's not gone away, but the old heavy-duty racism which used to dominate the estate has largely disappeared, he believes.
27 'My mum's Irish and my dad's Indian', he explains. 'They came here in 73. They got a bit of stick back then. Not any more. Most people with two brain cells to rub together are OK'.
28 'It's the Muslims in Highfields who don't mix', he sniffs, 'They're the ones who cut themselves off. A shame, really, because if people knew them better, they might understand what they're going through.'
29 'I don't think we realise how lucky we are. Everyone else around the world raves about Leicester and its tolerance. I've got relatives in Oldham and Bradford – they hate one another up there.'

30 Back in The Hastings, you can almost hear the crunch of metal furniture being rearranged as mother-of-four Anita Patel does a bit of arithmetic.
31 'I'm half Indian and my daughters have a white dad', says, Anita, tongue curled on to her top lip as she struggles with the sums, 'which makes them a quarter, no, three-quarters white. One's like you: blonde hair, blue eyes. The other's got dark hair and hazel eyes. My son's three-quarters Indian.'
32 'They're all different, but who cares? My little lad, Caidon, he's got a bit of Irish in him.'
33 'We're all mongrels', she smiles, 'but mongrels are the best aren't they? Go back a bit and everyone's got a bit of foreign blood in them.'
34 Steve Farmer nods sagely.
35 That's fine, but the people I spoke to in Westcotes (see below) seemed to think there was a problem in Leicester. They told me white people like them were starting to feel like strangers in their own city.
36 'That's them', says 54-year-old Steve dismissively. 'I'm white and I've lived round here 30-odd years. I can only talk about that.'
37 'It's better now than it's ever been. Everybody gets on. There's a good mix.'
38 The people in Belgrave 'welcome you like gold', reckons Harj's husband, Gurpit.
39 'Ghettoes? That's rubbish', says the 28-year-old Sikh, who grew up in Evington. 'They roll out the red carpet for anyone down there. I'm like the whites', he smiles, 'I don't speak any of the lingo either. But I've never had a problem with anyone in Belgrave or Highfields.'
40 'The thing about Leicester is that most people do get on. Trevor Phillips is wrong.'
41 Mr Phillips, chairman of the Commission for Racial Equality, has warned that Britain is sleepwalking to segregation.
42 Gurpit continues: 'We do a free homemade curry night down here on Thursday nights and they love it. Black, white, Indian, West Indian, whatever – everyone mixes together – and it's brilliant.'
43 You can't always translate lives into statistics. Most people in here haven't got lots of money and they wouldn't recognize a community-cohesion forum if it bumped into them on the landing. But they are integrating.
44 I like The Hastings. It feels like a nice place to be. In fact, I like it so much, I stay for another drink.
45 'I've got a boy and a girl by a Portuguese Indian from Goa', says a lady called Sharon, rummaging in her purse for pictures. 'And I've got another lad who's half-Indian.'
46 'They're grown up now', she says, 'but I'll always remember a thing in Humberstone Park when my daughter was little.'
47 'I was sitting on a bench and some kids started calling her a Paki.' I hate that word and I said: 'Excuse me, but do I look like a Paki?' They said no and I said: 'Well, I'm that girl's mother. A Pakistani is someone who comes from Pakistan. She comes from Leicester, like me.'
48 'That was ignorance, that was all it was', she shrugs. 'My kids never have any problems now. It's all changed. People are mixing. That old ignorance is disappearing.'

Text 2

Leicester Mercury
19 November 2005, Saturday
Section: p. 10
Length: 599 words

1 'Would I go to highfields?' Laughs one of the snooker team. 'Only in a tank'.
2 Westcotes Constitutional Club is in full, beer-fuelled session and their thoughts, if not exactly music to Trevor Phillips' ears, would probably raise a thin 'told you so' smile of vindication.
3 Last Saturday, the chairman of the Commission for Racial Equality appeared in this newspaper warning that Leicester was sleepwalking to segregation.
4 The city's multicultural fabric was unravelling as people retreated behind ethnic lines, he argued.
5 Lives overlapped less and less, and places such as Belgrave and Highfields were on their way to becoming ghettoes; no-go zones in the minds of many whites.
6 Anyone who said otherwise was in deep denial, said Sir Trevor. If you don't believe me go to Western Park or Westcotes and ask the white people there what they think, he said.
7 So here we are: Comfortably installed in the games room of a club which looks little changed since the portrait of Ted Heath went up in the 1970s.
8 It's telling, perhaps, that the main concessions to technology are the colour TV on the wall and the electronic security system on the front door.
9 A fifth of those living in Westcotes are from ethnic minorities, but they 'don't get many in here', says Steve Hill. He doesn't know why.
10 'I'll tell you why', says the barman to mumbles of disagreement, 'because they're not made to feel welcome.'
11 'We are not happy', says one regular. 'Put that in, put it in big letters and underline it.'
12 Why are they not happy?
13 Lots of angry, indistinct reasons – many of which don't stand up to much scrutiny.
14 There are too many 'coloureds', they say. The ethnics don't want to mix. They get everything handed to them on a plate. White people are becoming a minority in their own city – except they don't have any of the ethnic minorities' rights. If we're not careful – and you hear this time and again – there will be a civil war.
15 It's not nice, it might be completely unrepresentative of the way most white people in Westcotes (and everywhere else) view this city, but it's how they see it.
16 'Would I go to Highfields?' laughs one of the snooker team incredulously. 'Only if I was in a tank. Would I go down Belgrave Road at night? Forget it.'
17 Why?

18 'Because you wouldn't be made welcome', says Steve. 'If you walked into a pub in Highfields you'd feel the eyes boring into your back.'
19 Belgrave is a no-go zone, reasons the 48-year-old who's never lived more than 400 yards from this club. Why? Because he never goes there. He wouldn't want to.
20 It's the 'loony lefty' city council who's to blame, grumbles someone else.
21 'They've got all the kids learning about Hindus and Muslims and all that', he says. 'They should be learning our religion – not theirs. When in Rome, and all that.'
22 Downstairs in the lounge, a lady who wants to be known only as Mrs Smith, has a different view.
23 'I've not been to Belgrave for years', says the 79-year-old, 'but I wouldn't mind'.
24 'My mum lived in Belgrave and I can honestly say the Indians were lovely to her.'
25 Smiley Ernest Lee and Jocelyne Milsom try to get on with everyone.
26 'But', Ernest confides quietly, 'there are too many.'
27 Who?
28 'Coloureds', whispers the 82-year-old. 'It used to be 3 in 10. It's 9 in 10 now.'
29 'It doesn't worry me', says Jocelyne.
30 'It does me', he replies, drumming his fingers silently on the table. 'It's not safe to walk around town now.'
31 'That's not the coloureds fault', she replies hesitantly.
32 'I don't know. It can't help.'
33 'We're getting fed up because the whites are getting overrun', says Jocelyn. 'As far as I'm concerned it's our country, not theirs.'
34 * Census figures show Leicester to be 64 per cent white and 36 per cent black and Asian.

Text 3

Leicester Mercury
3 December 2005, Saturday
Section: p. 10
Length: 1228 words

1 **How do I look to you?**
2 Let's talk about what's happening in Iraq . . . Adam Wakelin watched students in a classroom discussing multiculturalism. Did they learn anything?
3 It might not be the most scientific snapshot, but Sam Nwanuforo's tutor group is a pretty fair summary of 21st century Leicester. Hindus rub shoulders with Muslims, blacks sit next to whites, a Chinese girl smiles shyly towards the front – and, right now, they all look as though they'd rather be somewhere else.
4 Trainers are scuffed beneath desks, fingers are knotted and designer-label cuffs are gnawed anxiously. A whiff of 'don't pick me' worry hangs heavy in the air.

5 'Come on, Gita!' urges Sam, chirpier than the dawn chorus. 'Tell us something about things from a Hindu perspective.'
6 'Errr, I dunno', she giggles nervously, eyes doggedly avoiding Sam's invisible spotlight. 'We celebrate Diwali an' that.'
7 'If I didn't know about Diwali, how would you describe it?' he cajoles.
8 'A festival of light', she shrugs, batting back further questions with a bashful smile.
9 This afternoon, Sam's class of 16- to 19-year-olds at Regent College are Swapping Cultures – an initiative aimed at promoting understanding and respect between Leicester's different ethnic and religious groups.
10 So far, despite the bubbly best efforts of their tutor, it's not going great – not helped, probably, by the fact that a man from the newspaper is sitting there making notes.
11 If someone does respond, it feels choreographed, an obvious politically correct comment dutifully trotted out for Sam's – and my – benefit.
12 It feels contrived and artificial, and to be brutally honest, it's living up to all the woolly, middle-class, do-gooder stereotypes which first surfaced yesterday when Swapping Cultures director Adam Newman Turner spoke of turning kids into 'community cohesion development apprentices'.
13 Paddy Ayres is asked to talk about aspects of white culture. This particular prospective community cohesion development apprentice couldn't look more mortified if his mum came in, spat on her hanky and started wiping his face.
14 I understand his predicament. I wouldn't have a clue what to say either. What's he meant to talk about? Roast dinners? Bingo? Shakespeare?
15 'I'd like to talk about what's going on in Iraq', says Haseeb Malik, waking everybody up after 30 fairly fruitless minutes.
16 'Just because there's a bunch of people who are extremists, it doesn't mean we're all like that.'
17 'How do you think most people see Muslims?' asks Sam.
18 'Terrorists', replies the 17-year-old.
19 'Why is that wrong?'
20 'Because', explains Haseeb, 'very few Muslims belong to that group. They're expressing their views in the wrong way. They're nothing to do with me, but that's how I'm seen.'
21 'A lot of people', says Leon Mattis, 'think black people are criminals and drug dealers and that.'
22 'I can see the worry in their eyes when I walk by them. I don't want to be put down like that. I want people to know that I'm getting an education and I'm bettering myself.'
23 'Black people stereotype white and Asian people as racist', adds Sapphire Thompson.
24 'They think white people see them as low-life. I'm black and I don't think like that, but a lot of black people do. That's a problem in this city. On both sides.'
25 'Lots of people on my estate are racist', ventures Ziggy Whitlock hesitantly. 'There's an Asian guy in the shop who's always getting his windows put out.'

26 'I don't like it', he shrugs, 'but there's not really much I can do about it.'
27 Finally, we're getting down to brass tacks.
28 And it is quite interesting hearing the ebb and flow of debate as this group of kids, who count themselves as friends, talk candidly about their experiences – good and bad.
29 It's something that Trevor Phillips, the chairman of the Commission for Racial Equality, believes that people in Leicester – like many other cities – are not doing enough of.
30 Birmingham's recent race riots started with a rumour, Mr Phillips told the Mercury – essentially that a black teenager was gang-raped by Asians. It was totally untrue, but it took hold, he said, precisely because the different communities no longer talked to one another.
31 A climate of fear and mistrust effectively allowed a poisonous whisper to gain such momentum that it exploded into bloodshed and murder.
32 If you think it can't happen in Leicester, he warned, you're living in a fool's paradise. Race relations is no longer a black and white issue, it's about getting every shade of opinion interacting.
33 Regent College, according to Sam, setting his ever-present smile to full beam, is modern, multicultural, 21st century Leicester in microcosm.
34 It's black, it's white, it's Hindu, it's Muslim, it's Sikh, it's Chinese, it's Somali and it's everything else in between.
35 Multiculturalism isn't something you learn out of a book here, he stresses. It's displayed in college fashion shows where students model the clothes of different cultures, it's experienced in the sharing of food and music, and it's celebrated by getting involved in one another's cultural and religious festivals.
36 'It's embedded in everything we do', says Sam, a nice man who's obviously brilliant at a job he loves. 'You can see it, you can feel it and you touch it.'
37 All of which is undoubtedly true, certainly in his tutor group. But, if Regent College is Leicester in microcosm it's still sending out some pretty mixed messages on race relations – at least to these eyes.
38 The place feels every bit as relaxed and safe as Sam says it is, but it's impossible not to notice that, by and large, students still gravitate to their own ethnic groups.
39 At lunch, a posse of Asian lads prop up one wall. Black teenagers stand, hands plunged deep into pockets, in another huddle. Muslim girls chatter away in their self-absorbed little gaggles.
40 It doesn't feel threatening, there's no 'us and them' eyeballing, and it's hardly surprising if kids who went through school together and come in on the same buses congregate with their mates at break-time, but it still feels like cosy coexistence rather than genuine interaction.
41 Which is why, according to Adam Newman Turner, initiatives like Swapping Cultures are so important.
42 'It is a structured way for young people to engage with one another', says the director, 'rather than just be ships that pass in the night'.

43 'I accept Trevor Phillips' argument that you can live next door to someone for 20 years and still know nothing about them. We need to get beyond that.'
44 'Children are the future of this city. We need to get them talking. The riots down the road in Birmingham have showed that we can't afford to be complacent about this.'
45 'Despite the awkward, self-conscious start to the debate in Sam's class, most of his students seem to share the same view.'
46 'Swapping Cultures is a good thing', says Mustafa Saleh. 'If you don't know one another properly, that's when conflicts break out'.
47 'If someone's your friend', he adds to nods and mumbles of agreement, 'you look at them different. They're not just a Hindu or a Muslim or whatever, they're a human being just like you.'
48 'I can't speak for anyone else, but I like socializing with people from different backgrounds', says Haseeb.
49 'This college isn't 100 per cent integrated, but it's better than pretty much anywhere else. You might not be best mates with everyone, but you say hello to them and you respect them. I think we're getting to know one another – slowly – and things like this help.'

References

Abercrombie, N., Hill, S. and Turner, B. (1980) *The Dominant Ideology Hypothesis*. London: Allan and Unwin.
Adler, M. and Longhurst, B. (1994) *Discourse, Power and Justice: Towards a New Sociology of Imprisonment*. London: Routledge.
Agar, M. (1985) 'Institutional discourse'. *Text*, 5(3), 147–68.
Althusser, L. (1971) *Lenin and Philosophy and Other Essays*. London: New Left Books.
Arnheim, R. (1969) *Visual Thinking*. Berkeley and Los Angeles, University of California Press.
Arnot, R. (1967) *The Impact of the Russian Revolution in Britain*. London: Lawrence and Wishart.
Atkinson, M. (1984) *Our Master's Voices: The Language and Body Language of Politics*. London: Methuen.
Bachrach, P. and Baratz, M. (1962) 'Two faces of power'. *American Political Science Review*, 56, 947–52.
Baker, P. (2006) *Using Corpora in Discourse Analysis*. London: Continuum.
Baker, P. and McEnery, T. (2005) 'A corpus-based approach to discourses of refugees and asylum seekers in UN and newspaper texts'. *Journal of Language and Politics*, 4(2), 197–226.
Barthes, R. (1977) *Image, Music, Text*. London: Fontana.
Barthes, R. (1973) *Mythologies*. London: Paladin.
Beard, A. (2000) *The Language of Politics*. London: Routledge.
Becker, H. S. (1958) 'Inference and proof in participant observation'. *American Sociological Review*, 23(6), 652–60.
Bell, A. (1991) *The Language of News Media*. Oxford: Blackwell.
Bennett, W. L. (2005) *News: The Politics of Illusion*. London: Pearson Longman.
Bennett, W. L. (2004). 'Transnational communication regimes and civic cultures'. *Annual Review of Political Science*, 7, 125–148.
Benwell, B. and Stokoe, E. (2006) *Discourse and Identity*. Edinburgh: Edinburgh University Press.
Bernstein, B. (1990) *Class, Codes, and Control, Vol 4: The Structuring of Pedagogic Discourse*. London: Routledge.
Bertrand, I. and Hughes, P. (2005) *Media Research Methods: Audiences, Institutions, Text*. Houndmills, Basingstoke: Palgrave Macmillan.
Bettelheim, B. (1976) *The Uses of Enchantment: The Meaning and Importance of Fairy Tales*. London: Thames and Hudson.
Billig, M. (1995) *Banal Nationalism*. London: Sage.

Bishop, W. and Jaworski, A. (2003) '"We beat 'em": nationalism and the hegemony of homogeneity in the British press reportage of Germany versus England during Euro 2000'. *Discourse and Society*, 14(3), 243–71.

Blunkett, D. (2000) Speech on Higher Education, 15 February 2000 at Maritime Greenwich University. Retrieved 28 August 2007, from http://cms1.gre.ac.uk/dfee/

Bond, B. (2002) *The Unquiet Western Front: Britain's Role in Literature and History*. Cambridge: Cambridge University Press.

Bordwell, D. (1985) *Narration in the Fiction Film*. London: Methuen.

Bourdieu, P. (1998) *Television and Journalism*: London: Pluto.

Bourdieu, P. (1991) *Language and Symbolic Power*. Cambridge: Polity Press.

Bourke, J. (1996) *Dismembering the Male: Men's Bodies, Britain and the Great War*. London: Reaktion.

Bromley, M. (1997) 'The end of journalism? Changes in the workplace practices in the press and broadcasting in the 1990s', in Bromley, M. and O'Malley, T. (eds), *A Journalism Reader*. London: Routledge, pp. 330–50.

Brown, G. and Yule, G. (1983) *Discourse Analysis*. Cambridge: Cambridge University Press.

Burawoy, M. (1979) *Manufacturing Consent: Changes in the Labour Process under Monopoly Capitalism*. Chicago: Chicago University Press.

Caldas-Coulthard, C. R. (2003) 'Cross-cultural representation of "otherness" in media discourse', in Weiss, G. and Wodak R. (2003) (eds), *Critical Discourse Analysis: Theory and Interdisciplinarity*. Basingstoke: Palgrave Macmillan, pp. 272–97.

Cameron. D. (2003) *On Language and Sexual Politics*. London: Routledge.

Cameron, D. (2001) *Analysing Spoken Discourse*. London: Sage.

Cameron, D. (2000) *Good to Talk? Living and Working in a Communication Society*. London: Sage.

Cameron, D. (1995) *Verbal Hygiene*. London and New York: Routledge.

Charteris-Black, J. (2004) *Corpus Approaches to Critical Metaphor Analysis*. Basingstoke: Palgrave Macmillan.

Cheshire, J. (1982) *Variation in an English Dialect: A Sociolinguistic Study*. Cambridge: Cambridge University Press.

Chomsky, N. (1999) *The New Military Humanism: Lessons from Kosovo*. London: Pluto Press.

Chouliaraki, L. (1998) 'Regulation in "progressivist discourse": individualized teacher-pupil talk'. *Discourse and Society*, 8(1), 15–32.

Chouliaraki, L. and Fairclough, N. (1999) *Discourse in Late Modernity: Rethinking Critical Discourse Analysis*. Edinburgh: Edinburgh University Press.

Clark, B. R. (1998) *Creating Entrepreneurial Universities: Organizational Pathways of Transformation*. Oxford: Pergamon Press.

Cohen, S. (1985) *Visions of Social Control: Crime, Punishment and Classification*. Cambridge: Polity Press.

Cohen, S. (1983) 'Social-control talk: telling stories about correctional change', in Garland, D. and Young, P. (eds), pp.101–129.

Cohen, L. and Musson, G. (2000) 'Entrepreneurial identities: reflections from two case studies'. *Organization*, (7)1, 30–48.
Cottle, S. (ed.) *Ethnic Minorities and the Media*. Buckingham: Open University Press.
Curran, J. and Seaton, J. (1977) *Power without Responsibility: The Press and Broadcasting in Britain*. London: Routledge.
Dahl, R. A. (1961) *Who Governs: Democracy and Power in an American City*. New Haven, CT: Yale University Press.
Dahl, R. A. (1957) 'The concept of power'. *Behavioural Science*, 22, 201–5.
Deetz, S. (1982) 'Critical interpretive research in organizational communication'. *The Western Journal of Speech Communication*, 46, 131–49.
Deignan, A. (2005) *Metaphor and Corpus Linguistics*. Amsterdam: Benjamins.
Deignan, A. (1997) 'A Corpus-Based Study of Some Linguistic Features of Metaphor'. Unpublished Ph D thesis, University of Birmingham.
Delin, J. (2000) *The Language of Everyday Life*. London: Sage.
Dorling, D. and Thomas, B. (2004) *People and Places: A 2001 Census Atlas of the UK*. Bristol: Policy Press.
Drew, P. and Heritage, J. (eds) (1992) *Talk at Work: Interaction in Institutional Settings*. Cambridge: Cambridge University Press.
Drew, P. and Sorjonen, M.-J. (1997) 'Institutional dialogue', in van Dijk, T. (ed.), pp. 92–118.
Du Gay, P. (1996) *Consumption and Identity at Work*. London: Sage.
Duguid, S. (2000a) *Can Prisons Work: The Prisoner as Object and Subject in Modern Corrections*. Toronto: Toronto University Press.
Duguid, S. (2000b) 'Theory and correctional enterprise', in Wilson, D. and Reuss, A. (eds), *Prison(er) Education*. Winchester: Waterside Press, pp. 48–62.
Edelman, M. (1977) *Political Language: Words That Succeed and Policies That Fail*. London: Academic Press.
Edwards, V. (1986) *Language in a Black Community*. Clevedon, Avon: Multilingual Matters.
Eggins, S. and Slade, D. (1997) *Analysing Casual Conversation*. London: Cassell.
Fairclough, N. (2003) *Analysing Discourse: Textual Analysis for Social Research*. London: Routledge
Fairclough, N. (2001) 'Critical discourse analysis', in McHoul, A. and Rapley, M. (eds), *How to Analyse Talk in Institutional Settings*. London: Continuum, pp. 25–41.
Fairclough, N. (2000) *New Labour, New Language?* London: Longman.
Fairclough, N. (1995a) *Media Discourse*. London: Arnold.
Fairclough, N. (1995b) *Critical Discourse Analysis: The Critical Study of Language*. London: Longman.
Fairclough, N. (1993) 'Critical discourse analysis and the marketization of public discourse: the universities'. *Discourse and Society*, 4, 133–68.
Fairclough, N. (1992) *Discourse and Social Change*. Cambridge: Polity Press.
Fairclough, N. (1989/2001) *Language and Power*. London: Longman.

Fairclough, N. and Wodak, R. (1997) 'Critical discourse analysis', in van Dijk, T. (ed.), *Discourse as Social Interaction*. London: Sage, pp. 258–84.

Ferguson, G. (1942) *Signs and Symbols in Christian Art*. London: Oxford University Press.

Fishman, M. (1980) *Manufacturing the News*. Austin, TX and London: University of Texas Press.

Flowerdew, J. (1997) 'The discourse of colonial withdrawal: a case study in the creation of mythic discourse'. *Discourse and Society*, 8, 453–77.

Foucault, M. (1994) 'Method', in Storey, J. (ed.), *Cultural Theory and Popular Culture*. London: Harvester Wheatsheaf, pp. 163–9.

Foucault, M. (1980) *Power/Knowledge: Selected Interviews and Other Writing 1972–1977*. New York: Pantheon Books.

Foucault, M. (1977) *Discipline and Punish: The Birth of the Prison*. London: Allen Lane.

Foucault, M. (1972) *The Archaeology of Knowledge*. Trans. S. Smith. London: Tavistock.

Fowler, R. (1991) *Language in the News: Discourse and Ideology in the Press*. London: Routledge.

Fowler, R., Hodge, R., Kress, G. and Trew. T. (1979) *Language and Control*. London: Routledge.

Gaffney, A. (1998) *Aftermath: Remembering the Great War in Wales*. Llandybie: Dyfed, Dinefwr Press.

Garland, D. (2001) *The Culture of Control*. Oxford: Oxford University Press.

Garland D, and Young, P. (eds) (1983) *The Power to Punish: Contemporary Penalty and Social Analysis*. London: Heinemann, pp. 101–29.

Galtung, J. and Ruge, M. H. (1965) 'The structure of foreign news'. *Journal of International Peace Research*, 1, 64–90.

Gans, H. J. (1980) *Deciding What's News: A Study of CBS Evening News, NBC, Nightly News, Newsweek and Time*. London: Constable.

Gee, J. P., Hull G. and Lankshear, C. (1996) *The New Work Order: Behind the Language of the New Capitalism*. St Leonards, NSW: Allen & Unwin.

Genders, E. and Player, E. (1995) *Grendon: A Study of a Therapeutic Prison*. Oxford: Clarendon Press.

Giddens, A. (1991) *Modernity and Self-Identity: Self and Society in the Late Modern Age*. Cambridge: Polity Press.

Giddens, A. (1984) *The Constitution of Society: Outline of the Theory of Structuration*. Cambridge: Polity Press.

Giddens, A. (1981) *A Contemporary Critique of Historical Materialism*, Vol. 1. London: Palgrave Macmillan.

Gledhill, C. 1995. 'Collocation and genre analysis: the phraseology of grammatical items in cancer research articles'. Zeitschrift für Anglistik und Amerikanistik 18, 11–36.

Goffman, E. (1961) *Asylums*. Reading: Cox and Wyman.

Goffman, E. (1959) *The Presentation of Self in Everyday Life*. New York: Doubleday.

Goodin, R. E. (1980) *Manipulatory Politics*. New Haven: Yale University Press.

Gordon, C. (1991) 'Governmental rationality: an introduction', in Burchell, G., Gordon, C. and Miller, P. (eds), *The Foucault Effect: Studies in Governmentality*. Brighton: Harvester Wheatsheaf, pp. 1–51.

Gramsci, A. (1971) *Selections from the Prison Notebooks*. London: Lawrence and Wishart.

Grant, D. and Iedema, R. (2005) 'Discourse analysis and the study of organizations'. *Text*, 25(1), 37–66.

Gregory, A. (1994) *The Silence of Memory: Armistice Day 1919–1946*. Oxford: Berg.

Gunnarsson, B.-L., Linell, P. and Nordberg, B. (1997) *The Construction of Professional Discourse*. London: Longman.

Gustafsson, M. (1975) *Binomial Expressions in Present-Day English*. Turku: Turun Yliopisto.

Habermas, J. (1987) *The theory of communicative action, Vol. 2: Lifeworld and Systems*. London: Heinemann.

Habermas, J. (1984) *The Theory of Communicative Action, Vol. 1: Reason and the Rationalization of Society*. Cambridge: Polity Press.

Hall, S. (1992) 'The west and the rest', in Hall, S. and Gieben, B. (eds), *Formations of Modernity*. Cambridge: Polity Press/Open University.

Hall, S. (1982) 'The rediscovery of ideology: the return of the repressed in media studies', in Gurevitch, M., Curran, M. and Woollacott, J. (eds), *Culture, Society and the Media*. London: Methuen, pp. 56–90.

Hall, S., Dobson, D., Lowe, A. and Willis, P. (1980) *Culture, Media and Language*. London: Hutchinson.

Halliday, M. A. K. (1985/1994) *An Introduction to Functional Grammar*. London: Arnold.

Halliday, M. A. K. (1978) *Language as Social Semiotic: The Social Interpretation of Language and Meaning*. London: Arnold.

Halliday, M. A. K. and Hasan, R. (1976) *Cohesion in English*. London: Longman.

Hallin, D. (1996) 'Commercialism and professionalism in the American news media', in Curran, J. and Gurevitch, M. (eds), *Mass Media and Society* (2nd ed.). London: Arnold, pp. 243–62.

Harcup, T. and O'Neill, D. (2001) 'What is news? Galtung and Ruge revisited'. *Journalism Studies*, 2(2), 261–80.

Hartmann, P. and Husband, C. (1974) *Racism and the Mass Media*. London: Davis Poynter.

Hatzidaki, O. (1999) 'Part and Parcel: A Linguistic Analysis of Binomials and Its Application to the Internal Characterisation of Corpora'. Unpublished Ph D thesis, University of Birmingham.

Herman, E. S. and Chomsky, N. (1988) *Manufacturing Consent: The Political Economy of the Mass Media*. New York: Pantheon Books.

Hobsbawm, E. (1983) 'Mass producing traditions: Europe 1817–1914', in Hobsbawm, E. and Ranger, T. (eds), *Inventing Tradition*. Cambridge: Cambridge University Press, pp. 263–308.

Hoey, M. (2000) 'Persuasive rhetoric in linguistics: a stylistic study of some features of the language of Noam Chomsky', in Hunston, S. and Thompson, G. (eds), pp. 28–37.

Hollingsworth, M. (1986) *The Press and Political Dissent*. London: Pluto Press.

Houghton, C. (1995) 'Managing the body of labour: the treatment of reproduction and sexuality in a therapeutic institution', in Hall, K. and Bucholtz, M. (eds), *Gender Articulated: Language and the Socially Constructed Self*. London: Routledge, pp. 121–41.

Hunston, S. (1985) 'Text in world and world in text: goals and models of scientific writing'. Nottingham Circular, 14, pp. 25–40.

Hunston, S. and Thompson, G. (2000) *Evaluation in Text*. Oxford: Oxford University Press.

Iedema, R. (2003) *Discourses of Post-Bureaucratic Organizations*. Document Design Companion Series. Amsterdam: Benjamins.

Iedema R. (1998) 'Institutional responsibility and hidden meanings'. *Discourse and Society*, 9(4), 481–500.

Iedema, R. and Wodak, R. (1999) 'Introduction: organizational practices'. *Discourse and Society*, 10(1), 481–500.

Jablin, F. M. and Putnam, L. (2001) *The New Handbook of Organizational Communication: Advances in Theory, Research and Methods*. Thousand Oaks, CA: Sage.

Jacques, R. (1998) 'Managing for the next century – or the last', in Mabey, C., Salaman, G. and Storey, J. (eds), *Strategic Human Resource Management – A Reader*. London: Sage, pp. 269–79.

Jewitt, C. and Oyama, R. (2000) *Visual Meaning: A Social Semiotic Approach*. London: Arnold, pp. 134–56.

Keat, R. (1990) 'Starship Britain or universal enterprise?', in Keat, R. and Abercrombie, N. (eds).

Keat, R. and Abercrombie, N. (eds). (1990) *Enterprise Culture*. London: Routledge.

Kellner, D. (1990) *Television and the Crisis of Democracy*. Boulder, CO: Westview Press.

Kidd, W. (1997) 'Memory, memorials and commemoration of war memorials in Lorraine, 1908–1988', in Evans, M. and Lunn, K. (eds), *War and Memory in the Twentieth Century*. Oxford: Berg.

King, A. (1998) Memorials of the Great War in Britain. *The Symbolism and Politics of Remembrance*. Oxford and New York: Berg.

Knowles, M. and Moon, R. 2006. *Introducing Metaphor*. London: Routledge.

Kohlberg, L., Kaufman, K., Scharf, P. and Hickey, J. (1975) 'The just community approach to corrections'. Journal of *Moral Education*, 4(3), 243–60.

Kress, G. (1983) 'Linguistic and ideological transformations in news reporting', in David, H. and Walton, P. (eds), *Language, Image, Media*. Oxford: Blackwell, pp. 120–38.

Kress, G. and van Leeuwen, T. (2003). 'Colour as a Semiotic Mode: notes for a grammar of colour', *Visual Communication*, 1(3), pp. 343–68.

Kress, G. and van Leeuwen, T. (2001) *Multimodal Discourse.* London: Hodder Arnold.
Kress, G. and van Leeuwen, T. (1996/2006) *Reading Images: The Grammar of Visual Design.* London: Routledge.
Labov, W. (1972a) *Language in the Inner City.* Philadelphia: Philadelphia University Press.
Labov, W. (1972b) *Sociolinguistic Patterns.* Philadelphia: Philadelphia University Press.
Lakoff, G. and Johnson, M. (1980) *Metaphors We Live By.* Chicago: University of Chicago Press.
Laybourn, K. (1997) *The Rise of Socialism in Britain.* London: Sutton.
Lee, D. (1992) *Competing Discourses: Perspectives and Ideology in Language.* London: Longman.
Leicester City Council (LCC) (2003) Multicultural Leicester, background briefing note 1. Chief Executive Office Leicester.
Leicester County Council (LCC) (2002) Community Cohesion: Beacon Council Scheme, pp. 1–13.
Lennon, J. and Foley, M. (2000) *Dark Tourism: The Attraction of Death and Disaster.* London: Continuum.
Local Government Association (2002) *Guidance on Community Cohesion Leicester.* Available at: www.leic.gov.uk
Louw, E. (2005) *The Media and the Political Process.* London: Sage.
Lukes, S. (1974) *Power: A Radical View.* London: Macmillan.
Machin, D. (2007) *Introduction to Multimodal Analysis.* London: Arnold.
Machin, D. (2004) 'Building the world's visual language: the increasing global importance of image banks in corporate media'. *Visual Communication,* 3(3), 316–36.
Machin, D. and Jaworski, A. (2006) 'Archive footage in news: creating a likeness and index of the phenomenal world'. *Visual Communication,* 5(3), 345–66.
Machin, D. and Mayr, A. (2007) 'Antiracism in the British government's model regional newspaper: the "talking cure". *Discourse and Society,* 18(4), 453–79.
Machin, D. and Niblock, S. (2006) *News Production: Theory and Practice.* London: Routledge.
Machin, D. and Thornborrow, J. (2003) 'Branding and discourse: the case of cosmopolitan'. *Discourse and Society,* 14(4), 453–71.
Machin, D. and van Leuuwen, T. (2007) *Global Media Discourse.* London: Routledge.
Machin, D. and van Leeuwen, T. (2005) 'Computer games as political discourse: the case of Black Hawk Down'. *Journal of Language and Politics,* 4(1), 119–41.
MacLaren, P. (1994) 'Multiculturalism and the postmodern critique: towards a pedagogy of resistance and transformation', in Giroux, H. and McLaren, P. (eds), *Between Borders.* New York: Routledge.
Mautner, G. (2005) 'The entrepreneurial university: a discursive profile of a higher education buzzword'. *Critical Discourse Studies,* 2(2), 95–120.

Mayr, A. (2004) *Prison Discourse: Language as a Means of Control and Resistance.* Houndmills, Basingstoke: Palgrave Macmillan.

Mayr, A. (1994) 'A study of slang in Barlinnie Prison'. Unpublished M Phil Dissertation, English Language Department, University of Glasgow.

McChesney, R. W. (2004) *The Problem with the Media: US Communication Politics in the Twenty-First Century.* New York: Free Press.

McKibbin, R. (1974) *The Evolution of the Labour Party 1910–1924.* London: Oxford University Press.

McLaughlin, G. (1999) 'Refugees, migrants and the fall of the Berlin wall', in Philo, G. (ed.), *Message Received.* London: Longman.

McManus, J. H. (1994) *Market Driven Journalism: Let the Citizen Be Aware.* London: Sage.

Mehan, H. (1993) 'Beneath the skin and between the ears: a case study in the politics of representation', in Chaiklin, S. and Lave, J. (eds), *Understanding Practice.* Cambridge University Press.

Mesthrie, R., Swann, J., Deumert, A. and Leap, W. (2000) *Introducing Sociolinguistics.* Edinburgh: Edinburgh University Press.

Michalski, S. (1998) *Public Monuments: Art in Political Bondage 1970–1997.* London: Reaktion Books.

Milroy, L. (1987) *Observing and Analysing Natural Language.* Oxford: Blackwell.

Milroy, L. (1980) *Language and Social Networks.* Oxford: Blackwell.

Moriarty, C. (1995) 'The absent dead and figurative First World War memorials'. *Transactions of Ancient Monuments Society*, 39, 7–40.

Moriarty, C. (1997) 'Private grief and public remembrance: British First World War memorials', in Evans, M. and Lunn, K. (eds), *War and Memory in the Twentieth Century.* Oxford: Berg.

Mosse, G. (1990) *Fallen Soldiers: Reshaping the Memory of the World Wars.* New York: Oxford University Press.

Mumby, D. (2001) 'Power and politics', in Jablin, J. and Putnam, L. (eds), pp. 559–623.

Mumby, D. (1988) *Communication and Power in Organizations: Discourse, Ideology and Domination.* Norwood, NJ: Ablex.

Mumby, D. and Clair, R. P. (1997) 'Organizational discourse', in van Dijk, T. A. (ed.), pp. 181–205.

Murdock, G. (1984) 'Reporting the riots: images and impacts', in Benyon, J. (ed.), *Scarman and After.* Oxford: Pergamon Press.

Niblock, S. (2005) 'Practice and theory: what is news?' in Keeble, R. (ed.), *Print Journalism: A Critical Introduction.* London: Routledge, pp. 73–82.

Niblock, S. and Machin, D. (2007) 'News values for consumer groups: the case of independent radio news'. *Journalism*, 8(2), 184–204.

Ochs, E. (1979) 'Transcription as theory', in Ochs, E. and Schieffelin, B. (eds), *Developmental Pragmatics.* New York: Academic Press, pp. 43–72.

O'Halloran, K. (2007) 'Critical discourse analysis and the corpus-informed interpretation of metaphor at the register level'. *Applied Linguistics*, 28(1), 1–24.

O'Halloran, K. and Coffin, C. (2004) 'Checking overinterpretation and underinterpretation: help from corpora in critical linguistics', in Coffin, C., Hewings, A. and O'Halloran, K. A. (eds), *Applying English Grammar: Functional and Corpus Approaches*. London: Hodder Arnold.

Orpin, D. (2005) 'Corpus linguistics and critical discourse analysis: examining the ideology of sleaze'. *International Journal of Corpus Linguistics*, 10(1), 37–61.

O'Toole, M. (1994) *The Language of Displayed Art*. London: Leicester University Press.

Owen, C. (2004) 'University recruitments: advertisements and textual shelf-life'. *Critical Discourse Studies*, 1, 153–7.

Panofsky, E. (1972) *Studies in Iconography: Humanistic Themes in the Art of the Renaissance*. Oxford: Westview Press.

Park, R. E. and Burgess, E. W. (1927) *The City*. Chicago, IL: University of Chicago Press.

Parker, T. (1995) *Mixed Signals: The Prospects for Global TV News*. New York: Twentieth Century Fund Press.

Partington, A. (2003). *The Linguistics of Political Argument: The Spin-Doctor and the Wolf-Pack at the White House*. London: Routledge.

Patterson, C. and Wilkins, L. (1994) *Media Ethics*. Dubuque, IA: Brown & Benchmark.

Pelissier Kingfisher, C. (1996) *Women in the American Welfare Trap*. Philadelphia: University of Pennsylvania Press.

Phillips, D. (1981) 'The social and spatial segregation of Asians in Leicester', in Jackson, P. and Smith, S. (eds), *Interaction and Ethnic Segregation*. London: Academic Press, pp. 101–21.

Piaget, J. (1958) *The Growth of Logical Thinking from Childhood to Adolescence: An Essay on the Construction of Form*. London: Routledge.

Polsky, N. (2005) 'Research methods, morality and criminology', reprinted, in Gelder, K. and Thorton, S. (eds), *The Subcultures Reader*. London: Routledge, pp. 217–31.

Preston, D. (1982) '"Ritin' Folklower daun 'rong"'. *Journal of American Folklore*, 95, 304–26.

Quinlan, M. (2005) *British War Memorials*. Hertford: Authors OnLine.

Rampton, S. and Stauber, J. (2000) *Trust Us We're Experts: How Industry Manipulates Science and Gambles with Your Future*. New York: Tarcher.

Rampton, S. and Stauber, J. (1995) *Toxic Sludge Is Good For You: Lies, Damn Lies and the Public Relations Industry*. Munroe, ME: Common Courage Press.

Remarque, E. M. (1996/1929) *All Quiet on the Western Front*. London: Vintage Books.

Reuss, A. (2000) 'The researcher's tale', in Wilson, D. and Reuss, A. (eds), pp. 24–48.

Reuss, A. (1997) 'Higher Education and Personal Change in Prisoners'. Unpublished thesis, University of Leeds.

Richardson, J. (2007) *Analysing Newspapers: An Approach from Critical Discourse Analysis*. Basingstoke: Palgrave Macmillan.

Richardson, J. (2006) 'Who gets to speak? A study of sources in the broadsheet Press', in Polle, E. and Richardson, J. E. (eds), *Muslims and the News Media*. London: IB Tauris, pp.103–15.

Ritzer, G. and Liska, A. (1997) 'McDisneyisation and post-tourism: complementary' perspectives of contemporary tourism', in Rojek, C. and Urry, J. (eds), *Touring Cultures: Transformations of Travel and Theory*. London: Routledge.

Roberts, C. (1997) 'The politics of transcription'. *Tesol Quarterly*, 31(1), 167–76.

Ross, R. and Fabiano, L. (1985) *Time to Think: A Cognitive Model for Delinquency and Offender Rehabilitation*. Ottawa: Institute of Social Sciences and Arts.

Ross, R., Fabiano, E. and Ewles, C. (1989) *Reasoning and Rehabilitation: A Handbook for Teaching Cognitive Skills*. Ottawa: Cognitive Centre.

Rudy, C. (1918) 'Concerning Tommy'. *Contemporary Review*, 545–52.

Sacks, H., Schegloff, E. and Jefferson, G. (1974) 'A simplest systematics for the organization of turn-taking in conversation'. *Language*, 50(4), 696–735.

Sarangi, S. and Roberts, C. (1999) *Talk, Work and Institutional Order: Discourse in Medical, Mediation and Management Settings*. Berlin: Mouton de Gruyter.

Sarangi, S. and Slembrouck, S. (1996) *Language, Bureaucracy and Social Control*. London: Longman.

Scarry, E. (1994) *Resisting Representation*. New York: Oxford University Press.

Scarry, E. (1985) *The Body in Pain: The Making and Unmaking of the World*. New York: Oxford University Press.

'Schools to promote "enterprise culture"', BBC News, Education, 18 June 2001. Retrieved 24 September 2007, from http://news.bbc.co.uk/1/hi/education/1394674.stm.

Scott, J. (2001) *Power*. Cambridge: Polity Press.

Scott, J. C. (1990) *Domination and the Art of Resistance: Hidden Transcripts*. New Haven, CT: Yale University Press.

Scottish Prison Service. (2002) *An Evaluation of the Cognitive Skills Programme 'Reasoning and Rehabilitation' in the Scottish Prison Service*. Edinburgh: Scottish Office.

Scottish Prison Service (SPS). (1990) *A Shared Enterprise: Outline Corporate Strategy for the Scottish Prison Service*. Edinburgh: Scottish Office.

Scraton, P., Sim, J. and Skidmore, P. (1991) *Prisons under Protest*. Milton Keynes: Open University Press.

Shapiro, J. (2005) *1599: A Year in the Life of William Shakespeare*. London: Penguin.

Sigal, L. V. (1973) *Reporters and Officials: The Organization and Politics of News Reporting*. Lexington, MA: Heath.

Silverman, D. (1997) *Discourses of Counselling: HIV Counselling as Social Interaction*. London: Sage.

Simpson, L. (2004) 'Statistics of racial segregation: measures, evidence and policy'. *Urban Studies*, 41(3), 661–81.

Singh, G. (2003) 'Multiculturalism in contemporary Britain: reflections on the "Leicester Model"', *International Journal of Multicultural Societies*, 5(1), 40–54.

Solomos, J. and Singh, G. (1990) 'Race equality, housing and the local state', in Ball, W. and Solomos, J. (eds), *Race and Local Politics*. London: MacMillan, pp. 95–114.

Sornig, K. (1989) 'Some remarks on linguistic strategies of persuasion' in Wodak, R. (ed.), *Language, Power and Ideology*. Amsterdam: Benjamins.

Stubbs, M. (2001) *Words and Phrases: Corpus Studies of Lexical Semantics*. Oxford: Blackwell.

Stubbs, M. (1996) *Text and Corpus Analysis: Computer-Assisted Studies of Language and Culture*. Oxford: Blackwell.

Stubbs, M. (1983) *Discourse Analysis: The Sociolinguistic Analysis of Natural Language*. Oxford: Blackwell.

Talbot, M. (2007) *Media Discourse: Representation and Interaction*. Edinburgh: Edinburgh University Press.

Tedlock, D. (1983) *The Spoken Word and the Work of Interpretation*. Philadelphia: University of Pennsylvania Press.

Teubert, W. (2001) 'A province of a federal superstate, ruled by an unelected bureaucracy – keywords of the Eurosceptic discourse in Britain', in Musolff, A., Good, C. and Wittlinger, R. (eds), *Attitudes Towards Europe*. Aldershot: Ashgate, pp. 45–88.

Thornborrow, J. (2002) *Power Talk: Language and Interaction in Institutional Discourse*. London: Longman.

Thrift, N. (1997) 'Soft capitalism'. *Cultural Values*, 1(1), 29–58.

Tietze, S., Cohen, L. and Musson, G. (2003) *Understanding Organizations through Language*. London: Sage.

Troost, G. (ed.) (1942) *Das Bauen im Neuen Reich*. Bayreuth: Gauverlag.

Trowler, P. (2001) 'Captured by the discourse? The socially constitutive power of new higher education discourse'. *Organization*, 8(2), 183–201. London: Sage.

Tunstall, J. and Machin, D. (1999) *The Anglo-American Media Connection*. Oxford: Oxford University Press.

Tyrwhitt-Drake, H. (1999) 'Resisting the discourse of critical discourse analysis: reopening a Hong Kong case study'. *Journal of Pragmatics*, 31, 1081–8.

Underwood, D. (1995) *When MBAs Rule the Newsroom: How the Marketers and Managers Are Reshaping Today's Media*. New York: Columbia University Press.

Van Dijk, T. A. (2001) 'Multidisciplinary CDA: a plea for diversity', in Wodak, R. and Meyer, M. (eds), pp. 95–120.

Van Dijk, T. A. (1998) *Ideology: A Multidisciplinary Approach*. London: Sage.

Van Dijk, T. A.(1997) *Discourse as Social Action: Discourse Studies, Vol. 2: A Multidisciplinary Introduction*. Newbury, CA: Sage.

Van Dijk, T. A., Ting-Toomey, S., Smitherman, G. and Troutman, D. (1997) 'Discourse, ethnicity, culture and racism', in Van Dijk, T. (ed.), pp. 95–120.

Van Dijk, T. A. (1993) *Elite Discourse and Racism*. Newbury Park, CA: Sage.
Van Dijk, T. A. (1991) *Racism and the Press*. London: Routledge.
Van Dijk, T. A. (1990) 'Social cognition and discourse', in Giles, H. and Robinson, W. (eds), *Handbook of Language and Social Psychology*. New York: John Wiley and Sons, pp. 163–86.
Van Leeuwen, T. (2006) 'Towards a semiotics of typography'. *Information Design Journal and Document Design*, 14/2, 139–55.
Van Leeuwen, T. (2005) *Introducing Social Semiotics*. London: Routledge.
Van Leeuwen, T. (1996) 'The representation of social actors', in Caldas Coulthard, C.-R. and Coulthard, M. (eds), *Texts and Practices: Readings in Critical Discourse Analysis*. London: Routledge, pp. 32–70.
Van Leeuwen, T. (1993) 'Recontextualization of social practice', unpublished manuscript.
Van Leeuwen, T. and Wodak, R. (1999) 'Legitimizing immigration control: a discourse-historical analysis'. *Discourse and Society*, 1(1), 83–118.
Verschueren, J. (1985) *International News Reporting: Metapragmatic Metaphors and the U-2*. Amsterdam: John Benjamins.
Vertovec, S. (1994) 'Multicultural, multi-Asian, multi-Muslim Leicester: dimensions of social complexity, ethnic organization and local government interface', *Innovation: European Journal of Social Sciences*, 7(3), 259–76.
Vidich, A. (1955) 'Participant observation and the collection and interpretation of data'. *American Journal of Sociology*, 60, 354–60.
Wales, K. (1996) *Personal Pronouns in Present-Day English*. Cambridge: Cambridge University Press.
Wasko, J. (1982) *Movies and Money: Financing the American Film Industry*. Norwood, NJ: Ablex.
Weber, M, (1914) 'The Economy and the Arena of Normative and De facto Powers', in Roth, G. and Wittich, C. (eds), *Economy and Society*. New York: Bedminster Press.
Webster, G. (2003) 'Corporate discourse in the academy. a polemic'. *Industry and Higher Education*, 17(2), 85–90.
Weiss, G. and Wodak, R. (2003) *Critical Discourse Analysis: Theory and Interdisciplinarity*. London: Palgrave Macmillan.
Wetherell, M. and Potter, J. (1992) *Mapping the Language of Racism: Discourse and the Legitimation of Exploitation*. Hemel Hempstead: Harvester Wheatsheaf.
Widdowson, H. (2004) *Text, Context, Pretext: Critical Issues in Discourse Analysis*. Oxford: Blackwell.
Widdowson, H . (2000) 'On the limitations of linguistics applied'. *Applied Linguistics*, 21/1, 3–25.
Widdowson, H. (1995) 'Discourse analysis: a critical view'. *Language and Literature*, 4(3), 157–72.
Wilson, D. and Reuss, A. (eds) (2000) *Prison(er) Education: Stories of Change and Transformation*. Winchester: Waterside Press.
Winstone, P. (1996) 'Managing in a multiethnic and multicultural city in Europe: Leicester'. *International Social Science Journal*, 147, 33–41.

Winter, J. (1995) *Sites of Memory, Sites of Mourning: The Great War in European Cultural History*. Cambridge: Cambridge University Press.

Winter, J. and Sivan, E. (1999) *War and Remembrance in the Twentieth Century*. Cambridge: Cambridge University Press.

Wodak, R. (2001) 'The discourse-historical approach', in Wodak, R. and Meyer, M. (eds), *Methods of Critical Discourse Analysis*, London: Sage, pp. 63–94.

Wodak, R. (1996) *Disorders of Discourse.* London: Longman.

Wodak, R. and Meyer, M. (eds) (2001) *Methods of Critical Discourse Analysis.* London: Sage.

Wodak, R. and Reisigl, M. (1999) 'Discourse and racism: European perspectives'. *Annual Review of Anthropology*, 28, 175–99.

Wolff, K. H. (ed.) (1964) *The Sociology of Georg Simmel*. London: Free Press.

Wozniak, E. (1994) 'A customer-focused prison service in Scotland', in Duff, A., Marshall, S., Dobash, R. E. and Dobash, R. R. (eds), *Penal Practice and Theory*. Manchester: Manchester University Press, pp. 147–58.

Index

Abertillery monument 134
accountability of institutions 28
'active' listening 41
'adaptability' 34
advertising and newspapers 86–8
advertising discourse at universities 22
'allies and friends' use of phrase 152–5
Althusser, Louis, on institutions of civil society 13
Anger Management 49
anti-immigration discourse 5, 91
anti-racism in British regional press 90–114
antonyms and synonyms 54
appraisal of university staff 38
'architectures' as metaphor 161
Art Deco style, monuments 130
Assertive Communication 53–9
assertiveness 28, 55
assimilation 99, 100

Bank of English (BoE) 141, 148–9, 152, 176
Barthes, Roland, semiotician 124, 125
BBC and news reporting 62
behaviour modification 59
binomial phrases 148–55
   in the D & D corpus 149–50
   'friends and allies' 152–5
   'men and women' 148–52
Bolshevik revolution, Russia 24, 120, 121
bombings on Bali, news item 66
Britain's legacy to Hong Kong 141
British National Corpus (BNC) 176

bureaucratic organization
   and news 79–83
   in prisons 47
business-related lexis 27, 34, 35

capitalism 3, 5
Cardiff National monument 129, 135
cartoons 132
categorization, by function or identity 103–13
'centres of excellence' 30, 31
certainty or non-certainty, in news pictures 69–71
children, 'Swapping Cultures' 99–100
class inequalities 5
classical style in art 130
classification 103–13
cognitive development theory 48
cognitive rehabilitation programme 46, 50, 52
Cognitive Skills Deficit Model 48–52
Cohesion (Systemic Functional Linguistics) 50
Collins Cobuild, 'Bank of English' *see* Bank of English
commercialization of news 65, 83–6, 91
commercial ventures, and Oxford university 29
Commission for Racial Equality 93–104
communication 24
   assertive 58
   barriers to 5
   importance of 100
   skills training 37–43
connotative meanings 125

199

Index

conscription problems 116
consent to social order 14
Conservative views on multiculturalism 96
construction materials for monuments 133–4
consumers, and accountability 28
control of news by organizations 83–5
Conversation Analysis (CA) 8
conversational skills, assertive 53
corpus building and analysis 24, 176–7
corpus linguistics 138–42
and CDA 140–1
Corpus of Professional English (CPE) 176
crime control discourse 49, 52, 59, 60
crime footage for news 71–2, 80–1
criminal decisions 48
criminal nature, knowledge about 15
crisis in Scottish prisons 47
criteria, 'unofficial' for news 75
Critical Discourse Analysis (CDA) 5–10, 49, 63, 91, 139
Fairclough's approach 9–10
of news texts 88–9
practical framework 16–21
critical left views on multiculturalism 96–7
cross, sacrificial symbol 131

data collection 167–71
deaths of young men in war, justification 115
defence discourse 115–62
defence speeches 24
denotative meanings 124–5
Department of Defense corpus 141–9
dependence on official sources, news 67
deprivation 24
design images 71
detail, removal of, in monuments 132
'discipline' (Foucault) 15–16, 49

discourse 1–2
definitions 7–8
and enterprise culture 26–9
-historical approach 92
institutional 4–7
as 'language in use' 7
as social practice 9, 10, 21, 163
technologies 16, 39
discourses of multiculturalism, *Leicester Mercury* 95–100
dominant groups in society 2, 3, 14
domination and inequalities, society 9
dramatization, in news stories 76

education
as business 27
as commodity 20–1
egalitarian workplace practices 5, 6
employability of students 34
Employability Policy and Strategy, Salford University 33–6
English and Educational Studies Lecturer job description 36
enterprise in the university 26–45
enterprising managerialism 26, 46–8
'enterprise culture' 26, 27–9
entrepreneurship, at Salford University 34
ethnic minority population, Leicester 90
European Journalism Centre Online 84
evaluation in negative terms 52
event selection in news 77
exclusion of factors in racial conflict 114

famous people, news on 75, 78
financial support at universities 31
financing of news organizations 83–4
'fire' as metaphor 157
First World War 115, 116
death numbers 119
'flood' as metaphor 160
Foucault, Michel, on disciplinary power 8, 14–15

Index

fragmentation in news stories 76, 78
functionalization, in society 102, 103, 112

'geopolitical criterion' 139
Getty, commercial-image archive 68–71
global economy 35, 84
government's role in tuition fees 32
Gramsci, Antonio, on hegemony 13, 14
Greek statues, inspiration 131

Habermas, Jürgen, on institutional discourse 5, 6
health, as business 27
hegemony (domination by consent) 10, 13–15
higher education, discourses 26–45
Hyde Park Royal Artillery monument 136

iconography and iconology 124–6
ideational function of language 17
identification, names 102–10, 112
ideological bias 139–40
ideological manipulation, war monuments 115, 116
ideology
   communication of, in news 88
   definitions 10–11
immigration, in Leicester 90–114
   and social housing, Leicester 93
inclusion, language of 146
inclusive and exclusive use of 'we' 32, 142–8
Independent Radio News (IRN) 65
influence of political institutions 82
information-processing for news 67
inscriptions on war memorials 116
institutional discourse 4–7
   analysis of 163–77
   productiveness of 6
institutionalization of news process 88
institutions 1, 4
   of civil society 13, 14

and language 4, 5
run on business lines 27
intellectual freedom, threats to 37, 38
interdisciplinary perspective 92
international news, criteria for publishing 73–4
internet, for research 165–6
interpersonal function of language 17
intertextuality 21–2
interviewing and transcription 171–3
Iraq invasion, government justification of 3
Independent Radio News (IRN) list of choices 77–8
Independent Television News (ITN) archive 71

journalism, redundancies 85
journalist role, view of 62, 63

knowledge
   from business world 27
   and power 15
knowledge-driven economy 3, 34–5, 38

labour market, and learning 34
'landscape' as metaphor 156–7
language
   and culture 17
   and education 5
   and images, analysis 118
   and institutions 4, 5
   and meanings 16
   'normal' and 'institutional' 138
   in US military speeches 139
Le Monde Group, France 84
learning, and labour market 34
Learning and Teaching Strategy, Salford University 34
left-liberal views on multiculturalism 96
legitimacy of dominant groups 14
legitimization of actions, by use of 'we' 146

201

Leicester Mercury 90–2
   and multiculturalism 94–100
   recontextualization 114
Leicester Multicultural Advisory
      Group 94
Leicester, non-white majority 92, 93
lexical cohesion 21, 52, 54
liberal views on multiculturalism 96
life-history of prisoner 59
'life world' and 'system'
   (Habermas) 5, 6
local government, as business 27
Loughborough University website 30
Louvain Corpus of Native English
      Essays (LOCNESS) 176

managerialism
   and prisons 46–61
   in education 26–38, 43–5
managerialist vocabulary 22, 38
marginalization 101
marketization of university sector 29
meaning and doing, in discourse
   7, 10
'meaningfulness' of news 74, 75
media corporations 5, 85
media, institutional setting 1
melting pot 99, 100
memorial statues
   Berlin Torchbearer 132
   gaze away from onlooker 133–4
   on pedestals 116
'men and women', use of
   phrase 150–2
metaphor, power of 123–4, 155–6
metaphorical association (Kress and
   van Leeuwen) 123–4
military, institutional setting 1,
   138–62
Model verbs 20, 68, 132, 146
Modality 19–20, 52, 54, 132
Modality scales (Kress and van
   Leeuwen) 68–70
monuments, analysis of
   meaning 126–37
mood in language 17
multiculturalism 23–4

   in Leicester 91–114
   models 96
multiculturalists discourse 98–9,
   106–14
Multimodal Discourse Analysis 7,
   117–19
   of war monuments 116–36
myth 125

Nazi Arian imagery 132
Negotiation Skills Training
   Course 38, 39
'negotiation' skills 39–43
neo-liberalism 5, 95
   in British regional press 90–114
New Labour corpus 140–1
   'new Behaviourism' 59
   New Capitalism 95
'new' universities, former
   polytechnics 30
news 62–89
   commercialization of 83–4
   lexical tailoring of 87–8
   as product of institution 63, 65
   as truth or bias 64
   values 73–9
news items, sources and derivation
   of 79
news media 1, 2, 23
   as power 12
news organizations, and news
   events 79–80
news stories
   dramatization 76
   fragmentation 76, 78
   methods of search for 80
   official sources 81
   personalization 76
newspapers 67–73
   reporting 'sensitive issues' 114
   shaping of events by 10
newsworthiness 67, 73
nominalization 32–3, 51
nomination 103–13

obelisk 130
observer's paradox 169

Index

offenders 51
  as objects of intervention 54
  rehabilitation; cognitive
    approach 48–9
    managerial approach 47
  as 'responsible' 48
  as Theme 52
official legitimation of war 116, 118
official sources for news 81–3
  definitions of news events 83
'othering' 102, 105

pacifist monuments 122
Panofsky, Erwin, on meanings in paintings 126
participant observation 49, 169–70
passive and active constructions 18
Patten, Chris, Governor of Hong Kong, speeches 141
peer pressure, resistance to 53
personalization
  of institution 150, 151
  in news stories 76
persuasive function of 'we' 146
persuasive texts metaphor in 155
Phillips, Trevor, Commission for Racial Equality 93–113
photojournalism 67–73
political ideology 63
poses of statues 134–6
power
  as discursive phenomenon 13
  as domination 12
  key concepts 11–16
  as persuasion 13–16
  and politics of institutions 1, 3, 24
press reliance on advertisers 95
prison
  as a 'total institution' 46–7
  discourse 46–61
prison, institutional setting 1
prison officers (Cognitive Skills Trainer) 49, 53, 54
prisoners' legitimate complaints 58–9
pronouns, use of 32, 142–8

Psychological approaches to deviance 48
public health and customers 13

Queen's University, Belfast 39
questionnaires 174–6

racism 10, 12
  of British press 5, 91
racist discourse 97–8
radio news 64–7
reading and research 164–5
Reasoning and Rehabilitation (Ross et al.) 49, 50
recidivism rates of prisoners 59
recontextualization 22, 23, 50
  of social practice 101–2
  of war 136
red for danger 123
reductionist modes of learning 43, 44
rehabilitation of prisoners 46, 59
relational processes 18–19, 146
research 31, 36
  of institutional discouse 163–77
resistance to managerialism 44, 45
responsibility, indication in language 18
returning soldiers, attitudes 121
Reuters news 84
Revensbrück Concentration Camp Memorial 132
rhetoric and persuasion in corpus 138–62
'risk' framework, prisons 48
role play, aggressive and non-aggressive 55–8
ruling elite of colonial powers 115, 116

Salford University, Manchester 33
Scottish Prison Service (SPS) 47
'sea' as metaphor 158–9
segregation in Leicester 93–4
self-control skills 49
'selling' knowledge and education 22
Sheffield Hallam University 36

203

simplification of news items 66–7
'skill' concept 40
'Social Actor analysis' (van Leeuwen) 102–3
social actors in *Leicester Mercury* texts 101–13
social and communication skills training 16
social control 48, 59
  in prisons 48
'social exclusion' 140
social practice, language as 8
social skills 49
'Social Skills' training 55
Socialist trend in Europe 120
sociological approaches to deviance 48
Soviet propaganda 132
spoken and written data, collection 173–4
spoken data gathering 167–9
Stadler, Arthur, image of crucified soldier 117, 137
'structuration theory', (Giddens) 6
students
  as consumers 35
  as marketable products 33
'Swapping Cultures' initiative 99
symbolization of reality, in news 68–71
synonyms and antonyms 21, 54
'synthetic personalization' 42
Systemic Functional Linguistics (SFL) 16, 49, 50

'teamwork', buzzword 37
team workers, control and power 6, 15
technologization of discourse 39
texts
  in machine-readable form 139
  from universities 30–43
textual function of language 17

Theme, SFL 50, 51, 52
  textual function 20–1
threats in news stories 76
transcription 171–2
  of Scottish dialect 60–1
transitive clauses 17, 18, 19
Transitivity, 18–19, 50, 51
Trinity Mirror Group 83
tuition fees 32
Tunbridge Wells war monument 128, 134

underclass, unskilled, Leicester 93
unemployment 24
universities as businesses 3, 22, 26
  entrepreneurial 29–43
United States defence speeches 138, 139
United States Telecommunications Act 1996 84

video archive collections 71
Viquesney, Ernst Moore 118, 134
visual communication of war monuments 116–18
visual meanings in advertisements 118
visual modality 132
vocational approach to education 35

war, legitimization, of 24, 118, 122
war memorials, official committees 119, 120
war monuments, discourses 115–37
war propaganda, monuments 119
Weber, Max, on authority 12, 16
'wind' as metaphor 159
working classes
  crime 72
  men in war 119
  uprising 121, 122